ROUGHY

Jarryd Roughead played 283 games for Hawthorn between 2005 and 2019. He kicked 578 goals, earned two All-Australian selections and a Coleman Medal, and won four premierships.

Peter Hanlon is an award-winning sports writer from Birregurra.

ROUGHY

THE AUTOBIOGRAPHY

JARRYD ROUGHEAD

with PETER HANLON

VIKING
an imprint of
PENGUIN BOOKS

VIKING

UK | USA | Canada | Ireland | Australia
India | New Zealand | South Africa | China

Viking is part of the Penguin Random House group of companies,
whose addresses can be found at global.penguinrandomhouse.com.

Penguin
Random House
Australia

First published by Viking, 2020
This edition published 2021

Text copyright © Jarryd Roughead, 2020

The moral right of the author has been asserted.

Cover design by James Rendall © Penguin Random House Australia Pty Ltd
Cover photograph by Julian Kingma
Typeset in Sabon by Midland Typesetters, Australia
Printed and bound in Australia by Griffin Press, part of Ovato, an accredited
ISO AS/NZS 14001 Environmental Management Systems printer

A catalogue record for this
book is available from the
National Library of Australia

ISBN 978 0 14379 566 7

penguin.com.au

*To all who have helped me and
been there along the journey*

Contents

Introduction   1

CHAPTER 1   In the Genes   7
CHAPTER 2   Parrots, Pranks, Please and Thanks   25
CHAPTER 3   Out of the Bush, into the Jungle   43
CHAPTER 4   Learning What It Takes   59
CHAPTER 5   A Fine Line between Premiers and Pain   67
CHAPTER 6   Backyard Legends   85
CHAPTER 7   'It's Melanoma'   103
CHAPTER 8   That Footballer with Cancer   115
CHAPTER 9   'I'm Not in a Good Way Here'   131

             DONNA MILNE *Nurse*   141
             GRANT McARTHUR *Oncologist*   153

CHAPTER 10   The Power of the Mind   161
CHAPTER 11   Just a Footballer Again   167

SARAH ROUGHEAD *Wife*   175

GEOFF HARRIS *Benefactor*   187

CHAPTER 12   'I Can See What's Coming'   193

CHAPTER 13   'This is What Dad Used to Do'   211

CAM ROUGHEAD *Brother*   229

JORDAN LEWIS *Best mate*   243

CHAPTER 14   'What Foot Do You Kick With, Amos?'   255

CHAPTER 15   Mates You'll Have Forever   269

Conclusion   289

A Note on the Co-Author   301

Index   303

Introduction

On Monday 16 May, 2016, these things happened.

In Mexico, 24 beached whales died, despite the efforts of many to move them back into the water.

In France, tens of thousands farewelled the world's largest cruise ship, *Harmony of the Seas* – 16 decks high and more than 360 metres long – as it set sail on its maiden voyage.

In Kentucky, Hillary Clinton teed off on the 'frightening' policies of her likely opponent in the US presidential race, Donald Trump.

And in Melbourne, I left footy training early, missing the review of the previous weekend's game (bonus), drove to Lansdowne Street in East Melbourne, parked my ute in the late autumn sun and walked into the old Peter MacCallum Cancer Centre.

Less than a year earlier a spot on my bottom lip had been diagnosed as melanoma. Most skin cancers spread as they grow, but this one grew down, like a carrot. Cutting it out meant losing a quarter of my bottom lip. But other than adding to my rugged good looks it didn't greatly impact my world – I only missed two games of footy, and at the end of the 2015 season I played in Hawthorn's thirteenth premiership, my fourth and our third in a row.

In January 2016 I'd married Sarah Dunn, the beautiful girl of my dreams. Surrounded by the people we love, our wedding was the best party ever. Three months later we were just starting a big renovation on our house in Hawthorn, building the place where we planned to raise our family. Life couldn't have been better.

Like anyone who's had cancer, every three months I would have a PET scan. That involved fasting after dinner, barely allowed to even drink water, then heading to Peter Mac the next day, where a glucose solution was injected through a cannula in my arm. I'd lie there for an hour, completely still, not even allowed to read a book in case the movement of my eyes or fingers upset the dye running through my system. Then my body would move through the machine, slowly, as if I'd been divided into sections and they needed five minutes to look at each chunk. If there was any hint of cancer, the dye would be drawn to it.

A week later I'd go back to get the results. Our club doctor, Michael Makdissi, would always be there when I arrived, just in case I needed him.

I was feeling good. We were seven rounds into the season and I still hadn't played a game, but the posterior cruciate ligament injury that had flared up in my right knee in January – and needed reconstructive surgery five days after our wedding – was just about good to go. My best mate Jordan Lewis was due to play his 250th game in a couple of weeks; it would be touch and go, but I was determined to run out with him.

Grant McArthur, my oncologist, greeted me by asking how my knee was. I said it was fine. And then he said, 'We're in a bit of trouble.'

My first thought was they must have picked up a spot on my arm or my back. Then Grant said, 'You've got four spots on your lungs.'

What do you do when your world collapses? For some reason I stood up and emptied my pockets, putting my phone, wallet and keys on Grant's table, and started pacing around the room.

I asked questions: 'How bad?' 'How big?' 'What do we do?' I asked if it meant no footy for the rest of the year. Grant said probably no footy next year either.

Shit. Two years out of footy. I'd be 30 by then, probably done.

I never asked the big question. I just didn't think it. It shows how conditioned you become to seeing everything in terms of football, that in that moment I still thought of it like a footy injury. That's all I'd known.

We walked out and Doc Makdissi asked, 'What do you want to do?' It was about 4.30 pm and I knew Sarah would have finished work, but I couldn't go home and tell her straight away. I didn't know what to say. So I did what I'd been doing my whole adult life – I drove to the footy club.

I drove along Brunton Avenue, right past the MCG – 'the office', the place where I'd experienced some of the best days of my life. I didn't know what to think, I was numb. I knew the boys would have finished the review by then, so I rang Jordy.

He was on the freeway, heading home, and I said, 'Can you turn back?'

He asked me why and I just broke down crying. 'I've got spots on my lungs. I don't know if I'm gunna be alright.'

There was a bit of traffic on the drive out to Waverley Park, not as bad as a normal Monday in peak hour, just people in their cars going about their lives. And me. I got to the footy club, parked in the underground car park and composed myself. Doc had worded up the key people – coach Alastair Clarkson, footy boss Chris Fagan – telling them that I was on my way, that it wasn't great news. There's always a coaches' meeting after the review's finished, but the players all leave right away, so at least I knew the boys weren't there. That helped.

I went upstairs and Jason Burt, who was the footy administration manager at the time, was in his office. I asked if he could go grab Clarko and the others. I was sitting in Jason's office with my back to the door when Jord walked in. I just lost it again, and then he started to cry.

Clarko and Fages came in, our fitness man Andrew 'Jack' Russell, the Doc, and we just sat there talking for 10 or 15 minutes. In a strange way it felt good because I was around people I was with every day, but then there was the unknown. And there was Sarah. She'd been texting me for an hour or so: 'Where are you?' 'Why are you late?' 'What are you doing?' I just kept replying, 'I'll be home soon.'

I rang my brother Cam and sister Emily and asked them to come around, said I had something to tell them. Sarah's sister Maddie is with my teammate Sam Grimley, so we got hold of them and said to come over too. Everyone I spoke to, I told them not to arrive until after a certain time.

When I walked in Sars was sitting on a couch in front of the TV. I asked her to turn it off and said, 'I need to tell you something.' Then I started crying.

'I've got cancer again. There's four spots on my lungs.'

I'll never forget the look on her face, the quiver of her lip, the tears. And I'll never forget what she asked me: 'Are you going to die?'

CHAPTER 1
In the Genes

Where do we find strength and resilience? Where does the will to keep fighting come from, to not give in when things are grim, to keep believing you'll be okay? What makes us who we are? For me, I can see a lot of that in my family history.

On Dad's side of the family there's Scottish blood from the Rougheads, and Irish and Welsh from the Griffiths. On Mum's side it's English from the Bells and Scottish from the Fairlies. My brother Cameron, sister Emily and I are the products of that melting pot, and you don't have to dig too deep to see that the qualities that have got me through tough times are on every branch of our family tree.

Mum was born in Camperdown in western Victoria, the youngest of four, with three older brothers. Her biological father was Kevin Bell, who worked on the railways. They moved around a lot when she was a little girl – she lived in Camperdown, Murtoa, Koo Wee Rup, Seymour, Ararat and Gisborne. When Mum was eight, her parents divorced and her mother, Gwen Fairlie, moved to Melbourne with all of the kids.

Gwen – my grandmother – grew up in Middle Park. When her father went to war in the Middle East, her own mother worked in a munitions factory in Port Melbourne, and she and her two brothers were sent to Kinglake to live with a family up there. She met my grandfather, Kevin, in Merino, over near Casterton, where she was working as a seamstress; Mum reckons Nannie could turn her hand to anything – milking cows, shearing sheep, churning butter, whatever was needed. She was good at tennis, great at lawn bowls, a real all-rounder. She's in her late eighties now, lives in Leongatha, and is very broad-minded. She calls a spade a spade and isn't afraid to tell you how it is.

As for Kevin, my biological grandfather, he was an alcoholic and a troubled man. He was from Beaufort, the youngest of 12, all of them decent sportsmen. Kevin was a good cricketer and a ruckman who was the most reliable player in the Merino-Digby football team.

After divorcing Kevin, Nannie married Ted Wigley, a plasterer from Mansfield, who I always knew as Poppy and who my mum calls Dad. Ted was a good athlete too: a runner who competed in fire-brigade competitions, where they run along tracks with hoses, climb ladders, that sort of thing. He ran at the Stawell Gift one year, in the 400 metres. My sister Emily has a great photo of him on her fridge, in full flight. She always says what a handsome man our Poppy was.

Mum was a sprinter when she was at school and Poppy was her coach. When I was young, before basketball and footy took over, Mum got me into an old pair of her spikes and she and Poppy taught me how to run properly – up on my toes – and how to start on the blocks. Mum says Poppy even showed her how to hold her fingers a certain way when she was running, making her hold a little stone in each hand to get it just right.

We used to train at the Leongatha footy ground, doing a mix of strength and endurance – sprint, walk back, sprint, walk back, over and over. At the start of secondary school I won the junior boys' athletics championships, which allowed Mum to boast that she'd passed her running talent on to me.

Both of my grandmothers are seriously tough women. On the Roughead side, Nan is getting on for 90 now. Blind in one eye, she's had both hips done and a knee replacement. She raised seven kids on a farm with no electricity at Mardan, about 10 kilometres east of Leongatha, with an alcoholic husband who suffered badly from depression. One of their five sons, my uncle Vincent, took his own life about ten years ago.

Sometimes Nan will admit to being in pain, but she just smiles and gets on with it. She hasn't had it easy, but she's been a superstar for the family and we all love her. She's just what you'd think a grandmother would be – loving, caring, will do anything to help you. Every time you drop in to see her or speak to her on the phone she's over the moon. I've never seen her sad, she's just such a positive person. I don't feel pressure or expectation from Nan, never have. She just accepts life as it is, which is a great way to be.

Nan reckons she gave us resilience, humour and optimism, which I can't thank her for enough. And she takes credit for our calm disposition – she says the temperament of previous generations of Rougheads wasn't the best! 'Quick to anger. Not a violent anger, but a lot of yelling and carrying on. Then just as quick to come back down.'

When Nan hugs me now she doesn't even come up to my chest, but she has a laugh that fills the room. She's the family historian, with shelves full of folders that she's put together containing birth certificates and wills and all sorts of documents, photos and articles from local papers that track our story. She's given each of her grandchildren a copy, which is a great thing to have.

The story on her side of the family, the Griffiths, is that Margaret Carey, the daughter of Catholic publicans, and Richard Griffiths, who was Protestant, must have eloped. They caught a boat from Liverpool in 1850 and by the time they reached Australia they already had Eliza. They made their way to Gippsland, built a house on the Seven Mile Road at Trafalgar, and called it Evan Vale, which is Welsh.

Eliza Griffiths was apparently a very big woman – six feet tall and broad – who could carry a bag of wheat on her shoulders. She had a younger brother named William who was so big and strong he could haul a bale of wool up a ship's gangplank by himself. Several more children came along, including my great-great-grandfather Patrick in 1855, who 30 years later welcomed Nan's father, James Joseph Griffiths.

Jim Griffiths was in the Australian 4th Light Horse Regiment in World War I, who are legendary for the Battle of Beersheba, in October 1917, when they charged the Turkish trenches on horseback, took more than a thousand prisoners and kickstarted the fall of Gaza and the enemy's retreat into Palestine. Nan says he never spoke about the war at home, but would sometimes talk to other men about what he'd seen if he'd had a couple of drinks at the RSL.

His children took him to see *Forty Thousand Horsemen*, one of several movies made about 'the charge of the light brigade', but he reckoned it was nothing like the real thing. The only legacy of his experiences that he let people see was a taste for dates and coconuts. There's a souvenir he sent home to his mother that's been left to Nan, which she keeps in a glass cabinet in her lounge room: a brightly coloured, beaded snake, made in Egypt or Syria, that's filled with sand and about six feet long if you uncoil it. It's more than 100 years old but still looks brand new.

Jim's war story wasn't talked about when we were kids. I'm not a big war person or a watcher of war movies. We studied Gallipoli one year at school and I couldn't get my head around being 18 years old and told you had to go to the other side of the world to fight people you didn't even know. I remember thinking, 'I'd just go to jail.'

Jim Griffiths was 30 when he went to war and in his forties by the time he married; Nan remembers him being older than the fathers of the other kids at school. After the war he was a union organiser and a big ALP man who ran the local Labor Party meetings. He worked as a road contractor, with his brother part of the same crew, and together they made a lot of the roads in our part of Gippsland – around Yarragon, down through Allambee and Mirboo North – using these big, primitive scoops that Nan's got a photo of somewhere. When the Depression hit in 1930 he moved to doing a kind of work-for-the-dole thing, building tree guards between Trafalgar and Warragul.

Nan's father had a great appreciation of music and literature, which he'd developed as a young man living in Kyneton with Irish aunts. He used to read his kids *While the Billy Boils* by Henry Lawson, and was a great reader of all sorts of things – he got sent copies of Hansard, the parliamentary record, and read it from cover to cover. He could play the violin by ear; Aunty Libby, who's the musician of the family, has his old violin in Adelaide. She had it restored after finding it with all the strings missing.

Then there's the other side of Dad's family, the Rougheads, who've made a bit of a mark around home since Alexander Roughead first came out from Edinburgh.

Think of Rougheads and you think of Leongatha, and vice versa. When you come to the T-intersection on the way in from Melbourne, if you turn right you're in the centre of town, but turn left and you're on Roughead Street. Although you might not know it if you're not a local, because the street signs have had a bad habit of going missing. Coming home from the pub one night I might have decided the Roughead Street sign would make a good souvenir and jumped up and hung off it until it gave way. I'm told that's what happened anyway – funny how the memory gets a bit hazy over time. I've heard a rumour my brother Cam's got one too. Must be a coincidence.

Alexander Roughead was born in 1825. His father, James, owned a newspaper in Edinburgh, and when he died his oldest son inherited the paper and Alexander and his other son got £1000. Alexander took his fortune and moved to Australia, where he ran a draper's shop on the goldfields near Bendigo, selling provisions to the prospectors. Nan reckons her lot, the Griffiths, were proper gold miners while the Rougheads were a bit more up-market.

Alexander and his family lived in Chiltern for a while, up near Albury, where one of his sons was killed in a mining accident. Eventually they made their way to Melbourne, then travelled by boat – with their horses – from Port Phillip to Port Albert in South Gippsland. From there they bashed their way through the bush on foot, north to Moe, where there was a railway siding, then south-west to Mirboo North and Leongatha.

They had a store in what's now Roughead Street selling all sorts of provisions, billy cans strung from the rafters, stuff everywhere. Nan's got a photo of Leongatha from the late 1800s and you can see the name on the building:

'GF [George Francis] Roughead', Alexander's son. The bush you can see in the photo, directly behind the shop, is where the Leongatha footy ground is now.

A bit of significant history comes into the story in the next generation. In 1915 George Charles, the son of George Francis, married Josephine O'Reilly, whose parents had moved from Tatura when Gippsland was opening up. Josephine was Dad's grandmother, and used to boast that *her* grandmother was one of the first white births registered in Victoria. A couple of years ago my Aunty Libby did some research and found that it's true. She rang Aunty Christine and said, 'You realise this means we're probably related to every Catholic in Victoria!'

When George Charles Roughead died, in 1960, he was the oldest ever Leongathan (born in Roughead Street, of course). His funeral procession was said to be the longest ever seen in town. An obituary in the local paper described him as a very keen judge of stock, renowned for his skill with a rifle, a great supporter of the football and cricket clubs, a passionate card player and one of the top draughts players in the old Leongatha club, which played competition matches all over Gippsland. See, sporting genes, us Rougheads.

Anyway, I'm seventh generation Australian, my daughter Pippa is eighth, and we're descended from some of the original settlers of Port Phillip. Sarah and Michael Curtis had 15 children who all lived to be adults, which was some feat back in the day. Sarah and Michael lived into their eighties, while their daughter Catherine married Tom O'Reilly and they both made it into their nineties. I've got hardy people in my family tree, which is a bloody good thing I reckon.

And none are hardier than Nan.

Ann Griffiths moved from Trafalgar to Leongatha to teach, and there she met Jim Roughead at a dance. Jim had been in World War II and was then working as a carrier for a local farm, driving a lorry, carting potatoes to the railway trucks. Nan says the busiest day of the week always seemed to be Friday, the day before football, but Jim never missed a game.

Nan's seven children were all big babies. Christine weighed 7.5 pounds, Paul was 10, Greg was 11. They told Nan they'd put her in early after that but nothing changed – Michael (Dad) weighed in at 10 pounds, so did Brendan, and then the twins came along and trumped the lot. Vincent weighed 9 pounds and Libby 7.5 – that's 16.5 pounds in one go!

People ask Nan, 'How did you feed all of those children?' Her answer is always the same: 'We survived.' Then she adds, 'And we always had sweets.'

Dad was the quiet one, he never said boo and was very good-humoured. He always did his school work but never got any commendation for it. Nan tells the story of a time when everyone else was already on the school bus but Dad refused to go. She was concerned, so went in to school and asked the nun who taught Dad if anything had happened. And the teacher said, 'To tell you the truth, I never notice him.'

Another time, on Christmas Day, they left him at church and didn't realise until they'd made it home. Nan reckons they had the twins, who were obviously a handful, and Brendan had terrible asthma and needed extra attention. In a busy house, sometimes Dad just got overlooked.

Nan had a lot to contend with, what with Jim's struggles with depression, seven kids to raise, a house and a farm to run. Their place had been a dairy farm when they bought it but evolved over time to sheep and shearing. Nan could – and did – do everything on the farm. Dad and his brother Greg would go rabbiting, and one day they checked their traps and found a feral cat. They weren't sure what to do, so of course the answer was, 'Go home and get Ann.' (At some point – nobody seems to know exactly when – all the kids stopped calling her Mum and just called her Ann.)

So Ann took off with the broken shotgun over her shoulder. They hadn't even told her where the trap was, they just sat there waiting and eventually heard a 'boom!' A while later Nan came back, the broken shotgun slung over her shoulder again.

Another time they saw a big snake up on the hill, so home they went to get Ann to sort it out. They all trudged back into the paddocks, Ann and her tribe of kids, a mattock over her shoulder. The snake heard them coming and tried to crawl into a crack in the ground, but Ann was too fast. She took to it with the mattock, but then she was worried that she hadn't done the job properly – Jim had always told her that when you kill a snake, you've got to crush its head.

Anyway, when Jim came in from shearing, Ann told him that she thought she'd killed a snake but wasn't sure she'd got the head. Jim got in the ute and drove off up the hill. A few minutes later he came back and said, 'I think it's dead, Ann.' The snake was in about six bits – of course it was dead!

There are stories of great care and tenderness from the farm days too. Out spotlighting one night, Jim found a kangaroo that had been shot and killed, and in its pouch was a little joey. He took it home, they named her Kang, and she became their pet. The kids bottle-fed Kang and nursed her through those early weeks and months. When she was big enough she headed off, but she kept coming back at night to sleep at the front gate.

If the front door was left open Kang would come inside looking for them. She liked having her neck stroked, like a cat. Dad reckons she took to them because they were such bloody good people, but it could have been because she had no one else. One time, when Kang was fully grown, she came home with an awful open wound on her leg. They couldn't work out what had happened to her, but she sat by the front gate and they'd bring her bread and other food. Eventually she was well enough to head off again.

As tough as things were at times, Dad and his siblings had a great childhood doing all the things you do on a farm, like chasing the lambs for Jim to mark, putting the rings on their tails and somewhere even more uncomfortable for the boys. Dad said you didn't have to run too hard to catch them after that, they went very quiet.

Nan's children were disciplined with a wooden spoon, or alternatively the black Tupperware spoon. Dad says they all worked out that getting a whack with a wooden spoon wasn't nearly as bad as it sounded – sometimes it would break, and they could fake that it had hurt like hell when in reality they'd hardly felt a thing. But if Nan or Jim picked up the black Tupperware spoon, they knew they were in strife – there was no way that thing was breaking.

There were also drying rods – dowel with a plastic covering – which were used for drying nappies in the old gas clothes dryer. The kids knew they were in trouble when those came out; Dad says it was worse when Jim grabbed them, then you knew you were going to cop it, whereas if Ann went and got the drying rods they were confident they could talk their way out of it.

Sport was the constant in their childhood – on the radio, the television when they got one, in conversation, everywhere. Nan drove her children all over the place to play footy in the winter, cricket in the summer, netball, tennis, whatever, and anyone from the neighbourhood who needed a ride would hop in too. They'd travel all over the Latrobe Valley in their Holden station wagon, kids all rattling around in the back with no seatbelts, the twins in a couple of baskets.

One of the boys Nan used to cart around to the footy told her one day, 'Mrs Roughead, it's a pity you're not a man, you could go down and sit with those coaches and tell them how good we are and that we should be in the interleague team!' I'm not sure what sort of talent scout Nan would have made, but she clearly had everyone's respect.

Dad's the only one of Nan's kids who is still in Leongatha. Christine is in Richmond, Paul (father of Jordan, who played for the Bulldogs and now Collingwood) is in Ballarat. Brendan had really bad asthma and allergies as a child and was told he'd benefit from moving; he went to Maryborough and lived with Nan's sister. Greg lives in Warragul and runs the Mirboo North pub. Libby is a medical professor who lives in Adelaide – every family needs a smart one.

Uncle Vince was in the army, spent time in Tassie, did a lot of different things. For a while he drove tourist buses, and he'd sometimes park the bus out the front of Nan's, tell the passengers he was just popping inside for a minute to see family, then leave them there for ages while he was having a cuppa and chatting to Nan.

He was a big boy, the biggest of the brothers. He was a bit of a drifter, and eventually he went north and just disappeared. Paul and Brendan went looking for him and a couple of bikies told them they wouldn't find him in a hurry. That's when they found out he'd taken his own life.

There's sporting talent everywhere in the Roughead family tree, and not just when it comes to draughts and cards. Dad's uncle Jack (Jim's brother) played senior football and cricket for Leongatha from age 14. As a full-back he was named in Leongatha's Team of the 1940s. As a cricketer, bowling right-arm fast, he was a serious handful on the matting wickets of the '40s and '50s, making Leongatha's Team of the Century after taking six wickets in a match an incredible 23 times.

He also taught dancing, both privately and in classes in the hall. Nan says all of the Roughead men were good at sport and good at ballroom dancing. Dad says not all of them, but Nan insists that if ballroom dancing had still been popular when he and his siblings were young, they'd have been good at that too. Jim shared Jack's passion for dancing, played cricket with distinction, and in footy was a ruck-rover renowned for his strength. He played in Leongatha's premiership team in 1951.

The footy and cricket skills were passed down to the next generation. Dad stopped playing cricket after I was born because he needed to work Saturdays for the extra coin, but everyone says he was very good. He was a left-arm opening bowler who as a kid had batted right-handed, but Nan made him swap so he was left-handed at both. Nan's never been able to explain that one to me – all her other sons were right-handed batsmen and you'd reckon in a family that wasn't flush with money it would have been easier not to buy another set of gear.

Dad once bowled to the great West Indian all-rounder Garry Sobers, back in the day when the touring team for the Australian summer played up-country games against local sides. There are two cricket teams in Leongatha – Town and Imperials – and all the Rougheads played for

Town. There's a photo from a premiership in the '80s where Dad was the star, taking five or six wickets in the final and making 30.

The other thing I've always remembered about his cricket was that he never wore a helmet because they couldn't find one big enough to fit his big head, so he batted in a white floppy hat.

As a footballer Dad was a ruckman who tapped the ball left-handed and kicked with his left foot. Nan says he and Paul (Jordan's dad) were naturals. Paul was apparently into doing the right things from a very young age; on car trips to away games they'd stop halfway so he could stretch his legs and have a banana for the energy.

Dad played 211 senior games for Leongatha, is a life member, and was named ruckman in their Team of the 1980s. He played in a losing grand final in 1980, then won flags in 1982 and '89. There were good footballers around home. Col Boyd, who played for Footscray and Essendon in the 1970s, coached Dad in the 1989 premiership. His teammates in 1980 included Ian Salmon, who'd played more than 100 games for Footscray, and Steve Wallis, who was about to embark on a 261-game career and become a Bulldogs great. His mother still lives next door to Nan and they're great mates.

Dad played one reserves game for Footscray, kicked three goals, but they changed the recruiting zone and all of a sudden Leongatha was zoned to Hawthorn and he never got a crack in brown and gold. Funny how things turn out, isn't it? Paul spent the 1974 season at Western Oval and is in that year's team photo, in the company of Footscray royalty like Gary Dempsey, Bernie Quinlan and Kelvin Templeton.

Dad left Leongatha in 1991 to coach Bena in the Alberton league, giving up playing senior footy because his young family needed the money. Mum played netball for Bena, but did a knee and never played again. She'd been a really good netballer, won a couple of best and fairests, and is rightly proud that the last of them came in a Leongatha premiership year when she was already a mother of three.

I think the Bena footy team won one game in the two years Dad coached them. He used to say to them, 'Why don't you merge with Korumburra?' They wouldn't have a bar of it, then two years after Dad went back to Leongatha they merged.

In the old Latrobe Valley footy league there's Morwell in Richmond colours, Traralgon who wear maroon jumpers with a white V, Maffra in red and black stripes, Sale are Collingwood, Moe wear Brisbane/Fitzroy colours, and Warragul in black with a red V. Then there's Leongatha, in our green jumper with a yellow V, and with our highly intimidating nickname: the Parrots. I don't mind what we're called, the Parrots will always be my footy club.

There's a photo of me running through the banner before Dad's 200th game, wearing my green and yellow jumper with the number 4 on the back that Dad always had because, growing up as a Richmond fan, he'd loved Royce Hart. I can tell that game was at Leongatha, even though in the photo you can't see the old grandstand with the function room underneath, where I had my twenty-first, and you can't see the tennis courts or basketball courts or the pool, the netball courts, the velodrome or even the chook sheds behind the goals at one end.

I know it's Leongatha footy ground, home of the Parrots. It's a special place to me. It's where my sporting life began.

CHAPTER 2
Parrots, Pranks, Please and Thanks

I was born on 23 January 1987, in the middle of the last Australian Open played at Kooyong before it moved to Melbourne Park. Being sports fans, Mum and Dad spent the days before the big arrival watching the tennis on the telly, where Sweden's Anders Jarryd made the quarter-finals of the singles and won the doubles with his compatriot Stefan Edberg.

'Rough, we should spell the baby's name like that,' Mum said to Dad on the couch. And that's how I became Jarryd.

Nan wanted it spelled Jarrod, the most common way, and wasn't happy at all. 'He's going to spend his whole life spelling his name!' she said. Nan reckons the spelling of names is a teacher's nightmare. Lucky she's not still teaching now!

Anyway, there's a few of us around now, and plenty of choice for Jarryd/Jarrod/Jarrad/Jared fans. *The Monthly* magazine runs a story every year on AFL player names, which includes an annual 'Jarrad census'. Last time I checked there were five Jarrods, four Jarrads, three Jarryds and one Jared.

The letter J pops up a lot in the Roughead clan. Nan was married to Jim (same name as her father), who had a brother Jack, and her eleven grandchildren include Joel, Jordan, Jess, Jake and Jarryd. My siblings and cousins say we're all equal in Nan's eyes, but I remind them every now and then that I can't see any of their faces on a magnet on Nan's fridge.

Mum and Dad were living on Brumley Street in Leongatha when I was born, but when Emily came along two years later and then Cam two years after that they moved their little family to Abeckett Street. The house we grew up in has been knocked down since and there's three units on the block now, but it will always hold those special memories of childhood.

Dad worked as a food distributor, driving around a refrigerated HiAce van, and Mum was a nurse at the local hospital. When I was a little bloke Nan would often look after me when they were both at work, or on Saturdays when Dad was playing footy and Mum was playing netball. Nan would walk me to the end of her street, where there was a tractor dealership, and I'd have to sit on every tractor before we could move on. She'd take me to all the playgrounds in town, and as we walked the streets I'd read out the number plate of every car we passed.

Dad says the big thing he taught us was respect and manners. He tells the story of taking us for a walk one day – Em in the pram, Cam and me tagging along. Every time someone stopped to say g'day I'd hide behind Dad. When we got back home he said, 'Jarryd, it costs you nothing to say hello. "Yes", "please" and "thank you" – it costs you nothing.' I've always remembered that.

For all three of us kids, one of the strongest memories of staying with Nan is the glass jar with the orange lid. Nan's still got it; Cameron calls it 'The Jar of Joy', because it's always full of her famous chocolate balls coated in sprinkles of coconut. They're great any time, but when Nan's just finished making them and they're fresh and soft I reckon they're just about the best thing in the world.

Dad says Nan spoilt us rotten. He left me at her place one Saturday night when there was a show on at the footy rooms, when I was about one year old. He picked me up on the Sunday morning, took me home and put me down for a sleep, and when he got me up for lunch he asked, 'So what did Nan give you for brekkie, mate?' A big smile came over my face and I answered, 'Ice cream!' Dad dropped in to see Nan the next day and told her what I'd said, and her response was deadpan. 'Well, that's what he asked for!' Apparently I wanted to go and live with Nan after that.

In photos of me as a little bloke, there's pretty much always a ball in my hands, and a lot of the time it's a round ball or something else that could be used as a basketball. The Roughead colouring is there from the start – fair skin, freckles and red hair. I never had any issues with it, I just looked like Dad. I did experiment with dying it one year, when I was away in Horsham with a mate's family in the summer holidays before Year 11. We went and got a bottle from the supermarket and ran a black rinse through my hair. I couldn't bleach it – imagine that! But black wasn't a great look either.

Emily's a redhead too, but Cam's dark like Mum. He was born with a hole in his diaphragm and they nearly lost him a few times; he was in hospital for six weeks from birth and still has a big scar from his chest right down to his stomach. He gets asthma pretty badly, but other than that he's good as gold.

When I was still a pre-schooler, Nan would take me to the footy in Leongatha, park up on the bank, and I'd make her kick a little brown plastic footy with me between the cars. At half-time all the other kids would jump the fence to have a kick, and I'd want Nan to do the same. I didn't see any reason why she couldn't just jump over the fence and get out there for a kick too.

We didn't need too much looking after as we got older, but as little kids we spent a lot of time at Nan's. We'd watch the same movies on her VCR over and over – *Jurassic Park* and Roald Dahl's *The Witches*. Another strong memory of Nan's place is the big lemon tree in her backyard. Me and a couple of cousins got in trouble one year when we couldn't find any balls to play cricket with, so we stripped the tree of every lemon we could find and used them instead.

———

Cam and I shared a bedroom in the Abeckett Street house until I moved to Melbourne. Everything revolved around the backyard. We had an above-ground pool, and as a kid you think you're doing alright if you've got a pool. It was a bugger to keep clean, but Dad looked after that.

The yard was your standard country set-up. The bike shed was in the back corner, at the end of the path, and next to that was a basketball ring – wooden poles and a Chicago Bulls backboard that I'd been given as a birthday present. We moved there in 1993, so everything was either the Bulls and Michael Jordan or Orlando Magic and Shaquille O'Neal.

At one side of the yard there was a gate that we'd use as goals in footy season, and the neighbour's shed wall was the goals at the other end. In summer the trampoline got tipped on its side and became the wicketkeeper and slips for cricket.

It wasn't all fun and games in the backyard – in winter there was firewood to be cut, split and stacked, and Cam and I would grab the wheelbarrow and get stuck in. Dad would cut wood at mates' farms with the chainsaw, bring it home and run it through the log splitter, then we'd stack it in the garage. We had two fires in our house – an open one in the lounge room and a firebox in the kitchen, so there was always plenty of wood to be sorted.

We were never allowed near the chainsaw, which was fair enough. Dad cut his leg one day, not too badly thankfully, but that's pretty standard for anyone who uses a chainsaw regularly. Damian Monkhorst, our ruck coach for most of my career at Hawthorn, has got little scars all over his legs from chainsaw mishaps.

I went to primary school at St Lawrence, then Leongatha Secondary College, which was a 20-minute walk from home. I enjoyed school because it was social – I was with my mates. I wasn't stupid, but I wasn't academic either. My reports had a pretty standard theme: 'If Jarryd applied himself to his schoolwork as much as he does to his sport he'd be a great student.' I've still got the report from when I was in Year 10 – it was a good one, which was mind-boggling at the time. PE and Outdoor Ed were my best subjects, and in VCE I did Biology, Maths and English too. I'm okay with straightforward numbers, but Pythagoras' theorem and all the trigonometry tripped me up.

When I was growing up there was no PlayStation, no iPhones, all you knew was sport. I played everything: footy, basketball, cricket, tennis, mixed netball. Anything that got me outside running around. There's a nine-hole golf course in Leongatha – you tee off from right behind the footy ground grandstand – and an 18-hole course just out of town. But I wasn't into golf at that age, I only really started playing a couple of years before my footy career finished, as a way of staying in touch with the young kids at the club.

But I had plenty of other sports to keep me busy. Two summers before I got drafted I even played competition tennis with Mum. When we were kids she told us there were two things she wanted us to do: learn to swim, so we could save ourselves, and play tennis. As a child who'd regularly moved from town to town, she reckoned tennis and netball were ways of being accepted.

I'd played cricket every year, but that summer Mum told me we were going to play a season together for Leongatha Tennis Club – Saturday afternoon competition, three men and three women in each team, and you'd play two sets of doubles and one of mixed doubles. Mum and I always played mixed together, and she used to joke that she didn't have to do much because I was like a big spider at the net. We argued a lot: 'That was your shot!' 'No, it was yours!' Or I'd yell at Mum, 'Run! Run!' But it was fun, and although for me it was just about getting out and playing another sport, even at 16 I knew it meant a lot to Mum.

Through my teens, as soon as school finished I'd race home, have a bowl of cereal, then play sport. I loved hanging out with my mates, and they were usually the kids I played sport with. Matt Atcheson and I were the basketballers (our dads had played together too), and we progressed to state level junior carnivals. The Atchesons had a farm a half-hour bike ride out of town, between Leongatha and Mirboo North, and that's where we'd often hang out, making our own fun.

There were a couple of other gun sportsmen from home – Luke Jones was an Australian champion motorbike rider, and Gerard Murphy a champion cyclist. They were in the same year at school as Matt and me, and the four of us were mates. Jonesy lived in town on a couple of acres, I could walk to his place. I wasn't a motorbike rider – I knew my expectations and my limitations and didn't want to get them mixed up – but I enjoyed watching Jonesy do his thing.

In between following our parents to their sport and playing our own, there wasn't too much time for us to become
ratbags. There were kids you'd always see on rollerblades
or skateboards, who were probably getting up to no good.
The only thing I really noticed about them was that none
of them ever had a ball in their hands; if you put a ball in
front of me I'd chase it all day.

When I was 16 or 17, we got up to a bit of mischief,
but I think that's the same for any kid, especially when
you've got the freedom of growing up in the country.
Our standard trick was to head out at night, line up a
street's worth of backyards and jump over every fence in
a row. Sometimes we'd grab a souvenir along the way.
We'd take bird baths and put them in places where they
couldn't be found, tie garden hoses across the street, just
stupid stuff.

We thought we knew what we were doing, that we'd
never get caught, but we always started at the same house
and ended up back there too. It wouldn't have been too
hard for the cops or anyone else to figure out. You know
what's right and wrong, and I ended up deciding, 'Nup, I'm
not staying involved in this.' The guys who were good at
sport had too much on the line. If you got caught doing
stuff like that, that'd be the end of your sport, and it meant
too much to me for that.

Dad says he never expected me to do anything with footy,
because basketball was my thing for so long. I always

played both, but in my mid-teens basketball had more of my attention – or at least demanded much more of my time.

To play high-level basketball as a kid from the country meant travel, travel and more travel. In 2002, I played for Vic Country in the national under-16 championships in Adelaide, and the same year went to Albury twice for country cups, plus Coffs Harbour and Port Macquarie. I was playing for Dandenong on Friday nights, which was an hour and a half's drive from Leongatha depending on traffic, as well as training there on Wednesday nights and Sunday mornings. Mum and Dad shared the driving with Matt Atcheson's parents; it's incredible to think of the miles they covered for us while we sat in the car and slept.

In summer I played cricket, but it was never a passion, more of a way to kill a few hours with your mates on a Saturday morning. I was a right-arm bowler, and a right-hand bat who they tried to turn into more of a bowler.

I was into cricket enough to play seniors before I moved to Melbourne, but not up to A-grade standard. When I first went to Hawthorn I used to go home a lot during summer. I'd train Saturday morning, jump in the car and shoot home, get there about 11 am, say a quick g'day to Mum and Dad, grab a feed, play cricket until 5 or 6 pm, go out Saturday night, laze around most of Sunday, then head back to Melbourne in the evening to be ready for footy training the next morning.

I played a couple of games for Town in 2006/07, then the next summer Cam asked if I wanted to have a hit with him and a few of his mates – at Imperials. This was seriously controversial, a couple of Rougheads defecting from Town. It had never happened before. Cam asked Dad if it would be okay, and he wouldn't give him an answer. He just said, 'You'll have to ask Nan.'

We eventually got permission from the top (thanks Nan), and I got to go home and play cricket with my little brother. The two grounds are at opposite ends of the school – Town have a turf wicket and footy club, whereas Imperials have only got a synthetic pitch because their ground has cows on it in winter as part of the school agricultural studies. Cows and turf wickets don't mix too well. Imperials' rooms are known as 'The Box' – there's no fence around the ground, but they have this funny tradition of putting up two poles and a little gate on game day, where you walk from The Box onto the ground. If you play for them and don't use the gate when you're walking on and off the ground you get fined.

One of the games the two of us played for Imperials was a 40-over game at Wonthaggi. That evening, when Dad asked Cam how the day had been, he replied, 'It was great!' Dad asked how many he'd made and Cam said, 'A duck!' Dad asked what was so good about that, and Cam said, 'Jarryd made a double century!'

I tell people Cam and I made 227 between us in a 40-over game, and try not to mention that he contributed a golden duck. I batted at three, went in early and hit 16 fours and 19 sixes using Cam's bat. He came in when I went out, I handed him his bat on the way past, and he was back a minute or two later. Still, that bat of Cam's averaged 113.5 from its two hits that day, which isn't too bad.

I still absolutely love my basketball, but I was never going to make a career out of it. I was a quick guard who could read the game well and was good at stealing, but I wasn't a jet at state level. By 2002 footy was starting to seriously compete for my time and attention. From March through September that year it was basketball on Monday, footy Tuesday, basketball Wednesday, footy Thursday, basketball Friday, footy Saturday, basketball Sunday. I was good at sleeping in the car, and then when I got my L-plates it was great for getting the hours up behind the wheel, but something had to give.

Money was a factor too – basketball was very much a pay-your-way sport, even at representative level. In footy if you played for Vic Country you were flown around at AFL Victoria's expense, you didn't have to pay for anything. For the basketball under-16 nationals in 2002, most of the Vic Country team had to meet a bus in Melbourne, then pick up the rest of the team in Geelong, Bendigo and Horsham along the way, and we paid for most of the trip ourselves through fundraising.

Fundraising meant asking businesses at home for 50 bucks to help send you to the nationals. We'd write letters and send them all round Leongatha; Mum and Dad did a lot of that, and I'd sell raffle tickets. Without that money, you weren't going. In footy, if you made the All Australian under-16 team there'd be an Australian Institute of Sport scholarship contract – you were actually getting paid.

Every dollar counted, so at 15, after spending three weeks of work experience working with a concreter, that became my school holiday job to help fund basketball camps or trips to big tournaments. Em and Cam got a job at the IGA – Em worked in the deli and Cam was more of a shelf stacker and trolley collector – but supermarkets wouldn't hire me because I couldn't be relied on for shifts in the holidays, I'd be going away for basketball.

Concreting paid $13 an hour with a local bloke, pouring big slabs, cleaning moulds, cutting all the reo and putting those little chairs underneath it. When they'd pour the concrete I'd be the one behind, shovelling, and then I'd have to clean up. They looked after their stuff really well so I had to do it right, washing everything with a hose so there was nothing left on the tools that could set. They were early starts – 6 am – and then working through until 4 or even 5 pm, but any time I needed a bit of coin I'd be off concreting.

I've still got all my junior basketball jerseys and it's nice to look at them and think back to those days. We won the bronze medal at the 2002 under-16 nationals, but that was my last tournament. I was getting sick of it by then – the driving obviously didn't help, and I was missing out on stuff like mates' sixteenth birthdays and other get togethers. Looking back you think that's just stupid, but that's growing up: everyone else was going to parties and I was playing basketball.

The six weekends prior to that nationals tournament in '02 were two weeks in Ballarat, two weeks in Bendigo, two weeks in Geelong, Saturday and Sunday every week. Every school holidays I was at camps, training weekends, rep games, travelling all over Victoria. Even in a 'normal' week when there was no extra stuff, I was spending nine hours a week in the car travelling to and from basketball. I started to become more aware of how hard that was for Mum and Dad, and for Atch's parents, all of those miles on the road. As the eldest of three, I felt like all the energy was going into only me. I was never comfortable with that.

After the 2002 nationals Dad said, 'If you quit basketball I'll coach your footy side.' I was fine with that. I'd missed getting picked for Leongatha when they won an under-16s grand final in 2000. I was only 13, skinny, and hadn't really grown yet, but I had been shattered. They beat Moe; a mate of mine who later became one of my groomsmen, Daniel Langstaff, got picked, and he still rubs my nose in it. Throwing myself into footy was the thing to do, but I only ended up playing four games under Dad in 2003, then things started happening.

It's not much of a stretch to say I grew up at the Leongatha footy ground. Mum would be playing netball and Dad footy, so I'd get $2 at the start of the day to get me through. I'd get there just before midday and walk around for five hours amusing myself. Two bucks got you three packets of chewy, and I'd buy that and try and fit it all in my mouth at once. I never even thought about a can of soft drink – we weren't allowed chewy other than at the footy, so Saturday was chewy day. I'd come home with dirt everywhere, because every break I'd be out there kicking the footy with whoever I could find.

When I was a bit older I'd do the scoreboard with a mate. You'd do the fourths, then some days you'd do the thirds boundary and be back in the scoreboard for the seconds and seniors. You got ten bucks and a free lunch for the scoreboard, and another ten bucks and a free lunch for the boundary. Twenty bucks and two lunches, that was pretty bloody good. The best lunch you could get was two sausage rolls and a chocolate Big M, and you'd have plenty of change left over.

The scoreboard is at the opposite end of the ground now, and the whole area has been redone. The Leongatha basketball court used to be in town, but that's a cinema now and the basketball court is next to the pool. If you go around the precinct there's the tennis courts, croquet club, pool, basketball courts, footy ground, chook sheds, velodrome and netball courts, plus the nine-hole golf course out the back of the old grandstand with the function rooms underneath. I used to have a key to the rooms and thought that was pretty special, but then I found out pretty much everyone had one.

Latrobe Valley footy was arguably the best country league in the state when I was growing up. When Dad went back to Leongatha and played seconds, the ones included Matty Mansfield and Adrian Campbell, who'd both played at Footscray, and another old Bulldog Barry Standfield came back and coached. When I was playing under-16s the senior coach was Andrew Dunkley, an old Gippsland boy who'd played 217 games for Sydney before moving back to Yarram. Hawthorn premiership player Paul Hudson was his assistant and was running around with the Parrots too.

Going into 2003 I started pre-season training with a couple of mates, doing swims and whatnot early in the morning. The idea of training and fitness making you better was sinking in. I'd train with the under-16s then hang around and train with the seniors too. It was Dunks' first year as player-coach, and after a few weeks he said to Dad, 'This boy of yours is going to be too good for under-16s, he could play seniors with me.' Dad's reply was, 'He's 16!' Which was nothing compared to Mum's reaction when he got home and told her. But Dad took her to meet Dunks and he told them, 'Don't worry, I'll look after him.' So that was it, I was in.

My first senior game was against Moe at Moe, and I kicked two goals five. Goalkicking! Yeah, maybe it was an issue my whole career. I could run a bit – I wasn't heavy then and played anywhere from forward pocket to flank and wing. Dad had worn number 4, which I'd proudly had on my little Parrots jumper as a kid. It was available when I got picked for the seniors and to run out in Dad's number was a huge thrill.

The next week we played Wonthaggi at home on a Sunday afternoon and it felt like most of Leongatha was there. I played on Dean Rice, who'd had a long career at St Kilda and Carlton before becoming player-coach of Wonthaggi. I kicked the first goal of the game, and another one near the end, and we ended up winning a tight game. Senior footy felt pretty good.

My third game was at Maffra, and we drove up in Dad's van. We had a few key players out, then Dunks pulled out with a back or hamstring injury. In the last quarter, I saw the ball switch and went to go in that direction. Their centre half-back saw me move, cleaned me up, and broke my collarbone.

Having said he'd look after me, Dunks wasn't even playing! Mum and Dad weren't happy at all.

It was a long, quiet trip home. Dad, Mum and I sat up front in the refrigerated HiAce, me with my arm in a sling and in tears because my footy world had just fallen apart. I'd done a few training sessions with Gippsland Power's TAC Cup team, and the Victorian under-16 championships were two weeks later in Bendigo. Things were just starting to happen and now I had a busted collarbone.

It's the only broken bone I've ever had, but there's not much you can do with a broken collarbone, just put the arm in a sling and rest. It was my left arm and I write right-handed, so I couldn't even get out of school. How stiff can you be?

I went up to Bendigo and watched the championships to be around the group, and then I got a letter from Vic Country saying I'd still made the team for the national under-16 championships. I was surprised, but you don't ask any questions in that situation. After six weeks out and with my shoulder healed I came back and played four games in the Leongatha under-16s, just so I could say Dad had coached me, then played the last two in the seniors and three finals.

We lost to Maffra, beat Sale in the preliminary final, and played Maffra again in the granny. There was a big crowd, utes backed up against the fence with couches on the back and blokes working their way through eskys full of beer, classic country footy stuff. I kicked the first goal of the game – Dunks gave me a handball, I swung onto my left and popped it through. I was feeling pretty good, thinking I was gunna win a senior premiership at 16. I played okay, kicked the last of the game too, but we fell about four goals short.

I didn't realise it at the time, but that was an initiation to the biggest day in any footballer's life, learning what goes into winning a flag. We had a good team – Dunks and Huddo, Mick Johnson, the Paveys who were very good – but we were old and sore. Before the game I watched the doctor jab blokes in the rooms just to get them out on the ground.

I had no idea how much more of that I'd see, how many other grand finals days I'd be part of. Playing in a premiership for your home town is the dream, simple as that. If country footy was still a bit rough back then I didn't notice, and I don't remember seeing anything that frightened me. I loved footy, everything about it – being around the older players at the club, sitting in the rooms soaking it all up as they told their stories.

There was a tradition when Leongatha won a footy premiership that was passed down from generation to generation and team to team. The train doesn't run through town anymore, but back in the day someone worked out that you could set off the level crossing at the start of Roughead Street by rubbing the tracks at a certain point with a pole. In the days after grand final wins, celebrating footballers would be walking from the rooms to the pub, or from the pub back to the rooms (you get the picture), and the lights would start flashing and the bells would ring, drivers stopped and wondered why there was a train coming at this time, and then out of the dark came half a dozen nude blokes running along the tracks.

I wanted to be one of those blokes, a Leongatha premiership player. Losing hurt, but at 16 I thought grand finals would happen every year. The AFL was a long way away, but closer than I realised.

CHAPTER 3
Out of the Bush,
into the Jungle

I didn't take much notice at the time, but somewhere along the way in 2003 some hype started to build. You're playing senior footy at 16, you make the Vic Country team, play in the under-16 national championships, end up in a grand final for Leongatha. Things started to get written in the local paper, people from other towns who we were playing against started to know who I was, a bit of expectation started to build.

Not that Vic Country set the world on fire at the national championships in Adelaide. I was vice-captain to Marcus Drum, a star junior from up around Bendigo who would have played a lot more than 22 games for Fremantle if he'd had a better run with injury. Brett Deledio (Richmond and GWS) and Dale Thomas (Collingwood and Carlton) were in the team, but we came home with an unwanted boast.

Our first game was against Vic Metro and we got smashed. Then South Australia at Football Park, we got done. Last we played Western Australia – the first time I came across a certain promising young bloke by the name of Lance Franklin – and lost that too. So there we were, the first ever Vic Country team to not win a single game at a national under-16 championships.

I didn't think I played all that well, but somehow I made the All-Australian/Australian Institute of Sport squad. I suppose you're just picked on talent – again, you certainly don't ask questions when you're in! They still sent out letters back then, and mine came with a handwritten 'Congratulations, well done' on the back of the envelope. I thought that was pretty cool, until I found out it had just been written by a mate who was doing an internship at the AFL who'd been asked to post the letters.

My All Australian teammates made a pretty decent side. It included Deledio, Shannon Hurn (West Coast premiership captain), Josh Kennedy (Carlton, Eagles premiership player), Buddy Franklin (Hawthorn premiership player, Sydney), Mitch Morton (Richmond, Sydney premiership player), Angus Monfries (Essendon and Port Adelaide), Ivan Maric (Richmond and Adelaide). Out of that group, Buddy, Josh Kennedy and myself are all in the top 40 all-time AFL goalkickers.

Through basketball I'd interacted with enough kids in these sort of situations that I wasn't shy meeting these young blokes from all over Australia. I roomed with Angus Monfries on the first camp we had, and we got on. Terry Wheeler was the AIS team coach and there was a focus on making the promising kids adopt professional habits at a younger age – weights training, core training, homework, kicking tuition. I just went with the flow and only realised years later how quickly things happened between the end of 2002 and the end of 2004.

Before Christmas 2003 we had a second camp in Melbourne where two players were placed at each AFL club. Toby Stribling and I went to North Melbourne. I'd barracked for North as a kid and a couple of my childhood heroes, Anthony Stevens and Glenn Archer, were still there. I had a couple of chats with Neville Stibbard, who was North's recruiting manager.

Articles started bobbing up about the AIS squad – who was training where, what their prospects were. I remember seeing one that mentioned Buddy, how exciting he was, and how 'another key forward, Jarryd Roughead, is training with North Melbourne', then talked about what sort of player they thought I'd become. I was thinking, 'How do they know this stuff already?'

For all of the focus on being professional, we were still kids. Around the same time we had a camp in Canberra, and the champion boxer Kostya Tszyu was up there preparing for a title fight. We were 16-year-old boys, carrying on and making noise – we didn't have a clue how important sleep is for an athlete. We were in someone's room one night, making a ruckus, and Kostya Tszyu walked in swinging his neck chain. He gave us a death stare and said: 'I'll give you two minutes to get to bed.'

'Yes sir, no worries sir.'

We were absolutely shitting ourselves. I hardly slept that night – every creak, every noise, I was convinced it was

Kostya coming to get us. He'd obviously made sure Terry Wheeler and the support staff knew, because the next day Wheels went right off at us. 'You little pricks have put a world-champion boxer onto me!'

Kostya hated us. When someone went up and asked for an autograph he said, 'No. You kept me awake last night, you're not getting a thing.' We were lucky he didn't belt the lot of us.

Around Easter in 2004 we played a three-test International Rules series against the Irish using the round ball. We lost in Brisbane, won in Melbourne playing as the curtain-raiser to a Bulldogs–Melbourne game, then won the decider in Perth when Mitch Morton kicked an over on the siren to get us up by a point. Or at least we thought we'd won – they hastily did a score review and decided Mitch's kick had come just after the siren and didn't count, so we lost by two points. We were all convinced they were worried the Irish wouldn't come back so they tricked up the result.

I played in defence in each game, and in the last quarter at the MCG I even played as goalkeeper – I don't know how that happened. After I came back from the AIS, Gippy Power played me in the backline for the first couple of games and I went alright, and the experiment continued for Vic Country in the under-18 nationals.

I was a bottom-ager in a team captained by Andrew McQualter. We lost to Vic Metro on the MCG with Travis Cloke and Marc Murphy among the opposition, then lost to South Australia down in Geelong with me playing either loose in defence or on Heath Grundy, who was a forward back then. In our third game, against WA at Princes Park, I was in the backline again and we had a win.

Back at Gippy Power, in the second half of the year our coach Lachy Sim shifted me forward and I started to take off. I ended up kicking 53 goals in the TAC Cup season, which was second or third behind Matt Little. The most I kicked in one game was six against Geelong Falcons, when I spent the game mucking around with Jordan Lewis, the Warrnambool boy who I'd first met playing representative basketball and became good mates with as a teammate at the under-18 championships.

I think everyone would say they were a different player as a kid, because you just play on instinct when you're young. Later it's all structure – for pretty much every scenario the game throws up it's more or less set in stone where you should be and what you should be doing. Good junior footballers who are allowed to just play can become unspectacular role players in the AFL system. I was lucky, I guess, that I was pretty much the same player all the way through, or at least my assets – agility, jumping, vision, a bit of nous – never really changed.

I didn't think I ever dominated at TAC Cup level, but I suppose if you've kicked six and a few fours you're doing something right. Ten minutes into the second half of a game against Sandringham Dragons at Morwell I had four goals, but it was so cold they called the game off. I was spewing – it was country footy in winter, what did they expect? But then, Sandringham's captain did get taken to hospital in an ambulance with hypothermia, wrapped up in foil like a big souvlaki, so I guess it was a bit colder than usual.

On 25 November 2004, I went to my high school graduation thinking that the next day I'd become a Richmond player. The Tigers had been to Leongatha and had a chat, articles in the paper had me heading to Punt Road, and on graduation night Greg Miller, Richmond's general manager of football, gave us a call. 'We're going to take you tomorrow at pick 4. Our president Clinton Casey would like to invite you and your family back to his house for a barbecue afterwards.'

'Cool, appreciate it. Thanks very much.'

I'd been told for a while that I'd go early in the draft, but that only heightened the uncertainty of where I'd end up. The first article I remember seeing about where I might go was centred around the Bulldogs – if they won their last game of the season they'd get pick 5, but if they lost they'd get 3 and 6. The theory was that with pick 5 they'd take Buddy, but with 3 and 6 they'd get Ryan Griffen and me. That was the country version of the paper, anyway; I found out later the city version was completely different, like they'd had second thoughts between editions and had another stab at it.

The draft order was established, the first six picks would be Richmond, Hawthorn, Bulldogs, Richmond, Hawthorn, Bulldogs. Other than that I really didn't know what would happen until they called out my name.

I'd been to draft camp in Canberra in the September school holidays, the week after Port Adelaide beat Brisbane in the granny. At the camp we were segregated by geography – Vic Country in a group over here, Vic Metro over there, SA there, and so on. But Buddy Franklin was always hanging out with the Vic Country blokes; we already knew each other from camps and championships, and we got along. I'd hit it off with Mitch Morton too, but he knew he was going father–son to West Coast so didn't come to this camp.

My testing results were good without being great – a 13 beep test, but a pretty bad 3-kilometre time trial at 11 or 12 minutes. I wasn't a bad endurance runner in the early days – I raced okay over 400, 800 and 1600 metres, but then I got heavy. At draft camp I weighed 89 kilos and within 12 months I was 99 kilos. My days as an endurance runner were over. I actually came back from the camp with an ingrown nail on my left big toe. It needed operating on, which completed the set after I'd had the right one done in about Grade 6. My toes are a disgrace – I pretty much haven't got any nails at all.

In between all the fitness testing I met with five clubs: Carlton, Adelaide, Melbourne, Hawthorn and the Bulldogs. The Dogs had already grabbed six Gippy Power boys one day at Morwell and interviewed us separately. In Canberra it was a bit more on-the-spot to see how you'd react.

There were always good stories about Port coach Mark Williams trying to nail people. As soon as I sat down in front of him he came out with, 'Redhead, hey? Name me a good redhead footballer.' I shot back with, 'Justin Leppitsch.' And Choco went, 'Yeah, good answer.' Then he asked me why I was wearing Puma runners, and I said I wasn't sponsored by Nike like his footy team. 'Good answer.' And that was it. As soon as he realised I could interact he moved on.

Neale Daniher and the Melbourne crew were funny. I sat down and Neale said, 'We're not going to draft you, we just heard you were a good bloke to have a chat to.' That was nice.

Gary Buckenara was Hawthorn's recruiter, and he interviewed me with Jason Dunstall and a couple of others. Bucky did the talking, Dunstall sat in the corner and listened. I knew Hawthorn was going to trek Kokoda a couple of weeks after the draft and I wasn't too keen on that. I didn't really know much about Hawthorn growing up either – Dad was Richmond, the Tigers had played in a preliminary final a couple of years before, plus Terry Wallace was coach and you were confident he knew his stuff; Clarko was untried, hadn't coached before. Bucky had never come to Leongatha to see me, and I just didn't have any reason to think I was going to Hawthorn.

So after all that, at graduation I spent the night telling everyone I was going to Richmond. I was in the suit and tie, with a shark-tooth necklace on stretchy elastic around my neck. We had a few, got to bed about 2 am, and by 7 am I was up and on the road to Melbourne.

The draft was at Melbourne Park, but in 2004 it wasn't

the full-on television production that it is today. Only about half a dozen of us were invited – me, Bud, Brett Deledio, Richard Tambling, Danny Meyer who went to Richmond with pick 12, and Johnny Meesen who Adelaide took with pick 8.

Away we went: 'Selection 1, Richmond, player number whatever, Brett Deledio, Murray Bushrangers.'

Lids and I had gotten to know each other during Vic Country stuff over the previous year or so, and we'd already spoken about how our new lives as Richmond footballers would look.

'How about we live together with a host family? That'll make things easy, help each other out.'

'Yep, love to.'

Back home in Leongatha, my grandparents had decorated the house in black and yellow streamers in preparation for a 'Welcome to Tigerland' party.

Then they read out selection 2.

'Hawthorn, player number whatever, Jarryd Roughead, Gippsland Power.'

Dad looked at me and said, 'Um, that wasn't meant to happen . . .' I just sat there with no expression at all, knowing that whatever TV cameras were there were on me, but not sure what to do or think.

I was still in a daze as they read out Ryan Griffen to the Bulldogs at pick 3 and Tambling to Richmond at pick 4, then it was Lance Franklin to Hawthorn at pick 5. I knew Bud was sitting a couple of rows behind us so I turned around, and he just gave me this big wink. Very Bud.

The surprises weren't over yet. Tom Williams went to the Bulldogs with pick 6, then it was 'Selection 7, Hawthorn . . . Jordan Lewis, Geelong Falcons.'

Lewy had been convinced from the talks he'd had with clubs that he was going to Port Adelaide at pick 11. Hawthorn had played it so well. They didn't speak about who they were going to take, but they'd sucked Richmond into thinking they'd take Tambling at 2 by saying he was the second-best player in the draft. The Hawks had assumed Richmond would take Bud at 4, but they went for Tambling instead. Hawthorn's plan all along had been to get a key position player first, but in the end they got two of them: Roughead and Franklin.

Bud and I quickly put the white Hawthorn polos on, had photos taken with Clarko – the new coach and his new draftees – did a quick press conference, then headed to the old social club across the road from Glenferrie Oval. Sam Mitchell was the first new teammate I met, he just walked in and said g'day, and before long I was getting texts and calls from other players to say welcome aboard. Eventually we headed back to Leongatha, took the Richmond streamers down and had a party.

The club had told me someone would come and pick me up the next day, and I spent all of Sunday with my bags packed, ready to go. About 8 pm there was a knock at the door – it was Clarko and Damien Hardwick, who'd been signed as player development manager and forward coach. They gave Dad a bottle of Scotch, Mum a bunch of flowers, pretty much said, 'Thanks for giving us your son, we'll look after him,' then chucked me in the back of the car and off we went.

I don't think Mum and Dad were prepared for that – at the start of the weekend their first-born hadn't graduated high school yet and was still living at home, by Sunday night he was gone. Welcome to the AFL.

My first proper task as a Hawthorn footballer was to walk the 96 kilometres of the Kokoda Track. I'd never had a passport, but one appeared as if by magic. I don't remember having to get immunisation jabs. Everything just got pushed through, and in early December, less than two weeks after draft day, we were off to Papua New Guinea.

I'd spent the first couple of nights after leaving Leongatha with Clarko and and his wife Caryn, whose third boy, Matty, was only about a month old. Then Bud, Lewy and myself spent the couple of weeks before Kokoda with the Buckenaras, Gary and Annette, and their children, Andrew and Elysha.

I hadn't really been training prior to the draft, just playing a bit of basketball back home and cricket on the weekends. At my first training session, at Dendy Park, we did 100 metre sprints, and I ran with Spida Everitt and another good redheaded new boy, Josh Thurgood. At school I'd done some bushwalks and rock climbing in Outdoor Ed as part of PE, but I wouldn't say I'd had the greatest preparation for what can be a pretty daunting six-day trek through the PNG jungle. We'd all been given a book to read about the history of Kokoda, but us draftees had no idea what we were in for. I'm surprised by how well I got through it – I'm not saying Kokoda was easy, but I wasn't lagging. Somehow it didn't rain the whole time either, which was bloody lucky.

Kokoda was the best thing for us as new arrivals at the club. The 2005 playing list was set and, other than Tim Boyle, who was recovering from a broken leg, and one or two others, just about all of the 44 players slogged across the Owen Stanley Range, where the Japanese and Allied forces had fought a brutal battle during World War II.

Everyone was paired up with a different partner each day – I had Ben Dixon, Shane Crawford, Nick Holland, Richie Vandenberg and Spida Everitt – and that was a great way of bringing everyone together. Crossing creeks, sometimes more than 20 times a day, scaling up and down narrow mountain paths, going through swampy ground, you had to be there for each other. We bonded with our new teammates, and completing something so demanding, doing it together, gave you a belief that you could stand beside them and hold your own.

There were some funny moments. Bud stood out as someone who was asking to be stitched up right from day one – bringing a framed photo of his girlfriend when we were trekking Kokoda didn't help. He ate all his food on the first day and from then on relied on people feeling sorry for him and sharing their rations with him. The boys were all over him. Someone would distract him while someone else shoved rocks in the bottom of his backpack, and he wouldn't realise until he emptied out his gear at the end of the day. It was an initiation of sorts, and the rest of us newbies were just lucky that Bud was there to take the heat.

One thing that stayed with me from the trek was the dinner we had on the last night. Everyone had a few beers, and Clarko instigated a group exercise where we went around the tables and everyone had to say something. When it got to Crawf he broke down. He'd just turned 30, had played for 12 years without getting close to a premiership, and he was coming off a season he'd started with a chronic back injury and in which he broke an arm that became so badly infected he was in and out of hospital. He'd given up the captaincy at the end of 2004 too. And here he was in Kokoda, crying his eyes out and saying, 'I just want to win, that's all I want to do.'

One of the first things I remember Clarko saying picked up on a connection that had been made in the media: 'Second bottom on the ladder but second-highest pay bill.' Mark Graham got cut, Adrian Cox was cut, Nathan Thompson got traded. The club just decided, 'This is the path we've got to go down.'

All of this was going over my head as I settled in to my new life. Jordy Lewis moved in with a host family in Springvale that Crawf and Dicko had both lived with. Bud's parents moved over from WA to Box Hill to help him settle in. And I took up the kind offer of the Buckenara family to stay on with them in Camberwell. Being a bit older, Lewy was the only one of us with a licence, so we relied on him to drive us around. In January I got my licence and my first car, a second-hand Commodore, through the Gippy connection with Steve Wallis at Essendon Mazda. It copped a few dings as I got used to driving in Melbourne, touch-parking and whatnot, but that's the way it goes.

I hurt my ankle in pre-season but got over it well enough to play the first practice game, switching between centre half-forward and centre half-back. I didn't get a run in the NAB Cup games, though, and when Bud, Harry Miller and Josh Thurgood were all picked to debut against Sydney in round one, 2005, Lewy and I were left to bide our time.

I wasn't too disappointed – seeing AFL footy up close, training alongside these blokes, seeing the size of them, you were nervous as all get out. They might have only won four games the year before, but all I could see around me was Crawford, Everitt, Hodge, Mitchell, Vandenberg, Smith, Dixon, Barker, Holland, Jacobs, Hay, Croad. You're thinking, 'This is a good side, but for some reason they suck at the moment.'

When Box Hill took on Williamstown in the first VFL game of the season, a week after the AFL kicked off, I was ready to go. Simon Taylor, who was also taken in that draft, tapped the opening bounce straight to Lewy, who kicked it to me on the lead, and I kicked a goal. I was thinking, 'How good's this?' All three of us played well (Jordy had 28 touches, I kicked three goals), and the next week we all got picked to play our first AFL game at the G against Essendon.

I lined up on Dustin Fletcher. They say you never forget your first goal: 'Franklin (wearing number 38) kicks long towards the city end, Fletcher and Mark Williams create a contest, it spills towards the boundary, Roughead (number 35) picks it up, snaps on the left around the body, it goes through. Roughead goes nuts in celebration.' Probably a bit too nuts, in hindsight.

All up I had 12 touches, kicked 2 in the second quarter, cramped up, and was pretty happy – except for the result. Dean Solomon toe-poked a late goal that clearly came off Johnny Hay's boot. There was no goal review back then so that was the game, although the umpires later admitted they got it wrong, which was nice of them.

The next few weeks were a series of initiations. In my second game we beat Brisbane, who were coming off four grand finals in a row. Their backline included Mal Michael, Justin Leppitsch, Martin Pike and the Scott brothers. And you've got me, Bud and Harry Miller, with seven games and barely an armpit hair between us, walking down to take them on. It wasn't exactly intimidating for the Lions boys, but we had a crack. Leppitsch went at Bud and me from the start and ripped both our jumpers; we just tried to hold our own.

I got dropped after a quiet one the following week against North, but came back in for the Melbourne game in round eight. In the rooms Clarko got us young blokes together – Lewy, Bud, me – and said, 'Right, you're not taking any shit. I want you to go out there and start something. Take someone on before the first bounce.' Lewy got fined twice for wrestling, two $900 fines. I got fined for wrestling with Travis Johnstone and 'engaging in a melee', and that was 1500 bucks.

Things like that stay with you – not bowing down to someone who's been around a lot longer than you. Already, we were showing we could be pricks when we wanted to. Clarko would pump us up to do that: 'Just go out there and engage someone right from the start, show them you're not going to be pushed around.' And we were like, 'Righto, no worries.'

Bud, Lewy and me, the three young blokes, we had each other's backs.

CHAPTER 4
Learning What It Takes

There's no way I deserved as many games as I got in the early days, but you don't knock them back, not when you're young and trying to find your feet. Going into 2008 I'd played 58 out of 68 possible games since being drafted, but still didn't completely feel like I belonged as an AFL footballer. I didn't quite know where I fit, or what being comfortable as an AFL footballer actually looked like.

Late in my first season I got shifted to defence, where they like to send young blokes to learn the game. I started to flourish, and I earned a Rising Star nomination against Richmond in round 19.

Over the next pre-season I trained as a forward, and started 2006 in the front half. I was in and out of the team and we lost 11 out of 12 games through the middle stretch of the season, which made for a long winter.

It didn't help that I couldn't drive, having done my licence for 16 months by rushing back to training during the summer. I'd been feeling a bit homesick, went back to

Leongatha for a couple of nights, read the program wrong and only left at 11 am for the drive back to town. I thought training started at 2pm, but then the phone rang. 'Where are you? Training started at 11.'

I shit myself, of course, and sat there thinking, 'Don't speed, don't speed.' There were roadworks on the freeway and I missed the reduced speed limit signs – 94 in a 40 zone, see ya. Rick Ladson drove me everywhere in 2006. Cheers, Laddo.

Anyway, I missed a couple of games late in the season and then they said, 'We're going to play you in this new forward structure Clarko's come up with called "The Box".' They had a camera inside the coaches' box that was trained purely on the forward line, and they'd worked out a simple set-up that could make the most of the blokes we had up there. There was Bud, of course, and Ben Dixon, Tim Boyle, sometimes Johnny Barker, and myself.

Under this structure, there was no squeezing space up the ground, you'd just set up with four blokes inside 50 forming the corners of a square – two up near the arc, two back near the goals. The back two would lead up the ground while the two further up the ground would double back and cross over. The theory was it gave the kicker four options. Simple.

Boyler was a big part of where we were going. He could run and jump, was a beautiful set shot at goal, a bit different to match up on and great to play with. He kicked 32.25 in 2007. Then in round three the next year, against North, a pack went up for a mark, he was first to hit the ground, and was lying on his side when 100 kilos of Bud landed on him and crunched his pelvis. He was never the same again.

In round 20, 2006, I kicked four in the first half against Essendon, we won, went to Tassie and beat North, then we smashed Geelong at Docklands in Barks' last game. Willo kicked eight straight that day and got a bonus for getting to 60 goals for the season. For the first time it felt like, 'Right, something's working. Tick.'

We started 2007 by losing to Brisbane. I was playing forward, hardly touched it, and got dropped. The same happened after we beat Essendon in round six, then I came back and kicked three against St Kilda but went out of the side again after we beat West Coast in round nine.

Then something strange happened and I went on a run that left me finally feeling like it was happening, that I was fitting in and would make it as an AFL footballer. I was 20 and had played 43 games, so you'd hope so.

We were playing Port Adelaide over there on the Sunday, and I was playing for Box Hill against Williamstown on the Saturday. They told me to just go and get some confidence, enjoy my footy. I played well and headed home via a drive-through bottle shop, grabbing a six-pack and getting ready to enjoy a night on the couch. I was leaving the bottle-o when I got a call from our footy manager, Mark 'Dougy' Evans. 'Croady's back's gone, you're flying to Adelaide first thing in the morning.'

So home I went, put the beers in the fridge, washed my clothes (I was a bit fussy in terms of socks and whatnot), had an early night and flew over next morning. I'd played every minute of the game the day before, as you did back then, but I felt okay. I didn't exactly set the world on fire and only had three touches, but we won easily, and I got Shaun Burgoyne with a run-down tackle that still gets a run on old highlights every now and then.

I kept my spot, did enough against Sydney the next week to stay in, and the following Friday night I kicked five in the first half against Carlton in front of more than 53 000 at Docklands. Bud was injured and didn't play, but we still won by 100 points. That was the first game where I played really well as a forward, the moment I felt like it had finally started. The next week we beat Collingwood and I took a mark on Nick Maxwell, a big hanger that was on the back page of the papers, and pretty soon on the wall at Nan's house.

Other than getting towelled up by Max Hudghton and not kicking any in my fiftieth game, I went on a bit of a run with another couple of five-goal bags and, in the lead-up to September, four weeks in a row where I kicked three goals.

We played finals for the first time since 2001 and beat Adelaide in a cracking elimination final. Bud kicked seven and I had another three just after quarter-time. In a tight game you don't want to be the bloke who misses the chance to win it and I missed two – lead out, Joel Smith hits me, I hit the post; lead out again, Rick Ladson hits me, miss again. Thankfully there was time for one more surge, and Bud marked and kicked his seventh.

For a young side that was effectively our grand final; we got smacked by North the next week. Hodgey, Lewy and

Crawf all cracked everyone in sight, and were all watching from the stands in round one the next year after getting done for striking. Hodgey got a week, Lewy two – then another one as soon as he came back in round three – and Crawf three.

We were disappointed to bow out, but we'd played finals and made an impact. The belief that was building became even greater when Geelong went on to win the grand final; we'd beaten them twice the year before and again the one time we'd met that season. We were starting to see the benefit of what we were doing, and personally I was starting to feel like a forward. I kicked 40 for the season, Bud kicked 73. We were starting to click.

The team was growing too. The year I'd started Crawf had given up the captaincy, but even though he wasn't in the leadership group he was still an obvious leader, even three years later. Richie Vandenberg had taken over and he and Mitch really drove the new culture. Joel Smith was part of that too. Our leadership group was young – Hodge, Mitchell, Tim Clarke, Changa Bateman – but together they set the standard.

Through that period of building we were still young, and a few of us needed a kick in the arse. There were plenty of blokes in the coaching set-up happy to give one. Clarko, obviously, but if he didn't whack you then you had Damien Hardwick, Todd Viney and Ross Smith as his assistants – hard men. There were no ex-Hawthorn people, which in hindsight was exactly what we needed. Everyone would ask us, 'What's Dermie like? And Dunstall?' But other than first-game jumper presentations and the like, you didn't see those blokes. Credit to them for staying out of the way and letting Clarko forge his own path.

There were no camera phones back then – thankfully, because we got in a bit of trouble a few times. We were young kids getting free-drink cards, going out to the places in the city that were the hot spots of the time. Lewy was living with Campbell Brown, so we became close to Browny's mates. At times there'd be 10 young kids out on the tear together; it was never going to go quietly every time.

The club was trying to create a culture, so any time someone was late to recovery or training we'd all be hauled off down the beach. Bud and Jord broke curfew in our first year – we were all to be home by midnight and they got caught out after pumpkin hour. We all got summoned to the beach for a 6 am session, turning up with shorts and towels and walking to the end of the Kerferd Road pier, thinking we were all going for a punishment swim. Then they said, 'Right, Lewis and Franklin up front, in you go – up around that buoy and back again.'

It was the middle of July, not even dawn yet. Lewy jumped in and started swimming. Bud jumped in and he was yelling, 'Wait up! Wait up!' Lewy just took off. As soon as they each jumped in you heard that shocked inhalation of breath, the water was so close to freezing. Lewy's a very good swimmer, and he made it out and around the buoy in no time. Bud isn't a great swimmer and seeing him struggling in near-freezing water got the message through. Nobody broke curfew again.

Not that we didn't still push the boundaries. After beating St Kilda early on, I went out and had a few drinks, then on the Sunday had a few more. We went to the Geebung and Hodgey found out we were there. I said I'd had three or four, knowing it was actually a few more.

So myself, Bud and Lewy got called to front up to the leadership group, who would interview us one at a time. Jord went first and when he walked out of the room he whispered to me and Bud, 'Don't lie, don't lie.'

There was no time to collude and get our stories straight before Bud had to go in. A couple of minutes later he walked out, cool as a cucumber, and I knew he'd just lied through his teeth.

I went in and told the truth. Hodgey went through me. He still wasn't perfect at this stage of his career, so when he was having a crack at me, in my head I was going, 'Mate, you can rip me all you want, but I know what you get up to.' I only thought it, because I didn't feel like I was established enough to actually say it.

We copped our punishment, I can't even remember what it was, and I apologised on the quiet to Hodgey. I said, 'I'm sorry I kinda lied to you.' And he said, 'It's gunna take more than that.' Other than communicating for footy, we pretty much didn't talk for 12 months.

It came to a head in 2008, in the backyard at Croady's one Saturday night after a game. We're very similar, which Hodgey pointed out that night – both country kids whose parents had split up, both stubborn and not willing to give ground easily. I told him, 'I just feel that what's good for you is okay, but if we do it you come down on us for exactly the same thing.' We agreed, and everything was good from then on.

You forget sometimes that you do a lot of growing up within a footy club – you arrive straight out of school and enter an environment of routine and discipline. Of course there are times when blokes push back against that. We were no different, and I'm sure it helped bond us in ways that contributed to the success we had.

These were blokes who I loved playing with. Vander and Mitch drove the culture, and we had Hodge, Guerra, Lewis, Croad, Osborne, Brown – blokes who loved getting physical on the footy field. I started to realise I was surrounded by blokes who made you walk taller just because they were your teammates. When you've got each other's backs, and you're up for a fight, good luck to the other mob.

CHAPTER 5
A Fine Line between Premiers and Pain

You sit through a lot of game reviews in a 15-year footy career, but not too many that make you sit up and go, 'What the . . . !?' That's what happened when Clarko walked into the theatrette at Waverley one Monday afternoon in late July 2008.

He stood in front of us and said, 'We can win the flag.'

That Friday night we'd lost to Geelong by 11 points, but knew we weren't too far off the mark. Geelong went into that year's finals 21–1; they were a pretty good team. A couple of days before we played them, Hodgey's wife Lauren had given birth to their first child, Cooper. Hodgey was all over the place and we played a bit that way too.

Clarko gave his reasons why we could be premiers, said we just needed to train a few things, fix some areas of our game, not try too hard, just do the simple things. He's a really good storyteller, he can make you believe in something you doubted. He'd sell things so well to us that the entire group would buy in. And this was a pretty big sell, because there's no way any of us went into the 2008 season thinking we were going to be premiers. No way.

But the off-season had brought a couple of big wins: getting Cyril Rioli in the draft and luring Stuey Dew out of retirement. I didn't know much about Cyril (although the excitement of playing alongside him kicked in quickly), but I was really happy about getting Dewy, who as a Port Adelaide player had run circles around us and made us look stupid a couple of times. I thought he was a gun. Bringing a premiership player into a group that didn't have any could only be a good thing.

Then we heard the rumours of what he looked like, how unfit he was. I didn't see him during the pre-season – he was doing these secret sessions with Jack Russell and Clarko, while Dimma Hardwick took training. They hadn't officially picked Dewy in the draft yet, so they'd go off and train him without anyone knowing. There were stories about him training wearing garbage bags so he'd sweat more, Jack making him do two sessions a day. By all reports he needed to, because he was as big as a house.

I said to Dimma one day, 'Are we gunna get him?' And he said, 'Yep. You'll love leading to his left foot.' As a forward, when you've already got Hodge and Mitchell, guys who can hit you from anywhere, you love hearing that.

Bud and I were 21, Jord was 22. We'd all played more than 50 games and were getting our heads around what it took to compete with and beat the best. Things were coming together, but it was still a nice surprise when we won our first nine games of 2008. We dropped our first game in round 10, against the Bulldogs down in Tassie.

Clarko was drilling attention to detail into us – he wanted us to always remember that the little things are important. When we were manning the mark for an opponent's kick, we were instructed to come right up and point to the spot where the mark is. It's such a small thing, but you'd see other teams not bothering to do it and giving you half a metre. In reviews, Clarko was constantly at us to give them nothing. 'Get right up there, point to the blade of grass, pinch an inch if you can.'

He talked a lot about electricity in the feet. You could tell in the first five minutes of games that we were switched on, especially when we set up to defend the kick-in after a point. Everywhere you'd see blokes who were on their toes, ready to strike, not just standing flat-footed waving their arms in the air. When you're pointing and turning and talking – every one of you – it's intimidating for the opposition; they start to feel like they're outnumbered.

The way we played soon got plenty of publicity and attention, because it was different from what the rest of the comp was doing – as the season wore on, we increasingly used a zone set-up that became known as 'Clarko's Cluster'. Only the forwards and midfielders played the zone initially, and we were given most of the year to get it right. Then, from the round 18 game against Collingwood on, the six defenders were brought on board and we used it through the finals.

One of Clarko's mentors was a bloke named Phil Gartside, who was a long-time chairman of Bolton Wanderers in the

English Premier League. Clarko would head over to England every off-season and come back with something new each time. Then he'd bounce it off David Rath, who was a big ideas man – game scenarios, trends, ball movement, statistics – and they'd develop it further.

At the end of 2007 Clarko had been to Bolton and talked to their coaches about guarding space rather than guarding men. The idea was that if you could guard space, but remain within striking distance of a player, you could protect more of the ground. Then the next defender could fall off a little bit and guard space too, and so on up the ground.

Originally four of us in the forward line would form a diamond in defence whenever the opposition were kicking in from a point – one guy on the mark, two either side of him, and one in the middle behind the guy on the mark. We would guard all of that area and the wingers would fall in behind the two on the outside of the diamond. Your other two tall forwards would be behind the wingers, just outside 50, in case the attacking team kicked it long.

Patience was key. If the opposition got through the first layer of defence, maybe even the second, you couldn't panic. Because by the time they'd get to the third or fourth layer they'd also have pressure from behind, so you got them either way. And if they got through the whole lot you tipped your hat, well done.

Lindsay Gilbee was arguably the best kick coming out of defence in the comp, and the Bulldogs got through us once or twice. We'd be asking ourselves, 'Are we off today? Or have they worked us out?' But our focus would come back to being diligent on defence, and soon we realised that the times they got through were becoming the exception.

Not everyone could pick it up right away. Defenders like Trent Croad had spent their whole lives being drilled to stick with their man, body on body, to climb over him and spoil. Now they were being asked to guard the space in front of him, which was a huge change. There were teething problems, but we'd review it heavily every week and work on it in training. Then we'd go inside and review training.

Done well, it meant you weren't as focused on any particular opposition player, because at its heart the zone was about cutting the head off. 'Don't worry who the player is, just do what you need to do.'

We trained hard, until it became second nature. Tuesday morning sessions we'd do goalkicking, then have light training that was full of scenarios. Coaches were out on the field and would say, 'Right, the ball's here, how would you set up?', and everyone had to know their spot.

In the meeting the day before the Collingwood game Clarko had said, 'Righto, defenders, you're joining the zone.' He called the back part 'the trap', and the rest was just the zone. You only had to be out on the ground to realise its power – you could actually feel it working. When you won a turnover, you wouldn't just immediately bomb it straight back inside 50 to a tall, because you'd be able to hit a short 45. You could see the opposition defence thinking, 'What just happened? Where'd he come from?' There was no waiting for the option to be there, it was just there. In the following decade the game evolved to be all about turnovers, and we were kind of the start of that.

We got to the finals and Clarko said, 'You only have to be the best team *now*.' We played the Bulldogs on a Friday night and everything just clicked – Bud kicked eight, I got three. It was over by half-time.

The week off was interesting, because we had so many young blokes in the team. There was an expectation that you'd look after yourself, but it didn't go as far as a drinking ban. I had a working bee on my garden in Burwood – Xav Ellis, Sewelly and a few of the boys came over and helped build a retaining wall and a new front fence. Then we sat down and had quite a few beers on the Saturday night, watching St Kilda beat Collingwood in the semi-final.

We trained well the next week and with obvious spirit and energy, belted St Kilda, and hey presto we were in the grand final against Geelong. The great thing was, there was no directive to shut off the world and hide. The message was: 'Enjoy the week.' There were certain commitments you had to meet for the media and the host broadcaster, but we were told to relax and enjoy it. That was simple – you don't know what you don't know, so we just took it all in.

I'd played in a grand final for Leongatha, and even though this was a bit different – 100 000 people at the ground and millions watching on TV for starters – the approach was genuinely to treat it as just another game.

Dewy was a big help. He was introduced into the leadership group with a few rounds to go, just so he could formally add his voice about what to expect. It wasn't as if he'd get up in front of everyone and say, 'We've gotta do this and this.' It was just little bits of advice, knowledge.

On the Monday night I went to the Brownlow Medal for the first time, taking Jordy Lewis as my date. We sat there drinking water, and as soon as Adam Cooney was announced the winner we were out of there.

The only other thing that stands out from that week was Clarko taking us out to dinner at Geppetto, an old Italian restaurant on Wellington Parade, just across from Yarra Park. After we'd eaten we walked through the park to the MCG, went inside and stood on the ground. Then we went down into the change rooms we'd be using that Saturday. 'Next time we're here, you could have the cup,' Clarko told us. I was 21 and hadn't really thought too much about what it all meant, but that got my mind racing.

Hawthorn hadn't played in a grand final for 17 years, so training was big, but everything through the week went smoothly. I think I went and got some beers for my place, because I had mates coming to stay and I knew we'd be back there at some stage no matter what happened.

We had the belief to win. We'd played Geelong six weeks earlier and they just got us, but our record against them was good. I don't think they wanted to play us – they were more comfortable facing St Kilda or the Bulldogs.

———

In the rooms before the game Clarko delivered his famous 'kill the shark' message. He'd drawn a shark on the white-board, not a bad one either, and told us that sharks couldn't swim backwards. 'If they get caught in a net, they die.' Our net was our 18-man zone, and we were ready to catch a big shark.

We started the game okay without getting a lot of ball in the forward line, but just watching things unfold I knew we were on. After the game a lot was made of the fact that 11 of Geelong's 23 behinds were rushed, but that wasn't a strategy, more a release that got the game back on our terms. Brent Guerra rushed a heap and Mark Williams even kicked one through from about 30 metres out – marked the ball, turned around and kicked it straight through their goals, which is obviously a point. It was different, and prompted a rule change the following year, but it worked for us that day.

When Cam Mooney famously missed a goal from 10 metres out after the half-time siren, Hodgey said to Birch and Browny, 'Don't go at him. Say nothing.' I've spoken to Moons about it since and he says he was just going to run straight through anyone who said anything, but Hodgey read the situation too well. He was mature by then, he knew what to do. Not doing or saying anything got under Mooney's skin even more.

It was a game of memorable moments; Cyril on the wing in the third quarter, beating Corey Enright and Max Rooke with repeat efforts to win the ball. I actually thought at the time Rooke didn't have prior opportunity and might get a free, but thankfully the umpire saw it differently. Then two minutes later 'Junior' swooped on one in front of Bud and kicked a goal.

I wasn't thinking about winning yet, because it was Geelong, but I was like, 'This is interesting, this is good.'

Dewy got one when Harry Taylor slipped over and dropped the ball. Michael Osborne gave it to Dewy, and he turned and off one step went *whack*! Goal.

Then Dewy and Willo created a goal out of nothing. I ran through the middle of the ground and kicked long to a two-on-two, the ball hit the deck, and it turned into three Geelong players against Willo and Dewy. Somehow they just handballed it back and forth until Willo got enough space to kick the goal. And I'm like, 'Shit, this is really bloody interesting! We're a good chance here!'

Geelong got one back, but then Dewy kicked another one, a snap from the pocket, and it felt like we'd broken them. They just didn't know what to do. When Bud kicked the first goal of the last quarter, the way he celebrated, we knew we were home. Mitch kicked one out of his arse on the left foot and Rick Ladson got one from a Tom Harley 50-metre penalty. Tom probably shouldn't have been out there after I'd tackled him just on half-time; his head hit Willo and he was knocked out.

I kicked our last goal and then shifted into defence on Mooney, so I was at the Punt Road end when the siren went. I know everyone has a different take on how that moment feels, but for me it was just relief. 'We've won!'

The next five or ten minutes, straight after the siren in a granny, is the best feeling you can have on a footy field.

I carried on too much on the lap of honour, yelling and screaming. I wouldn't do that now, but I was looking at supporters crying, seeing how much it meant to them.

And so the party started, and it didn't really stop for about five weeks. I hadn't realised how crook Lewy was – he ended up in hospital after the game. It was something viral, he couldn't even eat, but he battled to get up for the granny. He was supposed to go travelling with me and Dewy but had to stay home and recover.

We missed him, but not having him there didn't exactly slow us down. In three weeks we went to Hong Kong, London, Amsterdam, Paris, Barcelona and Croatia. Dewy was a good organiser – I'm much better at it now, but back then it was all Dewy, 'This is where we're going, this is what we're doing.'

Everywhere we went we bumped into Aussies who'd congratulate us and want to have a drink. We were staying mostly in backpackers, without a care in the world, and we were happy to raise a glass with anyone and everyone.

When we got home we went to Adelaide for the races and spent a bit of time in the pub Dewy part-owns. I soon learned that when you've won a premiership you're flavour of the month, and that means getting invited to lots of things – the races, other sporting events, anything that's on in Melbourne, really. I didn't need post-season surgery so I was keen to get going again and stuck into pre-season for 2009, but I was keen to celebrate too.

It turned out I wasn't the only one. When the team came back for training and they did the mandatory skinfold testing, Jack Russell reckoned if you added them all up there was an extra person's worth of fat. Clearly we'd enjoyed it too much.

The 'premiership hangover' tag is real – we'd won it and we just weren't as hungry the next year. In 2007 we'd been on the rise, in '08 we'd won it against expectation, and in '09 we thought we'd just keep going. It doesn't work like that.

A few things went against us, not least a heap of injuries. Willo did his knee in Perth and only played 13 games for 16 goals, Xav Ellis played 11, Stephen Gilham 10, Guerra 16, Clinton Young five, and Croady didn't play any after a broken foot had ended his granny a couple of minutes in.

Crawf had retired a month after we'd won the flag. I was back home in Leongatha playing a game of cricket when I found out. I was out in the middle, batting, when we lost a wicket and the next bloke came in and told me, 'Crawford's retired.' I was like, 'What?' We hadn't heard a thing.

By the start of the season other teams were on to the zone we used and came up with their own versions; St Kilda tweaked it and made it a defensive weapon. Whereas we'd been the number-one scoring team, they had a system that ground you down. We didn't adapt and just tried to do the same things we'd done the year before.

We didn't start 2009 disastrously, we were 6–5 after eleven games. When I kicked eight against Carlton in round six the media started speculating about whether I'd be the next bloke to kick 100 in a season, after Buddy had kicked 113 the year before.

But our 2009 never really got going. When we lost to Brisbane in Tassie in round 12 we dropped out of the eight and never got back in. We were so hellbent on the idea that players coming back into the side would fix things. 'If we can just get this bloke back, and this bloke, we'll be right. Croady's not far away . . .' The reality was Croady never got back on a footy ground again.

I hurt my knee against St Kilda in round 19 and when we played Essendon at the MCG in the last home-and-away round, needing a win to make the finals, Bud and I were both watching from the stands. He'd hit Ben Cousins a couple of weeks before and was suspended, so we sat there and watched Matty Lloyd clean up Sewelly – all hell broke loose.

After we lost there was a sense of, 'Thank Christ that's over, now we can move on.' But we were still caught in a mentality that all we needed was to get all our players back. Everyone else had been working to get ahead of the game and we stayed where we were. Our training, our running program, our game plan – they were all exactly the same as 2008. It was as if we were thinking, 'All the cattle's back, we've got the talent, we'll play exactly the same way.' We started 2010 1–6.

It's been thrown around since and I reckon it's right – Mitch's tackle on Shane Tuck in the dying stages against Richmond saved Clarko's job. If we'd lost that game in round eight, Kennett probably would have sacked him on the Monday. Instead things started to turn around, with some old-school thinking at the heart of it.

At 1–6, after a narrow loss to West Coast at Subiaco, we were ready to try anything. So we settled on having beers after games. We flew home from Perth on the Saturday night and on the Sunday everyone met at the Geebung and got on it. The next week we beat Richmond, so we did it again. The next week Carlton, on it again. Sydney – let's go again. We won seven in a row.

Jack Russell masterminded the whole thing, but Clarko was right in on it. It worked and we just let it roll. We'd finish the game, get changed and go for beers. Win, have beers. Win again, more beers. By the time we thrashed Adelaide down in Tassie to get back to 6–6 and into the eight, Clarko was challenging us to make the finals. He used Kingston Town as an analogy; the thoroughbred won his third Cox Plate in a row even after the race caller Bill Collins, 400 from home, said he couldn't win it. Clarko always told us that if we could get to the finals, we could do some damage.

But I think we knew where we were at: we just weren't good enough. We did make the eight, and were within three goals of Freo in the elimination final heading towards time-on in the last, but Clarko reckons he knew we were shot at three-quarter time.

On the following Wednesday we had a post-season meeting where as a group we went through a heap of stats and identified what we'd done well and what we hadn't. Clarko had a go at me and Bud, said something like, 'We're paying you the big bucks and you're missing goals.' I'd kicked 53.46 for the season, Bud had kicked 64.42. He nailed us, gave us the challenge that we needed, and we had to cop it because he was right. We should have kicked more goals, simple as that.

Overall, 2009 and '10 were bad years. We were still playing okay footy, better than okay at times, but in reality we were just making up the numbers. Those years were the kick in the butt Clarko needed too – I think he realised he'd got a jump on the competition in 2008 but since then everyone had caught up and some had overtaken us.

We always have the Crimmins Medal, our best and fairest night, on the Saturday after the grand final weekend. In 2010 Collingwood and St Kilda played a drawn granny, so the club arranged for us all to go to the replay before jumping on a bus to the best and fairest. Sitting there in the hot sun, watching someone else win the premiership, competitiveness kicked in. I'd been there and I desperately wanted to get back there.

Our list was developing – that year Josh Gibson had come across from North Melbourne to shore up our backline, Shaun Burgoyne arrived from Port, players like Liam Shiels and Luke Breust were becoming really important, Ben Stratton, Matt Suckling and Taylor Duryea were drafted, and in 2011 Paul Puopolo and Isaac Smith were recruited – mature-aged and ready to go – and David Hale also joined us from North.

Just as important was another tweak to the way we played. With David Rath and the other coaches, Clarko worked on the premise that we'd put together a group of players who were very good with the ball – we could hit targets and maintain possession. It's pretty simple: when you've got the footy, they don't.

Midway through 2011, I ruptured my Achilles. It was my first serious injury.

At the start of that year we had a stretch that was like some sort of ruckman's curse – Stephen Gilham did his knee, David Hale had back and knee issues, Brent Renouf did a hamstring, and Max Bailey was still working his way back from a reconstruction. So starting with the St Kilda game in round eight, I was our number-one ruckman.

I enjoyed it right away. I'd never played in the ruck before, except maybe a little bit as a junior because every big kid gets a crack there in the juniors. From a team aspect, it was another example of the versatility we were starting to see – having people who could play multiple positions.

The rule change that meant the ruckmen had to start in the circle for centre bounces was made for me, because I could just go – *one, two, three, up*. I could jump off either leg, which was a basketball thing. Around the ground it was about trying to be another midfielder – if it hits the ground, back yourself to be better than them. Help your mids out as much as you can, then if you get the ball you know you can use it better than most ruckmen.

I was playing good footy but it wasn't about kicking goals – I was laying tackles, putting on blocks and shepherds, winning contested ball in tight. There was a pressure rating at the club and before long I was leading it by heaps. I only kicked 16 goals in the 11 games before I got hurt, but I was loving playing another role. As a forward it can be a graveyard down there when you're not winning games.

I'd had a sore Achilles for a few weeks before it eventually went. In the off-season I'd played a bit of basketball with mates, just going for a weekly shootaround. I didn't play as much basketball towards the end of my career, but even through the hat-trick years, on our day off I'd go to a court with some mates and shoot hoops – that was my weekly release. In hindsight, going from hard courts to softer grounds probably didn't help my Achilles in 2011.

On the Tuesday before the Geelong game in round 12 I had a scan done and it looked fine despite the soreness. So much of my game was spring and agility, which obviously impacts your legs, but I was still only 24 and had youth on my side.

There was a boundary throw-in and as I ran to contest it, it felt like I'd been kicked in the back of the leg. James Kelly had been behind me last time I'd looked and initially I thought it must have been him. But when I turned around, he wasn't there. I'd heard the stories about how doing your Achilles feels like you've been kicked from behind, and you want to turn around and spray whoever did it. I hailed the cab straight away, grimacing and thinking, 'Yeah, I know what I've done.'

I had great support from all sorts of places following the surgery. Chris Fagan had a connection with Russell Robertson from their time together at Melbourne, and he got in touch and told me what he did to get over the same injury a few years earlier. I caught up with netballer Sharelle McMahon a couple of times and talked about what she'd done. David Beckham had just done his, playing for AC Milan, and I read as much as I could about his recovery; it was the only time I looked at Google for an injury.

Stephen Gilham had done his knee the year before and travelled to Bolton soccer club as part of his recovery, so I asked the club if I could go to Barcelona, where my mate Joe Ingles was playing basketball, and continue my rehab over there. They were up for it, but then the wound from my surgery got infected. I'd rub it and pus would come out of the little holes where the stitches were. I was like, 'That's not right.'

I spent a week in Box Hill hospital, where they did a second surgery to put a PICC line in. I never got an answer as to why it got infected, just unlucky I guess – maybe tape cuts, maybe a blade of grass was in there. I woke up from surgery in plaster, and that stayed on for eight weeks. So I'd done my Achilles in June and was still on crutches during the finals, but it was a quick recovery after that second surgery and I was back running by December.

The boys made the preliminary final and I watched from the coaches' box, I reckon for the first time as a player. I'm nervous as all buggery watching. We had lost to Geelong, beaten Sydney, then got Collingwood in the prelim. I was sitting there thinking, 'If they win they're gunna play in a granny, and I'm not playing.' I wanted them to win, because I love the boys, but it's a bugger of a thing watching. You feel like you can't win either way.

The last three minutes of that game go for half an hour in my mind. I was on crutches, but they'd put a heel in the plaster like I had a mini stiletto on; I was pacing the back of the box like a caged animal. Bud kicked a goal that put us four points up – unreal. Then Luke Ball kicked one, the siren went, and we'd missed out.

Not playing, not being able to do anything to help, that probably hurt as much as any of the 105 losses I was actually part of. Thankfully, better times were just around the corner.

CHAPTER 6
Backyard Legends

There's a common denominator in the greatest era in Hawthorn history that I'm happy to take credit for: those three premierships all started and ended at my place.

It began the morning after we lost the 2012 grand final to Sydney, with beers and vodka, and bacon and egg muffins. It was a group that stuck together, determined not to have that much regret about a game of footy ever again. We never did either, and those post-grand-final Sunday mornings the next three years were some of the best hours I've had in footy.

The ritual started simply enough. Sars and I live not far from the spot where the bus would pick up the players on the Sunday afternoon after each grand final we played in. That would take us to Glenferrie Oval, to be presented to the fans, and from there we'd head to a pub somewhere and end up wherever we ended up. But before all that, it always started at my place. In grand final week I got used to buying beers for that Sunday session. Heading to our house those mornings became such a routine we kept it going even when we didn't make the granny – following whatever happened to be our last game of the season, the next morning the boys would all roll around to Roughy's.

We live in a dead-end street with great neighbours. Over time they got involved too – there'd be a barbecue cooking out the front of someone's house and local kids handed sausages in bread to the boys as they went past. Sometimes there would even be someone dishing out Beroccas, which was good thinking.

Shane Crawford turned up each year to do a quick live-cross for *The Sunday Footy Show* and would always thank us for our time with another couple of slabs. One year there was a chopper flying overhead trying to get footage of the boys; they should have been there the year that Stratts, who lived nearby, rode a bike up and down the street wearing a wetsuit.

But the best part was that when we were at my place it was just us, sitting out the back, away from the world, sharing the spoils of victory.

When we lost the grand final to Sydney in 2012 we had been hot favourites. Ask Clarko or any of the boys and they'll say we played some of our best footy as a group that season. We just couldn't get it done when it mattered most. All year we had an edge about us; we won 13 out of 14 going into the granny, including the game against North in Tassie when Bud kicked 13 goals. We were playing great footy and belting teams – rock up, win, repeat.

We got to the finals and only just beat Collingwood, without playing great, then got past Adelaide in the prelim by five points. We didn't realise how stuffed we were as a group. Sometimes you get to the end of the year and you're just cooked. A lot of us were feeling like that, and a few of us – me included – didn't have a great game. We were expected to win, played like absolute crap, and lost by 10 points. We won pretty much every stat, just not on the scoreboard. Hats off to the Swans – as we knew from 2008, there's nothing like winning a grand final when you're not expected to.

That's the game that hurts more than any other in my career, simply because it's the only grand final we lost. I don't want to feel that again. At the time, it felt like the worst thing in the world had just happened. But we got a reminder of perspective straight away, which was some-thing Clarko was so good at. We trudged off the MCG and down into the rooms, all miserable and feeling sorry for ourselves, and he spoke about Jill Meagher. She was an Irish woman who was living in Melbourne working at the ABC and she'd gone missing on the previous Saturday night. They had found her body on grand-final eve. Clarko basically just said that even though it's a grand final and you're feeling like crap because you lost, there's a lot worse things going on in the world.

Then Jason Dunstall came in and sat with us. I can't remember what he was saying, but he just made us laugh. The mood picked up pretty quick. We went to a supporters' function at Crown and for some reason we just all ended up back at my place after that. Everyone drifted home in the early hours, but I told them all to come back on Sunday morning and we'd go to Glenferrie from my place. Bring some beers, whatever – at least we'd be together.

A few came around by themselves, then we rang some-one else, and someone else, and soon pretty much the whole side was there – by 10 in the morning. It was decided that the youngest bloke would have to get bacon and egg muf-fins from Maccas, another ritual that stuck. We didn't have anyone in their teens that year, so Jack Gunston copped Maccas duty as our only 20-year-old. There was nothing exceptional to what we were doing – a group of footballers sitting around drinking at the end of a long season – but it was important. We hadn't cracked the shits and splintered, we stayed together.

People always ask me, 'How did you win three flags in a row? Why were those teams so good?' Honestly, I could pick it apart forever and not come up with an answer.

Like every club we tried different things behind closed doors in a bid to get an edge. Through 2012 and into that stretch we had a Navy Seals theme driving the group. It was all about being mentally tough. Clarko had us doing certain challenges designed to get into our heads and make us believe that footy games aren't as hard as they can seem in the moment.

One was underwater swimming. The pool in the base-ment at Waverley is 25 metres long and you had to get in, swim to the other end underwater, get out, walk back to the other end and do it again – ten times. Some boys

(Shauny Burgoyne and Liam Shiels for two) just couldn't do it; swimming isn't everyone's bag, especially swimming underwater. But what are you going to do? You can't force someone – we might still be there now, or we might have lost someone. But it made us understand that when it got tough in games – feeling like we were losing to Geelong every time, for example – don't fall back into that mindset of, 'Here we go again.' Work your way through it, understand it's not as tough as it seems.

Somewhere in the week after the 2012 grand final loss we reviewed the game, which was hard. We saw so many little things that we knew we could have done better, and if we had, we'd have won. We realised how hard it was just to get there, let alone win it, and then it got thrown away just because we played like crap.

A key change in mindset was that we realised we had been playing for ourselves. We went on a pre-season camp over that summer to Mooloolaba, run by Ray McLean and his Leading Teams program. Ray asked us what we were doing well. By that point I was part of the leadership group, and we said we couldn't put our hands up and say we'd been doing the right thing, because it had been a matter of, 'Do as I say, not as I do.'

Luke Lowden had been at the club for four years but was yet to play a senior game; he was still only 21. He put up his hand up and said, 'We've heard this all before boys – what's going to change?' Hearing a young kid say that, it had an impact. We knew we had to be harder on ourselves.

Certain things get swept under the carpet when you're winning. The key thing that happened after the 2012 loss was that we didn't point the finger at anyone else – the playing group, and the leaders in that group, took responsibility. We said it was our fault, not anybody else's. The leadership group was Hodge, Mitchell, Lewis, Gibson, Sewell and myself – we made it clear we needed to be hard on each other and from there it could filter down to the rest of the playing group. Other than Sewelly retiring at the end of 2014, that leadership group stayed the same for the next five years. It was a beautiful group that bonded so well.

The 2013 season started with another loss to Geelong, by seven points after we'd led by five goals. That took their winning streak over us – dubbed the 'Kennett Curse' – into double figures. We lost to them again later in the year and had an off day against Richmond in round 19, but won every other game for the season.

We caught Geelong again in the preliminary final, and were 20 points down at three-quarter time. Andrew Mackie, who was one of the better lippers I played against, was quick to tell us, 'We've got you blokes again.'

Somehow, the thing that had happened seemingly every other time we played them since 2008 just flipped. We got our noses in front through a Shauny Burgoyne goal and with five minutes to go they were trying to kick torps up the middle of the ground. Under pressure, they went away from everything that had worked for them, which is what we'd been doing whenever we played them.

The Kennett Curse, for anyone who needs reminding, had become a thing after our president, Jeff Kennett, said something several years earlier about their players not having the psychological drive that our blokes did. He added that Hawthorn beat Geelong when it mattered. When we were underdogs in the 2008 grand final and knocked them off, their players apparently made a pact never to lose to us again, which Paul Chapman later spoke about in an interview. The next 11 times we played them, they won.

They were incredible games of footy – the smallest crowd for any of them was 63 476. Other than two meetings in 2011, which they won by 19 and 31 points, every other game was decided by less than two goals. There were crazy momentum swings within games. A couple of times we lost games that we'd led by five goals. In 2012, we got in front after trailing by 51 points, only to lose to a Tom Hawkins kick after the final siren. Jimmy Bartel kicked a point for them to win after the siren in my one-hundredth game in 2009, after we'd led by 28.

Through that period, it really was like there was every other game and then there were Geelong games. We just knew each other so well, knew how the other was going to play. The draw would come out and you'd scan down to see when you were playing Geelong.

In-house, the reviews of those losses were hard, because the coaches would think we'd learnt from the loss and then we'd lose the next one anyway. But it wasn't just us – they were bloody good. I've always said how lucky I am to have played with so many Hall-of-Famers at Hawthorn, but that Geelong team had a few too: Selwood, Ablett, Bartel, Johnson, Ling, Enright, Scarlett. There were a few decent players on the next rung as well.

All of us would say the same thing – they were great games to play in, it's just that we kept losing them. It wasn't that we were playing shit footy, they really were awesome games to watch and be a part of. If you see one of them on *Footy Flashbacks*, you'll sit down in front of it for sure. For that Hawkins game, there were maybe 15 Hall-of-Famers on the ground at once. That just doesn't happen anymore, and I don't reckon it'll happen again.

Why did they keep winning them? It's something you can't explain, I'm just very grateful that I got to play against maybe the second-best team ever. I played Geelong 25 times for nine wins, and I played in Hawthorn's greatest era ever; they were a seriously good team.

On the field, I always felt like if I could have a joke and muck around with someone, get them off guard a bit, that was how I was going to beat my opponent. I'd get Harry Taylor most times, he was a good fella, we'd talk. I don't think the Geelong boys were arrogant. They didn't like Lewy, but there was generally a healthy respect – as distinct from the absolute hatred some players have for certain teams, like Dermott Brereton and Essendon.

From the outside it was known as the Kennett Curse, but inside the club it was never spoken about. It was just about trying to beat Geelong, and eventually we did. Before that 2013 preliminary final, Clarko got a kilo bag of flour, stabbed a hole in it with a pen, poured it in a line on the floor, and said that anyone who stepped over it had to be ready to give everything they had to get the job done. It was a nice visual trick, and we were all on board.

The five-point margin over Geelong was the same as we'd beaten Adelaide by in the prelim the year before. The following year we beat Port by three points in the same game; nothing like a close prelim to keep you on your toes. There's a reason people reckon they're harder to win than grand finals.

After beating Geelong in 2013, it was us against the Dockers in their first ever grand final. Everyone was talking about the pressure they put on you, about how manic they were. Chris Fagan, who was a legend for just going quietly about his business as one of Clarko's lieutenants, came in during the week and said, 'I've done all the stats on pressure boys – us and Fremantle – and we're still ahead.' So we just sat back and listened to everyone talk Freo up. For a lot of us it was our third grand final; we knew how to enjoy the week and what to do at the end of it.

The story of coming out after half-time against the Dockers has been told. We were 23 points ahead, Hodgey got us in his captain's huddle, and he said, 'I hope they kick the first four goals.' He stuffed up – he meant to say something about how we'd been challenged before, let's see if they can challenge us again. But that's how it came out, and it almost came true! They kicked four of the first five, I got the other one, and suddenly it was back to three points.

It still felt like we were in control, and when Smith, Breust and Hill goaled in the first 12 minutes of the last quarter we were five goals clear and as good as home. The 10 minutes after the siren in a winning grand final – having that feeling again, five years after we'd done it as young blokes, was somehow even sweeter. You get older, things just mean more to you.

Buddy Franklin still hadn't told us where he was going, or even if he was going to leave Hawthorn, but the story of him most likely going to GWS on a record deal was so loud you almost had to believe it. But on the Sunday morning after the granny, he was sitting on my couch playing PlayStation with my brother Cam, drinking beers.

There was Gibbo, Stratts, Gunners and me to start with, and the phone calls started again. Brad Hill brought the Maccas (he was the youngest that year), and then off we went.

On the Tuesday Bud came to my place again and told Jordy and me he was going to Sydney. We hadn't seen that coming.

In 2014 we lost five games, but I was suspended for two of them, which meant I only played in six losses in two years. Even so, that season felt different, if only because we went through a fair bit of shit along the way and still got there in the end. Gibbo hurt his pec against Sydney and missed a lot of footy, Mitch did a bad hammy, Cyril did a hammy late.

Clarko got Guillain-Barré syndrome and was really crook in hospital; he was unable to coach for five weeks.

It was in Adelaide in May, for the Port game (which I missed with suspension), that he told people he couldn't feel his feet, which was pretty scary. Brendon Bolton stepped in as coach and we won all five games that Clarko missed. Bolts had his own spin on things, but he still pushed the same mantras as Clarko. It was another example of how everyone was on the same page when it came to how we played.

Every time a change had to be made, someone just stepped into the hole. Lewis played midfield and had his best year, winning the best and fairest. Ryan Schoenmakers came back from a knee and played, Kyle Cheney stepped up in defence, Brian Lake got better and better. We never relied on one bloke. Bud had left, but I kicked 75 goals, which was three more than I'd kicked the year before. Gunners kicked more goals, Punky kicked more and was All Australian for the first time. It just didn't matter – we had such a good system, everyone knew what to do. The line you often heard was, 'Lose a soldier, replace a soldier.' Or, 'Squads win premierships, not players.' Same thing.

Grand final week was just another example. Joffa Simpkin, who'd stood up whenever he was called on, got dropped for Cyril Rioli, who had played three quarters of the VFL granny for Box Hill the previous Sunday and was right to go after his hammy. Jonathon Ceglar played in the prelim for us but was replaced by Ben McEvoy, who had also been named for the VFL grand final but was withdrawn late to keep him fresh.

That meant Brad Sewell – who was dropped after playing his two-hundredth game in the qualifying final win over Geelong – couldn't force his way back. Just to keep the tension up, Sewelly was still a chance to replace Jordan Lewis, who had been subbed out of the prelim with a corked thigh. But Lewy got up, and Will Langford held his spot too, kicking three goals in the best day of his 72-game career. Sewelly missing out was hard – for him, for Clarko, for everyone. But that was how it was. Squads win premierships.

Sydney were clear favourites, with Bud in their colours and playing such good footy. Like us after losing in 2012, their blokes will say that group played their best footy in 2014, but on the biggest stage they just didn't turn up. It was over by half-time. I had a good finals series, and realised that everything they say about the pride you get from performing in big games is true.

And so, again, Sunday morning we were back at my place.

There was never a spoken rule about who from the playing group would be there, but most of the boys who hadn't actually played in the grand final would give those of us who had played in the game a few hours to ourselves. Some would come, and they'd be welcomed, but others felt a bit awkward and stayed away. In 2014 Joffa Simpkin – who'd won a premiership the year before, and played 18 games for the season before he was dropped after the prelim – came along and made the day. Every time you turned around he'd be into Hodgey, who'd won his second Norm Smith Medal the day before, about how the

Swans had put it on a platter for him like it was a pie on a plate. It went on and on, until Hodgey eventually took his sunnies off and said, 'That'll be enough, Joff.' And that was enough.

We'd won two flags, but all everyone wanted was to win another one with this group. People took pay cuts to stay together. We would hear about blokes at other teams being on a million bucks a season, but we didn't have anyone on that sort of money. Clarko would always say, 'You'll make it up at the back end, with the careers it'll open up for you.'

There was never any arrogance in the group – that was one of Clarko's biggest strengths. If anyone did fall out of line, they were pulled back into shape straight away because of the people we had in the change rooms. And Clarko was able to keep us on edge, no matter who we were playing. We'd be playing Gold Coast or GWS for the first time and he'd say things like, 'Scar 'em, boys.' It was all about leaving such a deep impression on teams that if the time came that we weren't as good anymore, they'd still remember us that way. Games we might have gone into thinking we'd win no matter what, he'd have us so fired up we'd win by 80 points. You were almost asking yourself, 'What are we doing getting worked up for this?' But that was his strength.

Going into 2015 there was a sense of invincibility, but not arrogance. We'd just won back-to-back flags and only lost eight games in two years (eleven in three years if you count 2012, when we only lost three, including the granny). After we beat Geelong in round one – smashed them by ten goals – all the pundits were saying, 'Give them the flag now, it's a three-peat, it's all over.'

Next thing, we were 4–4. We'd win one, lose the next, win one, lose the next. They weren't saying 'give it to them now' anymore.

We'd topped up by recruiting James Frawley from Melbourne, and Ryan Schoenmakers came back in and played good footy; ultimately, those two in for Matt Spangher and Will Langford were the only changes to the previous year's premiership side. It wasn't a premiership hangover, we just weren't playing good footy.

But as it turned out, losing games was a good thing, because it took the spotlight off us. After a wobbly start, we still finished top four.

In the first week of the finals we went over to Perth and got done convincingly by West Coast. When we got back to Melbourne, people were writing Hodgey off, saying he was old and slow. The footy world had already had him in in their sights, ready to pull the trigger. In the lead-up to the finals he'd been suspended for bumping Port Adelaide's Chad Wingard into the goal post at Docklands; while he was sitting out he went around to a mate's place one night and had three beers while they were playing cards, thought he was right to drive home, got stopped, and blew just over the limit. He shouldn't have done it – he knew it, everyone knew it.

After West Coast, Hodgey's response to the criticism of his on-field performance was to boot two in the first quarter against Adelaide at the MCG and four for the game. We brained them.

We went across to Freo for the prelim and were in front for most of the night, only for them to come charging back, bringing themselves to within nine early in the fourth quarter. The Subiaco crowd was going off. Enter Cyril, who bobbed up like a sprinkler head after one of their blokes tried to switch it in the backline and kicked a goal. That broke them.

We weren't favourites going into the granny. West Coast had beaten us two weeks before and everyone was talking about them, how Adam Simpson's 'Eagles' Web' – their defensive set-up that could apparently control our forwards – was going to bring us undone.

It was a hot grand final day, 30 degrees, and everything just went right. It was as good as over at half-time. When I kicked one a couple of minutes into the last quarter, we were 55 points up. To spend the last 25 minutes of a grand final knowing you're going to win – there can't be many better feelings in footy.

One reason we were so good is that Clarko was able to drive us. But the other was we just wanted to win. We'd experienced what a loss was like in 2012 and we didn't want to be back there again. The chance to win back-to-back, the second Hawthorn team to do it, first time to three-peat, that motivated us too. We wanted to make the most of our chance. We were humble in the way we did it, but you can be humble and still driven.

There were always blokes who hadn't won a premiership, and when you've won one yourself you want your teammates to have that feeling too. Spangher in 2014 – he'd been part of squads at West Coast (2006) and Sydney (2012) when they won flags, but hadn't played in a premiership. Pup Shiels is best mates with Schoey – he had two premiership medals going into 2015 and Schoey didn't have any.

In 2008, on grand final eve, Stuey Dew had sent me a picture of his 2004 premiership medal that he'd won with Port Adelaide, dangling the carrot and saying 'let's do this'. So the night before the 2013 grand final I did that in a message to Gunners, the next year I did it with Spang, and the night before 2015 I sent a picture of my three medals to Chip Frawley and said, 'Let's just get you one of these tomorrow.'

We didn't have many major injuries that year, so we played a lot of footy together. At any given time, we knew exactly what each bloke was going to do, which way he'd roll with the footy, that sort of thing. You try and teach players now to know their teammates. If they're a left-footer they'll roll one way, right-footer the other way. So if Gunners had the ball, I knew where not to lead, knew how he'd turn to open up his right foot. It was art, really. We'd just watch the play unfold and know what was happening next. Blokes didn't even have to look half the time.

If that's the best era Hawthorn ever has, you'll only have to look at the teams we were putting out to understand why. At times in 2015 we had eleven blokes running around who'd already been All Australians: Birchall, Breust, Burgoyne, Frawley, Gibson, Hodge, Lake, Lewis, Mitchell, Rioli, Roughead. Gunston became one soon after. I'm a stats man; that type of thing is cool to look back on.

I'm happy, too, to think those three premierships in a row were the three best years of my career from a performance perspective. I hardly missed a game and consistently kicked goals. Only Shauny Burgoyne and Luke Breust played more games for the club over that time.

It was the best period of my career, but it's almost easy to do that when you look around you and see the blokes you're playing with. It's arguably the best team ever. Some of them will be AFL Hall of Fame Legends – Hodge, Mitchell, Franklin, Burgoyne, Clarkson. They won't just be Hawthorn legends, they'll be legends of the game.

To stand in that forward line, the connection we had – there was a reason we kicked all those goals. Our approach was 'give up a good shot to take a great shot', and I benefitted from that as much as anyone. Sometimes it was your turn to play a sacrificial role, to take your man away from the ball. Other times it was up to me – I was a leader, the main guy to go to when shit was going wrong, and the ball was coming to me regardless. The old saying was, 'You'll get your lick of the ice cream.' People would say to you the one thing they noticed about our team was, 'Jeez, you share the ball.' It didn't matter who kicked the goals.

Three of us kicked at least 50 goals, which was huge credit to the guys we were leading to, and seven blokes kicked 20-plus, which is an amazing spread. In 2008 us forwards had been excited to have Stuey Dew join the club, because we all knew what a great kick he was. By 2015 there were so many blokes you were happy to see heading your way with the ball in their hands: Mitchell, Lewis, Hodge, Suckling, Birchall, Hill, Smith, Shiels, and even Breust, Gunners and Poppy in the forward line.

By the Sunday back at my place in 2015 most of us had matured – we didn't go too hard, because we knew there were long days and weeks of celebrating ahead of us. We took the bus to Glenferrie and greeted the fans, then me, Lewy and Stratto went back to my place, got changed, and headed down to Circa in St Kilda.

On the way we dropped into a tattooist on Fitzroy Street. Stratto and I walked in and this pommy bloke added the '15 to the tatts we already had (mine's a big hawk holding the premiership cup in its talons). The tattooist had no idea who we were, which was pretty funny. He was asking why we were getting the work done, and meanwhile there was a bloke sitting there waiting, reading the Sunday paper, with all of us celebrating on the front page.

Seven years had passed since I got the original tattoo done. That day, the tattooist had asked if I wanted the '08 put on the cup itself. I had a look, could see there was only room for one year, so I said, 'Nah – just in case we win more.'

You never know what's around the corner, which I was about to find out in the most frightening way.

CHAPTER 7
'It's Melanoma'

I wasn't a beach kid. I'd go for a swim on basketball camp in Coffs Harbour or Port Macquarie, and every now and then we might make the 20-minute drive from Leongatha to Inverloch if it was really hot. I had mates who would tan up and have really dark skin by the end of summer, but that clearly wasn't my go. I slip-slop-slapped, got burnt a couple of times, as you do, peeled, got used to wearing a rashie.

When I arrived at Hawthorn there were blokes like Shane Crawford, Ben Dixon and Trent Croad who had good rigs, nice tans, and spent more time with their tops off than on. I knew there was no need for me to be doing that. I never even trained in singlets, always t-shirts. I never took my top off because I knew I'd be burnt in no time.

Our club doctor through my first seven or eight years was Pete Baquie, who came from down my way at Foster; he actually delivered a few mates of mine. I'd regularly ask Pete to check if I had any bad spots and he'd say, 'You've got a couple, I'll take them out and send them away.' One day he took three or four in one hit – little jab of local, cut them out with a scalpel, one or two stitches and on your way. I'd train the next day and the stitches would pop out because I was running, sweating and tensing, but it was never a big deal.

I can still find the small scars on my arms where Pete cut little dark moles out. I'd come in after training two days later and he'd say, 'All good Rough, you're fine.' Between them being cut out and Pete telling me I was okay, I wouldn't give a single thought to the possibility that something might be wrong. I didn't have a clue how bad skin cancer was because I just didn't think about it. There were still solariums on Glenferrie Road in those days. It was a different time.

Towards the middle of 2015, I noticed what I thought was a blister on the right side of my bottom lip. I showed Sarah and she thought the same as me – that it would be gone in a couple of days. But it didn't go away, and I was always knocking it when I was drying myself after a shower and making it bleed. This went on for close to two months, which is clearly way too long. Eventually I asked the docs at the club to have a look at it. They didn't seem too alarmed, but referred me to a skin specialist named Jeremy Banky to go and have it checked.

On the Thursday before we played Essendon in round 13, at the end of June, I went to Jeremy's rooms in Elsternwick. He did what's called a punch biopsy, where they put a needle into the spot and it acts a bit like an apple corer, penetrating the skin, punching down and taking a tissue sample on the way back out. I remember him saying there were three types of skin cancer, with melanoma being the most serious, 'but I don't think it's melanoma'. He said he'd call when he got the results and off I went without giving it another thought.

I played as a midfielder against Essendon at the MCG that Saturday afternoon and had a good day. We were tracking well in pursuit of a third premiership in a row and my form was good.

The following Tuesday Jordy Lewis asked me to give him a lift to Berwick, where he had to pick up a car. While I was driving to his place, I missed a call from Jeremy Banky, and I only checked the message once I'd met up with Jordy. Jeremy said, 'I need you to call me as soon as you get this – it's melanoma.'

Maybe trying to calm the mood, Jord's response was, 'Uh! At least now I know someone who's had cancer!' I looked at him and laughed too; as icebreakers go it wasn't bad! Neither of us took in what the news actually meant.

Our club doctor, Michael Makdissi, had seen the referral by this stage. He rang me with urgency in his voice. 'Rough, you need to come in.'

He told me I'd have to get it cut out and my reaction was to do a mental calculation of how to fit that around footy. I was thinking, 'I'll play against Collingwood this Friday night, go in Saturday or Sunday, have it cut out, and I should be right for Freo the following Sunday.' I could tell by the look on Doc's face that wasn't what was going to happen. He told me he'd already lined up a plastic surgeon, that I'd be getting it done as soon as possible.

'What, next Monday?' I asked.

'No, Rough. Tomorrow.'

We went upstairs and told Clarko and Fages, and that was when it started to sink in that it could be serious. With footy injuries, you pretty much know what's going to happen, how long you're going to be out for. This was different.

The next day I went into Royal Melbourne Hospital and met the man who would be my plastic surgeon, Anand Ramakrishnan. Anand is a ripper, an Indian doctor who's married to an Australian woman with whom he's had three children. He'd gone to medical school with Doc Makdissi, so there was a connection there. I felt comfortable with him straight away, which was handy given that he was about to cut out a big chunk of my lip.

They needed to work out if the cancer had gone into the lymph nodes, which meant while I was under for Anand's procedure, a different surgeon would also be going in through my neck. The punch biopsy had shown it was melanoma, but they still had to work out how much to cut away. I told Anand I'd shave my beard off, but he said he'd keep it so he could use it almost like a framework.

To work out how much to cut away, some other doctor put a needle either side of the spot on my lip and inserted a dye, which would reveal where they needed to cut the lymph nodes out. They reckon there's three places you don't want to have a needle stuck into you: your lips, the tips of your fingers, and you can work the other one out. They used a bit of frozen spray to try to numb my lip, then the needle just went *bang*! You've never felt anything like it – and then he took it out and stuck another in on the other side!

I had that test done on Thursday, 3 July, at Royal Melbourne, then that same night I went to Epworth Freemasons, near Fitzroy Gardens, to have the melanoma cut out. I'll never forget lying there, about to be put under for the surgery, and Anand was mucking around with something in the corner. I asked him what he was doing and he said, 'Just putting together my playlist.' Every time I've been for surgery since I've looked over and that's what they're doing – they're not looking at your scans or whatever, they're working out what music they're going to play while they're cutting bits off you.

They basically took a quarter of my bottom lip – it was 12 centimetres when they started and they cut out 3. I woke up that evening after surgery, grabbed a mirror and had a look at myself and thought, 'Oooh, jeez, that's not great.'

Then the doctor who'd gone in through my neck to check the lymph nodes came in. I hadn't even met him before the surgery. He said something like, 'That cut on your neck with the stitches, I did that.' It was a strange way to meet someone.

Cam brought Sars in to collect me. She burst into tears when she saw me. I don't think she realised it was going to be that bad – stitches everywhere, a quarter of my lip gone.

You never have to look too far for perspective though. The next morning, we woke to the news that Adelaide coach Phil Walsh had been stabbed at his home in the middle of the night. His son had been arrested and was about to be charged with his murder. A sore lip didn't seem like such a big deal.

For a couple of days I just lay in bed, sore and drugged. I couldn't eat, could only drink through a straw poked in through the corner of my mouth. But by Tuesday or Wednesday I was back out at the club, running around and feeling fine.

I had my first PET scan to see if the cancer was anywhere else in my body, and it came back all clear. I met Dr Grant McArthur for the first time and we discussed radiation therapy. That would most likely mean not playing again for the rest of the year – there would be burning, and the location on my face wasn't ideal – but thankfully they decided it wasn't necessary. I didn't need chemo either; didn't need any further treatment at all. It was basically just a matter of getting on with it.

I felt good and wanted to play the Fremantle game in Tassie that Sunday, but Doc Makdissi held me back. I went down there with the boys anyway and watched from the coaches' box. It was the game when Sam Mitchell and Nat Fyfe clashed as Mitch was putting on a block, and he was fined $1500 for raising his knee.

Watching just made me want to play all the more, and the next week the docs ticked everything off and I was right to go. I asked Anand if my lip would split if I got hit and he was confident it wouldn't. I played with gauze covering from my lip down to my chin, just in case. It wasn't a great look, but by then I was beyond caring. I was just happy to be in the clear.

My first game back was up in Sydney, at the Olympic stadium, and I had a good night. I'd missed a couple of weeks but my form had held up, which was a relief. At one stage I kicked a goal from the goal square and got pushed by a Swans defender, sending me sliding across the grass, into the gutter and over some bolts that had been left exposed when the fence was moved back after an NRL game. They ripped my jumper down the bottom of my back and scratched me up pretty badly, which caused a bit of a stir about player safety. But as Clarko said after the game, I'd overcome bigger challenges in the previous few weeks.

It was a strange situation – everyone knew what I'd just been through was serious, potentially life-threatening, but there was still a bit of lightheartedness in how it was discussed. I was interviewed straight after the game and the TV blokes had a laugh about my good looks taking a pounding. People weren't thinking 'this is something that kills', and I can't blame them, because I wasn't either. That was foolish and naive.

After the PET scan showed nothing untoward the doctors had told me the chance of a recurrence was low. Just to be safe, we increased the scans from every six months to every three. Other than that it wasn't talked about. We just got on with life.

For a while I had that annoying sensation you get when you've got a cold sore and your tongue is constantly drawn to the spot. Even now my bottom lip is still numb to a degree – not completely, it just feels different in the way scar tissue does. Anand advised me to get an electric tooth-brush and rub it over the scarred area to fire up the nerve endings, which I did for two or three months, but I stopped because it didn't feel like I was getting much of a result. Maybe if I'd stuck at it I'd have more feeling there now, but it doesn't bother me. I look at photos from before and after and I don't look vastly different anyway, just a bit more ruggedly handsome!

Plenty of people were going through tough times, some of them unimaginable. The night after we beat Geelong in round 20, Brett Ratten, an assistant coach at the footy club, lost his 16-year-old son Cooper, who was a passenger in a car that rolled in the Yarra Valley. Phil Walsh was dead. A year earlier, Clarko had been hospitalised with Guillain-Barré syndrome. You didn't need to look far for a reminder of our mortality; I saw it every time I looked in the mirror.

The week after we beat Sydney in my return, I hurt my knee playing against Carlton. I led out to Josh Gibson, his kick held up a bit, and Sam Docherty fell across my leg. It felt like a deep corky just below the knee, but it turned out I'd stretched the posterior cruciate ligament. I took the dog for a walk the next morning and was limping pretty badly. Bart, our physio, came around to my place, moved my knee around, and told me, 'You're going to miss two to four.' In the end I didn't miss a single game, didn't even have it jabbed to play, and after the first week or two didn't bother strapping it either. Some injuries you can just push through, even if on reflection you wonder how you did.

When we beat West Coast to make it three premierships in a row Clarko made a point of saying none of them had been easy. In 2014 in particular we'd had to overcome big injuries: Mitch missed two months with a bad hamstring, Gibbo was out for close to three months after tearing his pectoral muscle. In 2015 Hodgey had been caught drink driving right before the finals and, of course, I'd had a melanoma cut out of my lip in the middle of the season. As Clarko told us, good teams overcome. Sometimes I forget just how good a team we were.

I had another scan in October, and that was all clear too. I'd been careful around the sun beforehand and the only change was that I was now even more careful.

Sarah and I went on the International Rules trip to Ireland together, stopping off in New York for a couple of days for a training camp. It was a great trip made all the better by wives and partners being invited along, kids too, the whole lot. The flight over was a good window on what travelling with little ones is like. Eddie Betts and Dave Mundy both had their children on the plane, and we went Melbourne–Brisbane, Brisbane–LA, LA–New York, a seriously long haul.

During a long career in footy, you naturally get to know your teammates and their partners socially, but there aren't too many chances to get to know blokes from other teams other than bumping into each other from time to time. So that made the International Rules trip a really memorable time. Throwing everyone in together – footballers, wives, girlfriends, kids – in New York and Dublin, two of the great cities of the world, pretty much guaranteed a good vibe. There were plenty of Hawthorn faces too: Hodgey, Mitch, Grant Birchall, Luke Breust and myself were in the team, and Clarko was coach.

The first night was a catch-up drink and it went down a treat. The next arvo I knocked on Bob Murphy's door and said, 'Mate, do you want to have a couple of beers before dinner?' I hadn't even finished asking and he was out the door. Me and Bob and Hodgey went across the road to a pub, had a few pints, then the Hodges, Murphys and Rougheads went out. When I say 'the Hodges', Hodgey's wife Lauren was pregnant and had stayed in Melbourne, so Hodgey's little brother Dylan had taken her place. There's about ten years difference between Luke and Dylan, but it's like they're the same person. From day one in New York everyone was calling them 'the twins'.

New York set the scene for a ripper trip. Cath and Nick Riewoldt joined the party after flying up from Cath's family home in Texas. We got on really well, and the Riewoldts, Murphys and Rougheads made a pact to keep in touch back home, which we've kept.

My knee didn't bother me in New York or in Ireland, but in January, when I started training with the Hawks again, it flared up and I had to have a couple of weeks' rest. I was easing back into it, doing some straight line running along the boundary at Waverley, when I had a sensation like something had flaked off inside my knee. I thought, 'Shit, I know what this is.'

My knee blew up straight away. I went and had a scan, and it was going to be a PCL reconstruction.

Sarah and I were getting married on 30 January, and on the 29th they told me the date for the surgery. It meant we had to cut short our honeymoon in Noosa by a couple of days. The club had given me a few extra days off when everyone else was already back in full training, so I suppose we'd done okay.

I had the knee operation in early February, quietly ticked off my rehab week by week, and was hoping to put my hand up to come back through the VFL with Box Hill in mid-May.

Then I had another routine PET scan, the results came back showing spots on my lungs, and everything changed.

CHAPTER 8
That Footballer with Cancer

When they first told me I had spots on my lungs, my mindset was all about playing footy again. It seems crazy, but initially I was thinking, 'I'm a chance to play in a couple of weeks. Let's just cut them out and I'll be back before you know it.' That's how I regarded cancer from the word go: like a football injury. Tell me what it is, how long you think I'll miss, and what I have to do to get back to playing.

We were at Peter Mac in the office of Dr Grant McArthur, the oncologist who was about to become the most important person in my world. Doc Makdissi from the footy club was there and so was Donna Milne, who would be my nurse throughout treatment and recovery. She isn't far behind Grant in what she's come to mean to me, Sars and my daughter Pippa.

When Doc Mak's mood changed – asking questions about how serious it was, what we had to do next – I knew we were in trouble. Grant made it clear that if they started chopping bits out of my lungs, and then more bits appeared and they had to chop them out as well, pretty soon there wouldn't be anything left to chop. I was like, 'Yeah, fair enough.'

My knowledge of cancer was pretty limited. My grandfather on Dad's side had died of some form of cancer, but he had been an alcoholic. An aunty on Mum's side had it, and she'd also passed away. I'd known people who'd had cancer, but there wasn't anyone that close to me where you could say it had really had an impact on my life.

The only treatments I knew of were chemo and radiation. Pretty much all I knew was that chemo makes your hair fall out and radiation burns your skin. When I had surgery on my lip I was told I wouldn't need chemo, but they initially talked about doing some form of radiation. On my face, on my lip, that wasn't going to be pretty. Besides, there wasn't enough evidence that it would work, and in consultation with the experts we decided not to. Would I go back and get radiation again on my lip, knowing what I know now? Probably not, because the chances were so low that it was going to come back.

In the week between finding the spots on my lungs and having them biopsied, Grant told me that if the biopsy showed what he expected, the treatment he recommended was a form of immunotherapy that was so new it was still referred to as a clinical trial. There was only one other person at Peter Mac on it at the time, because it wasn't part of the Pharmaceutical Benefits Scheme and so was still really expensive.

But Grant said, 'There's been positive results with this, this is what we think you should do.' I didn't have any questions, didn't hesitate for a second.

I'm sure being an athlete helped with that. You have a history of being told, 'This is what's wrong with your ankle, this is what's wrong with your knee, this is what you need to do.' You're not the expert, they are. In my time in football I never saw a player kick back against a doctor or a physio and say, 'No, I don't think you've got that right.' It's what they're paid to do. If I was to give Grant goalkicking lessons I reckon he'd listen to me rather than thinking he had all the answers. Not that I was the greatest expert on goalkicking, but you know what I mean!

When they told Sars and me the cost of the immunotherapy treatment I was like, 'What!?' It was $36 000 for each treatment, and I'd need three treatments, so that was $108 000 for starters. After that it was $12 000 every two weeks for twelve months. I'll do the maths for you: that's $420 000 all up.

I knew we had a bit in the bank, as you'd hope to after a decade playing AFL footy, so I knew we'd be okay financially, but in a sense it was like, 'Who cares?' The results in the two or three years the treatment had been trialled were good. I didn't even ask how many people were on it; they had done their research and said it was having really positive results, and that was good enough for me. This was the best chance of making me better, I wasn't going to sit there and say, 'Nah, I'd rather have chemo and radiation and save the money.'

In hindsight it's amazing to have been part of the early days of something that's making such a difference – not to mention that it saved my life. Now, because it's been proven to work and is on the PBS, each treatment costs about $36.

In the week after the diagnosis I kept training. I felt fine. I could have played that weekend. I wasn't crook, or at least I didn't *feel* crook – I was a fit, elite athlete. I wasn't angry either, just confused and unsure what was going to happen next. I kept going to the club, did circuits with Hodgey, kept doing my weights, did skills sessions out on the ground with the boys. The thing I'd always known – the game – became my crutch to lean on, my release. I just wanted to be treated like normal, because that's how I felt.

I'd pretty much forgotten about my knee, which I guess is understandable. I've sometimes wondered how I would have gone if the cancer hadn't come back and all I had to deal with was an injured knee. PCL reconstructions for a big fella are pretty serious, but I would have made it back. It's funny the tricks your mind plays – could I have been the spark to help us win a fourth flag in a row? The boys were pretty cooked by the end of 2016, so probably not. But you never know.

I'd desperately wanted to be back playing for Jordy Lewis's 250th game, but as it turned out I had to be medically cleared just to fly up to Brisbane and sit in the stands. At that stage I still hadn't come out in the media about what was wrong with me, so there was speculation about why I was missing games. That made me an object of fascination I guess – I remember going through the security gates at the Gabba and people were stopping and taking pictures of me. I was just trying to be normal, but it was a window into what was ahead. It wasn't a great time. Lewy's family were all there, including his little boy Freddy, who was eight months old. We sat in the stats box, and I remember already thinking I'd become 'that sick person', even though I still didn't feel sick.

I found out about the spots on my lungs on May 16 and a week later they did the biopsy, which confirmed it was melanoma. One of the tumours was on the edge of one lung, under my right armpit, so that's where they'd go in for a sample. The scan had shown four green dots, each about the size of a thumbnail. You don't think that's very big, but three months earlier they hadn't even been detectable in a PET scan – that gave us some idea how fast they were growing.

Sarah took some time off work, trying to adjust to the change in our lives. Because I was determined to still go out to the club and train, during the day she was home on her own a fair bit. Sars thought it would help to have some company and decided we should get a cat. I've never been a cat person and wasn't too enthusiastic, but Sars found this grey thing in New South Wales, and next thing it was on a plane headed for our place. Why NSW? Don't ask me.

So the day of the biopsy started with me driving to Melbourne Airport to collect a cat that had flown in from another state in a little cage. I was running late, thinking about the surgery, feeling grumpy because I'd been fasting since the night before, trying to find the part of the airport where you collect animals. I suppose you could look at the bright side and say it was a good distraction.

Sars and the cat dropped me at the hospital at 3 pm, and I recovered from the surgery in the ICU. Because they'd gone in between two ribs, there was a bit of discomfort when I woke up. They'd cut me open, fished around between my ribs and cut a tumour off my lung, so it was understandable. The buzzer you press for pain relief becomes your friend pretty quickly, but I was home 22 hours after Sars had dropped me off.

About a week after the biopsy confirmed it was melanoma, around the end of May, I gave a media conference at the club. The media had been very respectful; we'd worried they might camp outside the house, trying to get footage and pictures to go with a story that nobody knew the ending to. But all the way through they left us alone, which was a relief. I'm grateful for that.

But as much as things were the same, I knew something had changed. I'd go for a walk around the neighbourhood and feel people's eyes on me. I wasn't the footballer anymore, I was that guy with cancer. My phone was going off, messages and well wishes pouring in from all sorts of people.

Fronting the cameras at the footy club was a way of hopefully showing everyone that I was alright, or at least that I was up for the fight. I said something about it not being like the weekend, when everyone barracks for different teams. In this battle, you know everyone is going to back you. That sense of being supported, knowing people were cheering for me, that was important. But nobody knew whether I was going to win.

I had my first treatment a fortnight after the biopsy, on 7 June. Before we started Grant took me through the technical names of what they were about to give me. The street names of the treatments are Yervoy (ipilimumab) and Opdivo (nivolumab) – I was getting a 100 millilitres of each fed slowly through a drip. Everything seemed to end in 'ab'.

The drugs were so expensive they'd wait until I arrived to start getting them ready. I used to try to ring and say, 'I'm on my way, can you start making it up?' And they'd say they no, if you get stuck in traffic or have a crash we'll have to throw it out, it'll be wasted. It seemed like nothing, they were just two little bags of clear liquid, but obviously they were way more than that.

I also sat down with Donna, my nurse, and she mapped things out for me. We first met when the spots appeared on my lungs, and pretty quickly she was preparing me for every step of the road ahead. She was basically my cancer PA. 'This is where you have to be, this is what you have to do, this is what you have to bring.'

She told me I always had to be open with her and to contact her every time there was any change, no matter how small. She and Sars hit it off, and she absolutely loves Pippa. From the word go Donna has been a star. She told me, very firmly, 'Any change in your body, any change in anything at all, you have to tell us. It's a trial. We've seen some side effects, we need to know if you experience any.' So I was literally in contact with Donna every day, ringing and telling her how I was feeling.

Because the treatment was still a trial and the body of evidence around what it could do to people was so small, they told me I might rash up, I might have diarrhoea, and that in truth they just didn't know what could happen. That's why I had to be open – if something changed, I'd ring Donna, she'd talk to Grant, and together they'd decide if I needed to come in. The thing was, I might have had a reaction they'd never seen before. They didn't know, I didn't know, and there was only one way to find out. Checking in with Donna each day was hopefully going to keep me alive.

When I rocked up at Peter Mac for the first round of treatment, I had people hugging me, patients coming up and saying thank you. I didn't need thank yous, but I had no choice – I was the poster boy for something I wished I didn't have.

Footy injuries had given me a bit of experience with hospitals, needles and all of that fun stuff. After I'd ruptured my Achilles and it got it infected, I'd spent a week in Box Hill Hospital. I've always been fine with needles, although being around an AFL footy club you're regularly reminded that not everyone is. Shaun Burgoyne hates them. He went through a stage where he needed painkilling injections in his ribs before games to play. I'd follow him into the medical room and take the piss, sit there holding his hand while he was getting jabbed, saying, 'Squeeze Shauny, squeeze, squeeze.'

The amount of jabs some boys would get to play – and the places they got them – would make you shudder. One time Robbie Campbell had a sternum injury and they'd get him to lie on his back on the medical table with his head flopped over the edge so Doc could stick the needle in from up near his throat, heading down towards his stomach. Footballers – easy life, hey?

That first session of treatment took the longest; they have to administer the drugs slowly in case you react badly to them. Sars took the day off work and we went in to the old Peter Mac in Lansdowne Street. You had to do an induction first, but Donna said, 'Just tell them you've already done it.' Because of the attention that came with being an AFL footballer starting cancer treatment, they tried to keep me out of the open and put me in a room somewhere quiet.

The first thing they do is give you a tourniquet, which is yours to look after for the duration of your treatment. Mine was blue, I reckon I've still got it somewhere. They quickly told me I had good veins, which made them happy – some people, especially the elderly, have to use heat packs to bring up a vein. But they took one look at my arms and were rapt.

The line for the first bag went in and it was so slow, not much more than 10 or 20 millilitres an hour; the actual drugs were in a saline solution. The whole process sped up as the treatment went on, but it still took six hours all up.

I had a couple of other patients come through, a young kid who I could tell was in a bad way. He might have been on chemo, I don't know, but he had the bald head and was in a wheelchair. He was younger than me, for sure. That was a bit confronting.

I'd been warned – Adam Ramanauskas had been through it after being diagnosed with cancer when he was playing with Essendon in the 2003. He told me, 'You might see some stuff that's confronting, you're just going to have to cop it. Don't be afraid of what you'll see.' It was good advice, but didn't make it any easier when it was happening right in front of me.

The whole thing can feel surreal, like it's happening to someone else. It helps to find some humour in it if you can. At one stage an old bloke from Bairnsdale, about 70, came into the room for his treatment. We were making conversation and I asked him what his story was. He told me he'd had tumours here, here and here, and was on this drug called Keytruda. It's the same one Ron Walker used, which lots of people mistakenly thought I was on. This old bloke said it had got him going again, kept him alive the last few years.

Then he asked about me and I said I'd had a melanoma cut out of my lip, and now unfortunately I had a few tumours on my lungs.

'You sound like that footballer,' the old bloke said.

And his wife, rolling her eyes, said, 'He *is* that footballer!'

There it was again: that footballer with cancer. The only way to shake that tag was to beat it.

If every cloud has a silver lining, mine came at the most ridiculously unexpected time: a bucket-list trip to America for ten days in between my first and second immunotherapy treatments. When Grant and Donna said they didn't know what side effects to expect, I'm sure going to the NBA finals wasn't among them.

I reckon if you ask most footy players, their dream sporting trips would be the Super Bowl, the soccer World Cup and the NBA finals. Because it's in early February, the Super Bowl you can just about get to – especially if you're an older player with a few credits up your sleeve. The World Cup happens in June and July, and the NBA finals are in June. No chance. For a basketball junkie like me, it was an itch I thought I wouldn't get to scratch until retirement.

That first treatment had gone well and I wasn't feeling any side effects at all. Out at the footy club one day I was talking to Hodgey and Stuart Fox, our chief executive, and I threw it out there. 'The NBA finals are on, in San Fran. I could just fly in, watch a game or two, fly out and be home in a week.'

It was a long shot. I certainly wasn't expecting them to reply in unison, 'Well, why don't you?'

I'd actually been a bit cheeky and already asked my mate Joe Ingles whether he'd like to go. But Joe's season with the Utah Jazz had ended when they missed the play-offs by a game, and he'd flown home to Melbourne for a break. Heading straight back over to watch the finals with me was a stretch.

But Joe said he could hook me up with some tickets through Andrew Bogut, whose Golden State Warriors were playing against the Cleveland Cavaliers (a team that included another Aussie, Matthew Dellavedova). I could get there and back in a week, and once I'd cleared it with Clarko and Fages, we were away. The tickets for the game cost $1000 each, but hey, you only live once. The stadium at Oakland, across the Bay Bridge from San Francisco, holds 19 500, and there would be a hundred million people watching on TV around the world. Bring it on.

Sars knew what it meant to me, and knew I'd come through the first round of treatment with no issues, so she was really supportive. My brother Cam is as big a US sports nut as I am, so he was my obvious travelling partner. He works for my management company, TLA, and hit up some connections in the States. Through an Aussie bloke from Sunbury who works on a basketball TV show in America we landed two media passes that gave us access to courtside and the changerooms. I was a bit hesitant about it all, but Cam has no shame.

While we were still in Melbourne, Golden State absolutely smashed the Cavs by a combined 48 points in the first two games, an NBA Finals record. It's a best-of-seven series and I was thinking, shit, this could be over before we even get there! The third game was in Cleveland and we were watching it at the footy club. The boys were all going, 'Rough, if they lose . . .' I was like, 'Yeah, I know, I know.'

Cleveland ended up winning game three, so we knew it was going to at least five. I didn't care who won – we were watching LeBron James, Steph Curry, Dellavedova, Bogut. And there was a chance Cam and I would be there to see Golden State lift the trophy.

Golden State won game four pretty much while we were flying over, making the series 3–1. Game five was in Oakland, which took about 40 minutes by train from San Fran. We got there early and picked up our media passes, and there I was, walking around the court with this thing on a lanyard that said: 'Jarryd Roughead, media.'

The woman who gave us our passes had told us to come into the green room at half-time, so we wandered in and there were Isiah Thomas, a two-time title-winning gun from the Detroit Pistons, and Grant Hill, a hall-of-famer who'd had a 20-year career with four NBA teams. They host a TV show now. We rocked up and had our photo taken with them, they asked where we were from and we chatted for a while. It was the greatest escape imaginable – they had no idea I was 'that footballer with cancer'.

Cleveland won 112–97 to make the series 3–2. We were hanging around after the game when Matthew Dellavedova walked out, which was pretty cool. I hadn't met him, but he knew what was going on. His family were there, and they know my uncle who lives in Maryborough, where they're from, so there was plenty to talk about. Andrew

Bogut hurt his knee in that game so I didn't get the chance to thank him for the tickets; I owe him.

We had a couple of days to kill before we flew out again and did a bit of sightseeing. Cam had been to San Francisco before, so he played tour guide. We tried to get into Alcatraz but it was booked out, and instead we hired some bikes and rode over the Golden Gate Bridge. I'd still been training, and we'd done a couple of gym sessions and been on the treadmill in the hotel gym. I thought I was in reasonable nick, all things considered, but when we set off on the bikes it wasn't long before Cam was pulling away from me, which doesn't usually happen. I was struggling.

That night, lying in bed, I had a really tight chest. Before we'd left, Grant had said that San Francisco was the best place for me if something went wrong, because he's got great connections with oncologists there. The tightness was gone the next morning, so I tried to forget about it and keep living the dream.

As it happened Stuart Fox was doing a course at Stanford University; he came down and met us and we went to a couple of baseball games. Game six of the NBA Finals was back in Ohio, and we watched it in this famous pub in San Fran called Green Bar, in the financial district. Foxy joined us, and while we're sitting there he says, 'What happens if it goes to game seven?' I said we'd be on a plane back to Melbourne. And he goes, 'You're here now – why don't you go? I'll allow it.' I remember thinking, 'You're the boss!'

It all unfolded perfectly while we're sitting there in the bar. Cleveland won 115–101, taking the series to a decisive game seven. Foxy said he'd take care of changing our flights and told me to text Bogut (who was injured and wouldn't be playing) to sound him out about tickets. I was thinking, 'Really, can I do that?' But like I said, you only live once.

Cam was the only sticking point. Game seven was on Sunday night in the US, but that was already Monday morning back home and he needed to be back in Melbourne first thing Tuesday for a really big work meeting. This is where it gets good: game seven was to start an hour earlier than the others, so we did the maths and ended up figuring we could make it. Bogut sent a message: 'I can get you two tickets.'

We needed two more nights of accommodation, and Cam said, 'I'll book it.' The place we were staying was full, so we checked out and headed to this other hotel he'd organised – to find we were in a room with one double bed. We'd shared a room for 17 years in Leongatha, but we'd never shared a bed before. Oh well, the things you do for love.

We had a driver pick us up and during the game he was waiting in the carpark with our bags. We watched the game, saw Cleveland make history by coming back from 3–1 down to win the series 4–3. The players ran onto the court celebrating and Cam and I were running for the exit. Into the car, raced to the airport, made our 10.30 pm flight and got back to Australia. That Tuesday morning, pretty much straight from the airport, Cam presented a proposal to his bosses and potential clients to take a group to the Super Bowl in 2017. He nailed it, got the gig, and we were done.

And that really was the end of the dream. A couple of days later I had a CT scan and a PET scan, ahead of starting the second treatment. I was sitting there waiting for the results when they rushed in looking really worried. 'How do you feel? Are you alright?'

Turns out I had a pneumothorax, which is when air leaks into the space between the lung and the chest wall. It's basically a collapsed lung. Something had obviously opened up as a result of the biopsy they'd done. They told me I had been running on one-and-a-bit lungs, which explained why Cam was pulling away from me on the Golden Gate Bridge. That's what I tell them when I do sportsmen's nights, anyway.

It was a jolt back to reality, but things were about to get a lot worse.

CHAPTER 9
'I'm Not in a Good Way Here'

Clearly, there's no good time to get cancer. But when you're lying in bed in one of the only three rooms left in your house, still freezing cold despite wearing a jumper and pants, having full body sweats, and your feet are swollen and either burning hot or completely numb, it does make you wonder if that dream renovation was such a good idea.

Even though they didn't know what exactly they'd be, the side effects Grant and Donna had warned me about had well and truly kicked in. Unfortunately at the same time, most of our house had been knocked down and replaced by a hole in the ground. That would turn into a two-storey reno, but until then we lived in three rooms for eight months, during which I was the sickest I've ever been in my life.

In one room there was a washing machine and dryer, a two-seater couch with a TV, a fridge with the microwave on top of it, and a freezer doubling as a TV table. We had an electric frypan, a toaster, a kettle, a rice cooker and a Weber on the front porch that was used as the oven. To do the dishes we'd take a big plastic bucket and hold it up to the drain hose while we were having a shower, then carry that out, wash the dishes, and set them out to dry under a little table. It was winter and the little heater we used to keep warm would trip the power all the time, so we'd constantly be outside at the fuse box turning it back on again.

We couldn't move out because we had the cat and the dog – good luck getting a pet-friendly nine-month rental. Most days I'd lie on the couch with a blanket or a doona, but some days I was so crook I'd just stay in bed. The builders were very good – they knew what was going on and let me be, and if they needed to ask me something they'd text first. If I was up for talking I'd come out and see them, but sometimes I'd have to text back, 'Sorry, we'll have to do it later.'

The initial stages were demolition and a lot of excavation, trucks moving piles of dirt. That was the tough two months, the dark days of immunotherapy treatment. Some days they wouldn't see me at all, I'd just be in bed with the dog and the cat.

They're not bad memories, it was just about getting through it. Sars was at work, which was good to keep some sense of routine and normality, and people would visit every now and then, dropping food off and checking in on me. I never felt alone, but it wasn't exactly a fun time.

The second treatment started in late June. Joe Ingles was still in Australia, having a break, and he came with me to the new Peter MacCallum Centre in North Melbourne and sat with me the whole time. Everything went smoothly, but the next day I woke up feeling like I had a massive cold – sneezing, body sweats, the lot. I texted Joe: 'Mate, do you feel like you've got the flu?' He was fine. I told him to be careful, that I had something but didn't know what.

I gave it a day, hoping it might come good, but the next morning I couldn't get out of bed. The sweating was out of control and I was freezing. All Donna could tell me to take was Panadol, which doesn't exactly do it for you when you've got cancer. I'd drag myself up, take a couple of those, and crash back into bed. I had no energy, just couldn't do anything. At night I'd change into new clothes and in no time I'd have sweated through those too. It felt like I'd played basketball in a jumper and tracky dacks.

I went in to the hospital and they did some blood tests. It was the start of the first big side effect: my liver wasn't functioning. They told me no alcohol, which wasn't exactly a hardship at that stage; I'd had a few for Lewy's 250 and a few in America, but it wasn't like I was in any shape to go on a bender.

The sickness that time lasted 15 days. By the end of most days I'd feel like I was slowly getting better, but the lack of energy, the sweating, it was out of control.

Wherever possible I tried to keep things normal. On 4 July Sars and I went to a barbecue at Nick and Cath Riewoldt's, along with Bob Murphy and his wife Justine. Nick and Bob had a few free days so they were keen to have wine with lunch, but they felt bad drinking in front of me because I was crook. It was an example of how illness takes over; I told them not to worry about me.

By the start of the third round of treatment, in mid-July, I was back to feeling reasonably okay. Jordy Lewis had a day off training and took me. I told him, 'Mate, you might see some things here, try not to stress about it.'

A couple of days after the treatment I thought I was fine, I had no symptoms at all. I was well enough to fly to Sydney with the boys when they played the Swans in round 17. I roomed with Lewy, and he woke up in the middle of the night to find me sitting on the side of the bath with my feet in cold water. I had pins and needles that were out of control. My feet felt so hot I'd lie on the floor and put the soles on the wall in an effort to cool them down.

Back in Melbourne I just nosedived. A couple of close mates from back home who now lived in Perth had flown over. We all got together for dinner at another mate's house, about a dozen of us. I rocked up with a Gatorade, a water and a fizzy drink. I was lying on the couch, but after a while I just said, 'I'm no good, I've gotta sleep.' I went upstairs and crashed in a bed.

I could hear them all having chats about me – seeing me like that, they realised how serious it was. They're my best mates and they were trying to work out how to support me. They'd done their research as well and I know they were asking, 'Is he going to go?' To see me in that state was confronting for them, as much as I didn't really think about it at the time. I ended up getting up at about 2 am and driving home.

That weekend was Sam Mitchell's 300th game; I was determined to be there and share it with him. By that point I was struggling to wear shoes properly – I'd slip them on but not be able to do the laces up, and I'd just drag my feet along the ground when trying to walk. The dog wasn't getting much joy – we'd try and go for a walk and I'd get to the end of the street and have to stop.

There were days when I'd have to ring the footy club and say, 'Nup, I just can't come'. But I dragged myself out there for 'Feelgood Friday', two days before Mitch's milestone. I thought I'd just try to walk some laps, so I chucked on a hoodie and shorts and headed out. It was a classic shit Waverley day: dark clouds, wind, and then the rain started to come. I stumbled back inside and David Rath said, 'What the hell are you doing, Rough?' I was gaunt and must have looked a sight. I replied, 'I just needed to feel something in my face, to make me feel like I'm still here.'

When I think about the lowest I got, that was it.

The next day they were shooting the tribute video to Mitch. I really like the milestone videos the club puts together, they're special, and I wanted to be part of it and do my bit to camera. But I was stuffed. I just couldn't get myself out there. Mitch understood – he told me later he knew things must have been bad for me to miss something like that.

I was still determined to get to the G on the Sunday, even just for a few minutes. I made it in there – I was still driving, God knows how – and waited for Mitch in the medical room. I was in my Hawthorn gear, a big jacket, shoes with the laces undone; I must have looked like shit. I said to Doc Makdissi, 'I'm not in a good way here, but I've gotta do this.' Mitch and Lewy came in, and that's when my eyes went.

My feet were no good, I had no energy, I was aching all over. I looked like I hadn't slept for days, my eyes were red and inflamed. Happy 300th, Mitch.

They've said to me since, 'You were there, but you were so crook.' I saw those two and Gibbo, but I didn't leave the medical room until the boys had run out. I sat in the coaches' box for the first half, but I don't remember a thing. At half-time I went down in the lift, got in my car and drove home. All I wanted was bed; I didn't even watch the end of the game on telly.

The next day, the Monday, I spewed for the only time. It was yellow, stinking bile, absolutely horrible. I rang Donna and she said to come in straight away. I had to ring Cam to take me, I was at rock bottom.

When we got there they put me on a bed in a kind of waiting bay. Sars came in from work. Grant arrived and they took some blood and tested it quickly. Then they said, 'Have some more Panadol.'

I cracked it. 'You're not listening to me! I'm stuffed! I've got nothing else to give!' I was so full of drugs, they were starting to turn on other parts of my body. My lungs had become inflamed, so there was something going on there too. I had no energy, couldn't even walk without dragging my feet, and I'd lost about 10 kilos. I'd tried to hide it as best I could – I didn't want to worry Sars – but I was getting desperate.

With the pressure of footy, I always had my releases. I was able to go out to dinner with friends, could have a few beers on the weekend, as well as actually training and playing the games. All of that had been taken away. I was in a big hole – mentally, physically – and didn't know what was going to happen.

Grant could see the state I was in and said, 'Right, we've gotta do something.' That's when they gave me the steroids. They were in tablet form and a pretty high dose to start – within two days I was feeling better. The steroids acted like an upper. As a footy player I think you're allowed a maximum of 50 milligrams a day for five days. In hospital they gave me 200 milligrams straight away. If I'd been drug-tested I could have gotten a four year ban! That would have made a better story, wouldn't it – four-time premiership player gets cancer and hits the 'roids!

By the end of the week I was back out at the club, that's how quickly it turned around. I weaned myself off the steroids over the next month, and after a PET scan in August they told me I was having a good response to treatment. The tumours were shrinking.

It should have been great news, but by then I was so consumed with what was happening with my feet that it didn't really resonate. They were alternating between being numb and feeling like they were on fire. My bedtime routine was to put a bucket of water on a towel next to the bed and when the burning sensation woke me up in the middle of the night I'd roll out of bed, dunk my feet in the bucket to cool them down, dry them off, fall back into bed and try to get back to sleep.

At the footy club I'd go and stand in the ice bath. I still couldn't walk the dog. It was driving me mad, and I must have been driving Grant and Donna mad asking them to work out what was going on.

It's not as if they weren't trying. Initially they started a treatment called immunoglobulin therapy, pumped into me through a drip, diluted in saline. I had four or five doses of that within a week of starting the steroids, but it didn't work at all. Next I saw a neurologist, who did nerve conduction tests. They put electric shockers on my feet and calves and tested my reaction time. It wasn't something I ever thought I'd be doing, and straight away the bloke said, 'You're a bit slow here.'

They worked out that the nerves in my feet were being eaten away. If the damage kept creeping up my body, I could have been stuffed for years before they grew back, if they did at all.

Of the few people who'd been through this kind of immunotherapy, this was the first time it had created this side effect. It was a pretty stark reminder that it was a clinical trial; we were in unknown territory.

The other thing they did to try and get feeling back into my feet was a big plasma exchange. I sat in a chair at Peter Mac with my feet in a bucket and they took the biggest needle you can get – they call it 'the fish hook' – stuck it in my arm and drained my blood. I sat there, trying to take my mind somewhere else, while my blood went up into a bag above my head then came back in through a needle in my other arm. I had to sit there squeezing a ball in my hand to keep it moving – if it didn't flow properly an alarm would go off and I'd have to adjust the tourniquet or sit differently so the blood would flow through the fish hook again.

By the end of it there was a six-litre bag of plasma hanging above my head. It was a yellowy liquid, a bit milky. That doesn't go back in you, thank goodness.

I had two or three of those sessions over a fortnight – sitting there for five hours at a time with my feet in a bucket of water. Of course, you have to go to the toilet at some stage, so they'd clamp the line, I'd pick myself up and walk to the toilet with all this gear hanging off me and a fish hook in my arm.

There were other patients in the room with me, getting blood transfusions and whatnot, and I'd chat to them. They were usually footy fans, so having me in there was a release for them, or at least a distraction. One fella was younger than me and he'd already had a heart transplant and was on a waiting list for a second one; he was a big Melbourne fan. Sometimes as a footballer it's just part of your job to talk footy, but it didn't feel like the right place. Still, if it helped someone feel better, that's the main thing.

Looking back, the side effects of the immunotherapy were such a weird and foreign experience, but I wasn't thinking about that at the time. My only thought was, 'I want to get my feet back.'

Eventually they tried a drug called Rituximab, which is used to treat certain autoimmune diseases and types of cancer. That was another bag, another drip through the arm. Lucky I had those good veins. I had three sessions of that, a few days apart, and my feet came back. By finals time I was walking properly again; three weeks earlier I hadn't been able to walk the dog.

I'd turned a corner. If I had any say in it, there was no way I was going back.

DONNA MILNE
Nurse

I've been a nurse since the early 1980s and have spent the last decade or so working in a melanoma role that's partly clinical, partly research-based. I missed the clinical stuff when I wasn't doing it – I enjoy the contact with patients. There's a sense of being able to help people, to do things for them.

I get satisfaction from feeling that I might have smoothed their pathway, even a bit – just made things a little easier. In research everything is so far down the track, it takes so long to get there, but at the end of a clinical day I can go home and think, I helped this person and this person and this person. There's an immediate sense of satisfaction.

We're in a very privileged position, because the people and families who we share this personal experience with – whether it's diagnosis or you're there with them when they're dying – they trust you enough to share in that time with them.

Death is difficult, but it can be a positive. When somebody doesn't respond to treatment, and you know they're going to die, it's not all bad. You don't say they're impressive deaths, but I've seen people whose lives have ended in a really positive way. Knowing their time is limited often makes people stop and do what's important for them, and that's pretty special to be part of.

It never ceases to amaze me how people adapt and cope with what you'd think is the most horrendous situation. They'll find something positive, or they'll do something they wouldn't have done otherwise. If there is that sense of helplessness, that's when we come in and say, okay, this is what we do next. And then you hope things will go well for them from there.

I first met Jarryd when he found out the cancer had moved to his lungs. He was very unemotional. You see a whole range of reactions to news like that – some people will cry, or they'll look at you like a rabbit in the headlights, totally overwhelmed, and you know you'll have to go over everything with them again when it can actually sink in. But Jarryd was switched on in that moment, very matter of fact.

There was a little bit of impatience from him, which I experienced a couple of times on our journey together. No time for mucking around, let's just do it. 'Okay, we can't change it, what do we do next? What do you need me to do, when do we start?'

At times I felt like I was almost there more to support Sarah. I remember one meeting she was in very early on. She was emotional, sitting there with a tear running down her cheek. All I wanted to do was put my arm around her. Just the way the consult had worked, Jarryd wasn't actually sitting next to her, so I said, 'Jarryd, why don't you come and sit over here?' I was so conscious of her sadness and worry. They sat together and held hands.

A lot of families come to appointments together, whether it's a consultation, treatment, whatever it may be. Jarryd would come with Hawthorn's doctor, Michael Makdissi, or his brother or a friend. I'd say to him, 'Does Sarah want to come?' And he'd say, 'Oh no, she's got to go to work, she's doing this or that.' I think it was a protective thing – he didn't want her to worry, and he didn't want to disrupt her routine. It became clearer as we got to know each other; Jarryd had been at Hawthorn for 12 years and known Doc all that time, he'd always been there with him for anything health-related, so it made sense.

When he told me that Sarah was pregnant, that was a beautiful experience. They came in when Pippa was only about 10 days old. I asked for a visit, and in they came, the three of them. I nursed Pippa through the whole consultation and they were so proud. It was just lovely.

Sarah and I have a fair bit of text correspondence, we got on well from the word go. It's tricky, because as much as you try to think of people in a family context, Jarryd is my prime responsibility. It's a fine line for me, supporting Sarah but not upsetting their way of being together. That was always very much in my mind.

There's not a lot of grey with Jarryd, things are black and white. I got the impression pretty early that if Jarryd said we were dealing with something a certain way, that's what we were doing.

One time they came in when of all the side effects from his treatment had started to appear. He was really unwell and he was as quiet as I've ever seen him, and also a bit grumpy. He was lying back on the chair with his eyes closed, very disengaged.

Sarah said to me in a quiet whisper, 'I'm really sorry, Donna, I don't like it when he's rude to you.'

I said, 'He's not being rude, I understand where he's coming from.'

He obviously heard and said, 'I'm not being rude, I feel like shit.'

I told him it was all good, I understood.

Jarryd was up there in my estimation before we met, I thought he was a great footballer and seemed like a hell of a guy. I always got the impression from afar that he was a fairly quiet country boy, and that was pretty accurate, but I wasn't prepared for him to be so organised. He's obviously been in control in his football, but he was really good at listening to what we said and then doing it.

He's a fantastic historian when it comes to his health – his memory is unbelievable. The nature of his treatment, a clinical trial, meant we didn't have a lot of real-world feedback, so a lot of our interactions were around him reporting symptoms. He could give me the rundown of everything – dates, times, dosages. 'I took those tablets for five days,' or, 'You told me to have a blood test on this day.'

Clinical trial patients are monitored heavily with scans and blood tests. At the time we were aiming to pick up on symptoms or side effects as early as we could, so we could intervene right away. We'd see Jarryd in person every three weeks, and relied on regular phone calls. Nine times out of ten it was him ringing me and asking, 'This has happened, do you need to worry about that?'

He listened – I'm sure because of his grounding in football. I was never concerned that I would tell him stuff and he'd ignore it. Some patients you can be speaking to them, telling them to call if they feel short of breath or have a dry cough, please ring me., and you know there's no way they're going to. But I felt very confident with Jarryd. Yes, he'd been coached before, but I got the impression that it was also a way for him to have a degree of control. Reporting symptoms, remembering things, telling me what was going on, it was his way of contributing to his own health care.

When he was unwell and the side effects were kicking in, he rang me and listed a number of things he was experiencing. I said, 'Okay, I think we need to do this and this.' And then he said, 'You know how you told me I need to tell you everything? I've got this really weird sensation in my big toe. It's probably nothing, but you did say to tell you everything.'

To myself I thought, 'Oh shit.' To Jarryd I said, 'Okay, that puts a bit of a different slant on things. I'll talk to Grant and get back to you.'

And of course it was something. It wasn't a common side effect – it was the first time I'd seen that sort of peripheral neuropathy with those drugs. He talked about having to stick his feet in cold water for relief and not being able to tolerate the sheet on his feet in bed at night. I think how lucky he was – and we were – that he was somebody who did do exactly what he was told. If he hadn't told us about the pins and needles, our response would have been delayed, and we don't know what the outcome might have been. It's an athlete's awareness of his body, too – that really helped. He knew the minute something was not right.

I was very worried about him, how much of a long-term impact that side effect might have. I was worried about his mortality from the beginning, of course, but the foot stuff, I was worried about it impacting his ability to play football again.

Grant had said to him, 'We'll get you back out there.' I think Jarryd pinned a lot of his hopes on that. I was a little less positive about that prospect – by that point I thought he'd survive, and have a normal life span, but I wasn't sure he'd be able to play footy again. Only because I'd seen the impact these treatments have on people, the way they knock their socks off, particularly around energy levels. If you're working in an office that's one thing, but you don't play AFL football with reduced energy levels.

I thought we'd be able to stop the sensation he was having in his feet from getting worse, but whether we'd be able to make it go back to normal, that was less certain. And his feet were pretty important to his career!

It took three lines of treatment to reverse that, and that was a concern to me. While we were doing that he couldn't have any more treatment on the actual cancer, which was an interesting conversation to have as well.

'This is making me better, when can I have more?'

'No, it's causing this side effect, if we give you more those symptoms might get worse or never go away.'

He was pretty good about it, to be fair, but it took a while before we knew that symptom was going to be resolved.

I actually barrack for Hawthorn – my dad lived in Glenferrie, used to go to training and all that stuff, so I grew up with them. I'd go to games with my mum and dad and sister; I was there when Jason Dunstall kicked 17 goals against Richmond at Waverley.

But I didn't tell Jarryd for a long time – I was very conscious of having a professional relationship. He never asked me, and I didn't say anything. We've got a connection with another football family, and they met Jarryd at an appointment. That patient's father said to Jarryd, 'You know Donna barracks for Hawthorn, don't you?' He looked at me and said, 'You didn't tell me!'

My son Lewis did work experience at Hawthorn, which Jarryd arranged. He had a great time. He didn't see Jarryd for the first couple of days, then saw him at a training session. Jarryd texted me saying he didn't have to ask who Lewis was, he'd picked him from a mile off because of the resemblance.

At the start of 2017, when Jarryd played his first game back, he made sure we were there. Grant took along a visiting professor from overseas, I took Lewis, and we sat with Sarah and Cam and all of his family. That was one of the best days, just seeing him run out there. The feeling when he kicked a goal, the excitement and pride . . . He drove in to Peter MacCallum especially to drop off the tickets; he didn't have to do that. I told him I'd pick them up, but he said, 'No, no.' And there he was in the foyer.

I've heard him call me his 'cancer PA', and I suppose that's true in so far as making things go as smoothly as possible for him. In my mind it was more about trying to maintain his privacy – my motivation was minimising how much he was exposed to the big hospital world. I was involved in the care of Ron Walker too, another big, tall man who was very recognisable in Melbourne. Those privacy issues are important.

Jarryd never asked me to shield him from the public, but I went into protective mode because I didn't want him to have to stop and talk to people all the time. He was there dealing with his own situation and I didn't want him to feel like he had to be the big, friendly footballer in those moments.

But he'd stop anyway. He'd walk in to Peter Mac and people would acknowledge him, say, 'Hey, Roughy, how are you going?' He was always so nice to people. He'd stop every time, never brushed anyone off.

And he'd always turn it back to the other person. They'd say, 'How's your treatment going, Roughy?', and he'd say, 'We're doing good things. What about yourself, what's up with you?' Some would tell him a little, others a lot. It was always the same interaction – giving minimal information about himself, but always making the other person feel important and special.

Sometimes, when he came for a consultation with Grant, instead of going to the waiting room I'd take him somewhere quiet. He'd text me to say he'd arrived, I'd go and meet him, and we'd disappear. I find that if I'm with him in the public areas it can deter people from coming up to him – you see people look, but they'll keep walking. For me, that's something small I can do to help him.

I met him at the desk one day when he came in for his PET scan. The woman there asked for his name and he said, 'Jarryd Roughead.' She asked him to spell it, then she found it in the system and got him to fill in the same form he filled in every single time. We walked away together and I said, 'Clearly didn't know who you are . . .' And he said, 'I love it when that happens.'

Understandably there's a degree of anxiety before those check-up scans, not that he lets on too much. I asked him once, 'How do you feel when you're coming in here?' His immediate response was, 'Fine.' Then he thought about it and said, 'Maybe a little bit nervous sometimes.'

Jarryd's had a positive attitude over his treatment, but it's almost like a no-frills attitude, too – very direct, get-on-with-it. That's just who he is. Positivity can be a really useful coping strategy, but I worry that when things go wrong – and it hasn't for him – that patients can feel like they weren't positive enough, that if they hadn't had that little bit of doubt, they might have been okay. So I tend to approach positivity cautiously, because otherwise it puts a lot of pressure on patients and their families to be positive all the time.

I tell patients they are going to feel shit, they are going to have bad days, they are going to feel like it's all too much. That's okay. It's okay to feel that way. But you just have to judge things – horses for courses. I remind people that being positive all the time can be hard work, so they shouldn't feel like they have to, but Jarryd was positive because that's who he is and that's what he does. You don't question that.

Back when I started nursing, there was a very clear line: they're the patient, you're the nurse. But I think you can't help but develop relationships with people when you're sharing such intimate experiences with them. You learn over the years to maintain the boundaries.

I guess we do have a friendship. Jarryd's always interested in me – he never sees me or texts me without asking, 'How are you? How's Lewis?' You connect with some people more than you do with others, and I think I would have connected with him and Sarah regardless of whether he was Jarryd the footballer. We've got similarities. I can deal with him – I can be just as bossy as he can! He trusted me and I trusted him. That was a really good foundation. There are some people you just gel with, and I just gel with Jarryd and Sarah.

We have conversations outside of his health and outside of football. He knows how much I love Pippa and sends me photos of her: 'You're gunna love this one.' He's so proud of her. I have this image of them leaving after he brought Pippa in one day, not long after she'd started walking. I'm watching them walk away, and she's reaching up so high to hold his hand, because he's so tall. A father and his little girl.

When he announced his retirement I texted him and said, 'Probably not very professional of me, but I'm taking advantage of the fact that I can contact you directly to say how delighted I am for you. As a Hawthorn supporter, thank you for all you've done for the club, and the joy you've given so many people. For being who you are.'

He immediately responded with, 'Stuff professional – we're friends. Thank you.'

When I was a little bloke, I pretty much always had a ball in my hand. Even as a pre-schooler, watching the footy in Leongatha, I'd ask to go on the ground at half-time to have a kick!

Dad played 211 senior games for the Leongatha Parrots. He's a life member and was named ruckman in their Team of the 1980s. I ran out with him for his 200th game, proudly wearing his number 4.

I practically grew up at the Leongatha footy ground. As well as watching my dad play, I used to run the boundary, do the scoreboard. I love it there; it's a special place. It's where my sporting life began.

I always played basketball as well as footy, and in my mid-teens it probably had more of my attention. I played for Vic Country in the national under-16 championships, but after that I quit – it was taking up too much time and money – and threw myself into footy.

In 2003, when I was 16, I got called up to play for the Leongatha seniors. I got to wear Dad's number 4, which was a huge thrill. After playing for Vic Country in the national under-16 championships in 2003, I made the Australian Institute of Sport squad, and that took things to another level. In 2004 I played for Gippsland Power in the TAC Cup and for Vic Country in the under-18 championships.

Playing for Vic Country against WA in the national under-18 championships in 2004.
(AFL Media/GSP Images)

Draft day, 24 November 2004, with Buddy Franklin and Alastair Clarkson. At the start of the day, I thought I was going to Richmond! Instead the Hawks picked me at number 2, and then managed to get Buddy at number 5. *(Fairfax/Sebastian Costanzo)*

My first AFL game: round three, 2005, versus Essendon. All up I had 12 touches, kicked two goals, cramped up, and was pretty happy with everything except the result – we lost it late.
(AFL Media/GSP Images)

TOP: I never had a coach other than Clarko. This is after my first AFL win: round four, versus Brisbane. BOTTOM: That first season Clarko's message to all us young blokes was to stand up for ourselves. In round six I got fined for wrestling with Melbourne's Travis Johnstone, but it set the tone. We had each other's back. *(AFL Media/GSP Images)*

In round 20 of the 2006 season, versus Essendon, I felt things really click for the first time, kicking four goals in the first half. *(AFL Media/GSP Images)*

By 2007 I knew I belonged. In round 12 I kicked five against Carlton in the first half and in the following round took a big mark over Nick Maxwell. *(AFL Media/Dave Callow)*

Winning the 2008 grand final showed me what it takes to win a premiership. I kicked our last goal and then shifted into defence – when the siren went, the overwhelming feeling was relief. After seventeen years, I knew how much it meant to our supporters.

(AFL Media/Lachlan Cunningham; AFL Media/Andrew White)

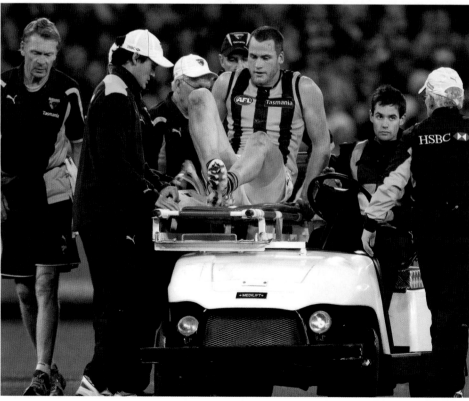

It's a fine line between premiers and pain.

OPPOSITE, TOP: In 2010 we lost the elimination final to Fremantle; our list was developing, but we just weren't good enough. *(AFL Media/Lachlan Cunningham)*

OPPOSITE, BOTTOM: Midway through 2011 I ruptured my Achilles and we lost to Collingwood in the preliminary final. Not being able to play that game and help the boys really hurt me. *(AFL Media/Michael Wilson)*

ABOVE: The 2012 grand final against Sydney was the most disappointing loss of my career – I never wanted to feel like that again. Thankfully better times were around the corner. *(AFL Media/Andrew White)*

In the 2013 grand final against Freo they came back at us after half-time, but we always felt like we were in control. Winning it a second time was somehow sweeter than when I was a young bloke. We didn't know yet where Buddy was going, or if he was even leaving, but it turned out to be my last game with him.

(AFL Media/Andrew White; AFL Media/Michael Wilson)

ABOVE: In the 2014 grand final, Buddy was on the other side, playing for the Swans. By this point Clarko's system was so refined, and everybody stepped up on the day, so the game was over by half-time. *(Fairfax/Joe Armao)* OPPOSITE: Jordan Lewis is my best mate and, after all we've been through together, looking back at moments like this is priceless. *(AFL Media/David Callow)*

OPPOSITE: In 2015, following the round 13 game versus Essendon, a spot on my lip was biopsied and diagnosed as melanoma. *(AFL Media/Sean Garnsworthy)*

ABOVE & RIGHT: After surgery, the scar was pretty scary, but I felt fine and by round 16 I was back, playing up in Sydney. *(AFL Media/Anthony Pearse)*

We'd lost to the Eagles two weeks before, but in the 2015 grand final everything just went right for us and we won big. The way we were playing was art, really – the connection we all had with each other. I'm proud to say that I hardly missed a game during the three-peat; they were the best three years of my career. *(AFL Media/Michael Wilson)*

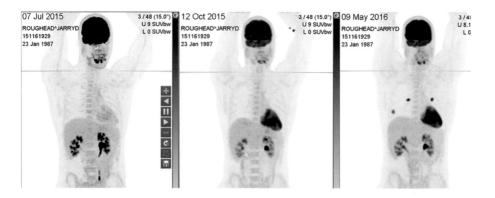

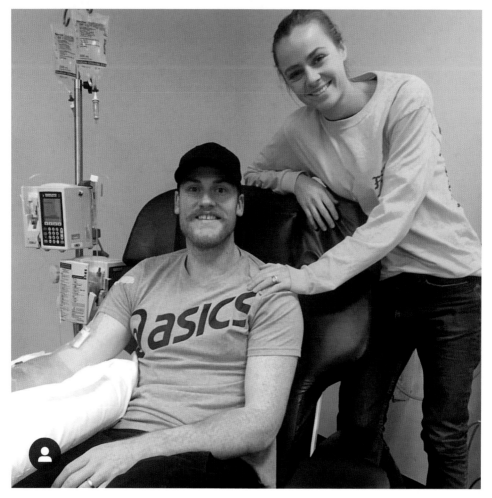

I'd just won my fourth premiership and married Sarah – the girl of my dreams – when, at the start of 2016, a PET scan showed I had lung cancer.

It was a difficult time for Sarah, but I was determined to be positive; I never thought about dying. The immunotherapy was brutal, including nerve damage to my feet, but I just thought of the cancer like a footy injury – I didn't know any other way. Whatever I needed to do to get back to playing, that's what I'd do.

TOP: Returning in 2017, I had a great sense of freedom – there was no expectation. Being named captain brought more responsibility, but to be honest: I wanted it. It was a tremendous honour to be captain of the club I love. *(AFL Media/Michael Wilson)* BOTTOM: Celebrating my first goal back, against Essendon in round one. *(AFL Media/Michael Trafford)*

TOP: Kicking the winning goal against the Swans in round ten made me feel like I was back to my previous level. *(AFL Media/Mark Metcalfe)* BOTTOM: Footy gave me mates I'll have forever. Whenever I played against Buddy and Jordan after they moved club, we'd go as hard as we could for two hours, like our friendships didn't exist, and as soon as the siren went it was back to normal. *(AFL Media/Quinn Rooney/Getty Images)*

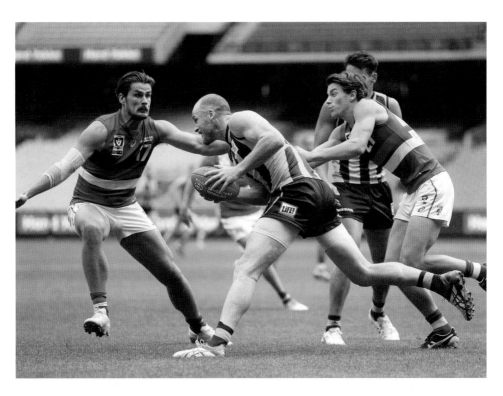

Playing for Box Hill against Footscray in May 2019. I'll always remember my last season fondly, and with no regrets that I played on. Clarko had flagged that at times I might find myself playing VFL, and while I wasn't happy about his decision when he did drop me, I enjoyed my time playing for Box Hill. It reminded me of what Dad used to do.

(AFL Media/Dylan Burns)

Our last home game in the 2019 season was round 22, versus Gold Coast. My instructions were simple: get the ball. I had a great time and kicked six goals – it was like I was having a kick in the park. I'll always be grateful that I had the opportunity to say goodbye as a Hawthorn player. *(AFL Media/Darrian Traynor; AFL Media/Michael Wilson)*

Sarah and Pippa mean everything to me. That's what I always raced home from training for: time with my girls.

GRANT McARTHUR
Oncologist

I'm a footy fan, I barrack for Carlton. I've followed footy all my life and in my younger days would go every week. When Jarryd asked me and I told him who I support, he said, 'Oh.' He felt sorry for me! That says something about Jarryd – he was always asking how other people are, even while he was going through this whole thing. As a Carlton supporter, he felt my pain in difficult times.

Before I met Jarryd I just saw him as a really successful sportsman, among the best. I remember being really intrigued by how Hawthorn would switch this big fella onto the ball when they were slipping in a game. He's not really a midfielder, but he was able to be put right in the mix of it when they needed to turn around a game. That he could do that says something special about a big bloke, a forward.

I was into sports big time as a kid, athletics and cricket. I never got anywhere near the elite level, but I represented my school in every distance from 100 metres up to cross country. I've discovered cycling in the last few years, with the body failing and the back going.

One of the things I love about sports, which I've noticed in my professional career, is what a great grounding it gives you in life. You learn teamwork, you learn how to deal with adversity, you learn how to really put yourself on the line and take risks. I think sports are a fantastic part of Australian culture, integral to the way we think about ourselves as a nation. When one of our elite sportspeople get struck down with something like metastatic cancer, it touches the nation.

I met Jarryd after he'd had surgery on his lip. It was a concerning melanoma, the features of it. Just by my reputation in the field, they came to me – I tend to see the high-profile patients when it comes to melanoma. Ron Walker was my patient, Jimmy Stynes too. After the melanoma was removed Jarryd was at risk of the cancer coming back, so we needed to put in place a plan where, if it did come back, we could deal with it as effectively as we could.

There's a bit of a tendency with cancer to say, well, it looks pretty good now, let's just get on with life and forget about it. But no, you want to maximise the chances of beating it long term. Unfortunately for Jarryd, that meant doing regular scans to see if it had come back, which can be stressful. It's a constant reminder, 'I've had cancer and it might come back.' And of course it did.

One reason I have such respect for Jarryd is because of the way he developed over this whole journey. When someone's first diagnosed with cancer, it's always very confronting. He was a bit quiet and intimidated at the start, but I've just seen him grow from there. To become captain of Hawthorn after coming back from a life-threatening illness, he just impressed me so much – as a leader, as a guy people look up to. He was always confident in his footy, but I think he learnt to be confident in other aspects of his life too.

Ten years ago the spots we found on his lungs would certainly have been considered terminal. But we don't consider it terminal anymore, because we have these new, breakthrough treatments.

The role of radiation therapy remains controversial for melanoma. There are some cancers where it works really well, but the thing about melanoma is its capacity for small cancers – and most of them are small when they're diagnosed – to spread relative to their size.

In Jarryd's case the cancer cells had escaped into the lungs and, in time, were detected on the scans. But at that point I was becoming pretty confident he'd get a good outcome. That's interesting, because in my field there are a lot of my colleagues who tend to be pessimistic. I was pretty optimistic, others weren't. When we plan treatment we confer on the case to get the input of multiple specialists, and one of my senior colleagues said, 'He'll never play footy again.' I remember thinking, 'Yes he will.'

It was in Jarryd's favour that it was just in the lungs, and we knew at that time the immune treatments did better if the cancer was only in the lungs. And of course you get better results in younger people. So I was quietly confident, although you never know for certain with that treatment whether there will be a good response.

The decision that had to be made was if we would give him the standard immune treatment or two treatments at the same time. There was data emerging that doing two at once produces a lot more side effects, but you might get better results. We had a chat about that with Jarryd and he said, 'Look, I'll leave it to you.' But he was tending towards, 'I think we need to really go for it here.'

We suspected that putting the two treatments together – the ipilimumab and nivolumab – was the way to go. We decided to go for it and look for a cure. Just a few years later – for a bloke of his age – we'd always use the two together, but that's really only emerged since Jarryd was treated.

The thing is, when you put the two treatments together, you do get a lot more side effects, and that's what happened to Jarryd. We knew the types of things that might happen, but you never know with each patient. Jarryd got hit pretty bad – a lot of people don't know quite how bad. It really knocked him around.

The issue with his feet was the most troublesome – the immune system had attacked the nerves in his feet. I was worried about that for a bloke who earns his living by precisely kicking a football, not to mention running huge distances. We went for it and gave him every treatment we could to reverse the nerve damage – and he's recovered 100 per cent. He's had all the formal testing and his nerves are completely normal.

As well as the nerve damage, his eyes were inflamed, which we worry about because it can affect your vision in the long-term. He also had a type of hepatitis, inflammation of his liver, and his lungs started to get inflamed. There he was, a fit bloke, an elite athlete, and he couldn't get enough oxygen into his body.

All four of those side effects were occurring at the same time. We stopped the immunotherapy and gave him treatment that reversed the side effects. We still don't understand the science behind this, but it's actually quite remarkable: you can turn off the immune system to make all those side effects better, but it somehow continues to fight the cancer and gets rid of it. That's what happened with Jarryd.

It's also interesting that, routinely, we'd been running that type of immunotherapy treatment for two years – so our expectation was he'd be out of football for that long. Getting all of those side effects, and not being able to continue with his treatment, that actually got him back to footy quicker.

His mindset helped, certainly – that very structured way of dealing with it. Because footy players obviously get a lot of injuries, he had a mindset that helped him deal with it. And the steely resolve. He wasn't going to focus on, 'This might kill me.' It was, 'Let's get on with it and deal with this.'

I went to Jarryd's first game back and took along a colleague who was visiting from the US, a leading expert from the Mayo Clinic. Hawthorn started alright but in the end the Bombers ran over the top of them. The final siren sounded and my American colleague said, 'Jarryd's the winner. Just to be back out there, after what he's been through, Jarryd was the winner tonight.'

I always get emotional, and I like that. It's my personal style and I think it helps me. I don't get emotional to the point where I can't calm down and make decisions, but I find it's a really good way of building a better connection with your patients if you get a bit emotional. That night was emotional. It was just amazing to see him back out there.

What was interesting is afterwards he told me, 'I'm fine.' I asked how his pre-season was, how it compared to other years. 'Pretty much as good as ever.'

During that first year back, rather than becoming fatigued he got better as the season went by. He was actually still recovering from the cancer treatment during the season, and it took him a while to get going. He played every game, which would have been a feat for anyone of his age but was just remarkable for someone who had just been through advanced cancer and endured all the side effects that had knocked his body around.

Another little learning for me: people talk about Hawthorn as the family club and they really are. Through Michael Makdissi I saw how the club supported him, and it was a real family approach. They were very impressive.

Jarryd has spoken to groups of patients for us here at Peter Mac. People want to hear his story, it brings a lot of hope to them. To see a bloke who's overcome what Jarryd has, it's hard not to be inspired. He's got better at talking about it with time, adding real gems of information about what he's been through. That's part of the growth I've seen.

When I first met Jarryd he didn't stand out to me as a guy who was going to have a huge career after retiring as a player. But by the end of all of this, having got to know him, I'm certain he's going to have a great career after footy. He's a great bloke, but he's also really eloquent and confident now and the way he can deliver messages to people is just terrific.

He became an ambassador for clinical trials for the National Health and Medical Research Council, and has been very generous with his time. To have someone of Jarryd's profile say he values clinical trials sends a strong message. It was through the clinical trials that we were able to identify the best treatment for him, so for him to give back in that way – he's just a super generous guy.

What got him through? Strong resolve, being well organised, disciplined – he brought that athlete's discipline to the treatment. You don't have to be Jarryd Roughead – an elite sportsman – to get through cancer, but he had some skills from sport that helped him for sure.

CHAPTER 10
The Power of the Mind

The day I told Sars there were spots on my lungs she asked if I was going to die. I said no and we never spoke about that possibility again. The first night she cried, but after that I never saw her in tears again either.

I know that sounds strange to most people – detached, cold even – but that was how we coped. And it wasn't an act, at least not for me. I never thought about dying. It's not like you're ever ready for it, but I knew I really wasn't ready. No way. I was too busy enjoying life. I'd just got married, we were renovating our house, were excited about starting a family. I'd played in four premierships so work wasn't going too badly either.

I've said it often since – from the day I found out, I just treated cancer like a footy injury. That's all I've ever known. My mindset was simple: 'Righto, we'll just get over this and then I'll get back to playing.'

Apparently it's quite normal for healthy people to think about their own funeral, to picture it in their mind. I've never done that, and it was certainly never spoken about when I was crook. I guess subconsciously I knew everything was in place; I already had a will, which had been updated when we got married, and I had life insurance, which is one of those things that is done through your management team as an AFL player. But I never thought about them coming into effect.

Sars definitely thought about it, but she hid it well. She told me one day she'd consulted Dr Google, which was a big mistake. The people who knew us well were more worried about her than me. I can understand that – I had the boys and the footy club to occupy me, and I could deal with it in my way. Whereas I don't think Sars had any idea how to: there's no guide to being a partner of someone going through cancer.

In my way I thought I was protecting her by not letting her find out too much. I was worried about her, but I couldn't talk to her about that either. It helped that she had full-time work, leaving home just after 7.30 in the morning and not getting back until 5.30 at night. And she was playing netball for Drouin, so each Thursday night she'd drive an hour and 20 minutes to train, then head back again on Saturdays to play. She had distractions too.

I imagine a lot of people thought I might die, but they never let me know they were thinking that way. I just thought I'd be in the percentage that got over it. People would ask, 'How are you?' and I'd answer, 'I'm alright.' It was bullshit, but only a few who I was really close to called me out on it.

Inside the footy club you're not going to get all 44 players constantly asking how you are, but I knew they were wondering. If Lewy asked I'd say I was struggling. Gibbo would rarely ask, but he'd always ask Lewy how I was – that's an example of how it worked.

Things were passed on from person to person. Donna was regularly in contact with Sars, and if Sars was really worried she'd talk to Cam, and Cam would come and see me. Cam was the only person in my direct family I spoke to about my condition – I deliberately hid the reality from Mum, Dad and Em. They'd ring and I'd just say, 'I'm okay, everything's fine – I have my shit days and my good days.' I didn't open up to them because I didn't want to scare them, but I also didn't want them dropping everything and coming up to Melbourne either. It hadn't been like that for the 10 years since I left home and I didn't need it to be like that just because I was sick.

I'd speak to Mum and Dad once a week, but they didn't see me at my worst. In fact, from the diagnosis in May until I started feeling better around September, they didn't see me at all. That was my doing, what I thought was best for all of us. We've never been a really close family in that way – we love each other, but we're not all over each other like some families are. I didn't want to be bombarded just because I was crook. I didn't want everyone putting a stop to their own lives and rushing to me. I didn't want, 'Poor Jarryd.'

Maybe that was something else I'd learned from footy: everything evolves so quickly, everyone moves on so fast, you can't stand still feeling sorry for yourself. You've just gotta get going or you get left behind.

My Aunty Libby was across it more than everyone else I reckon, because of her academic expertise in pharmacy. She knew what could happen, and occasionally she'd touch base and ask what was going on.

I only found out later that she had a conversation with Dad after they found the spots on my lungs. That was a wake-up call for him. They were talking, and Dad was saying everything would be okay, that I'd beat it no worries, because that's what I'd told him. And Libby said, 'Michael, it's melanoma. It kills people.'

When I was at my lowest, between the second and third treatments, I went and saw a psychologist. The club suggested it and gave me a nudge to make sure I went through with it – they knew how down I was and were trying to help. I saw a woman at a practice in Collingwood, and maybe it was because I went in there with a mind that was more closed than open, but I knew the questions before she asked them.

I don't imagine as a psychologist you get too many 29-year-old footy players coming in and saying they've got cancer and don't know how to deal with it. I told her I'd done what I was doing for twelve years, and during that time I'd always had my releases, but now I didn't have any. She said, 'Yeah, you're right.' I wasn't being a smart-arse, I just said, 'That's where I'm at. You can understand why I'm frustrated, pissed off, flat as a tack. I haven't got anything, nothing, everything has been taken away.'

I didn't get much out of it, to be honest. I guess I felt like I had enough people at the footy club – Jack Russell, Fages, a few others – who I could confide in if I needed to. I had to be patient. It was basically a shitty ten-week stretch where I just had to ride it out. I was like a little kid who'd had all his toys taken away and been left with only one block.

I don't know why people go to the negative straight away, in terms of injury or sickness. I genuinely don't understand it. Why do we think of the worst outcome first? Why can't we think, 'Right, how long's it going to take? What do I need to do to get better? Okay, let's do that then.'

If I've got a footy injury, I'm not thinking, 'Fuck, I'm never gunna play footy again.' I'm thinking, 'How long's it going to take?' They never tell you the best-case scenario – if it's serious, it's always, 'At least a year.' Well, why? Just because that's the way it's worked for most people doesn't mean that's how it will be that time. Everyone's different.

In 1998, Tony Liberatore played again for the Bulldogs 117 days after doing his knee – typically a 12-month injury. He did his knee in round five, had conventional reconstructive surgery, and played again in round 21. Why not? Ask any of the medicos at a footy club and I reckon they'd say the same thing: as soon as someone gets injured the attitude is, 'Righto, let's go to work to get him better.'

As for talking about death, I don't see the point. Say things don't go your way, you don't make it, and you've let the closest people in your life share that with you. Their last memory, what they're left with forever, is of this really sick person on death's door. I didn't want that.

I knew all along there were people thinking the worst. At the media conference at the club just after we found out, the questions were all, 'Are you going to retire?' 'Is this the end?'

And I was like, 'No!' I wasn't thinking I was going to die. I was thinking, 'I'm 29 with three years left on my contract. I've just got married. I love my life.'

You're not going to give that up. Not without one hell of a fight.

CHAPTER 11
Just a Footballer Again

A month after my feet were such a mess I couldn't even walk, I was out at the footy club running 10×100 metres. It was more of a jog than a sprint, out on the far wing with our rehab coach Phil Merriman, but I didn't struggle too much at all. Once they found the right treatment, my recovery happened fast, but it needed to – I needed my feet, they were important tools of my job.

Our 2016 finals campaign was a disappointment. We lost to Geelong when Izzy Smith missed a goal after the siren, then lost against the Dogs a week later. 'Punky' Bruest hit the post in the second quarter with a kick that would have put us up by 27 points. A goal might have buried them, but instead they got on a roll and came back, and the rest is Bulldogs history.

If the boys could have gone on to win four flags in a row they probably would have become the best team ever, and I would still have felt like I was part of that – a pretty big part. I absolutely wanted them to win, I was a fan, but when they lost to the Dogs, on one level I felt relief.

Every time anyone from the club fronted the media that season, especially as it wore on, they'd get asked about me. 'How's Rough? What's going on?' I'd go to games and sit in the box, and my mindset as a spectator was heaps better than it had been in 2011, when I'd missed games because of my Achilles. I guess it was because I'd been lucky enough to have won four by 2016. But in the box, the camera would be on me, and I didn't want that. I wasn't going to go and sit in the crowd, but I wanted to go to games and see my mates play well and win. When we eventually got put out, at least that all stopped.

Sars and I had a couple of weeks in Noosa, just kicking back. After a pretty ordinary year I was finally feeling good. Sars had just started a new job, so when we got back I headed over to the States. I was there for a bit less than a fortnight, the first half with Patty Mills in San Antonio, the rest with Joe Ingles in Utah. I got my NBA fix and saw each of them play two games, which was pretty cool. And because you don't bump into many Aussies in San Antonio or Salt Lake City, it was a really relaxing trip, which was just what I needed.

By that stage I'd been given an inkling that the tumours were shrinking, although I was also told not to get ahead of myself before the next scans. I was doing a strength program for my legs and knee, slowly building up fitness again, and was starting to feel good. I hadn't really lost weight when I stopped lifting weights, just a bit of definition, but that came back quickly too.

While I was in Salt Lake I went for a run on the tread-mill at the Utah Jazz facility, and got a bit worried when I was absolutely stuffed after 20 minutes. I had to stop and walk to catch my breath. Then I remembered that the city is more than a kilometre above sea level; it was a relief to realise it was because of the altitude, which I'd never exercised in before, and not me.

I had a PET scan around late November and was told to prepare myself for good news. The day in December when Grant said, 'You're cancer free,' it was strange. I know people would think it's the most incredible relief, but it wasn't, because that was always the plan, to get rid of it. That was the endgame all along, and to my mind there was nothing overwhelming about getting there.

The next day I got up in front of the boys out at Waverley and told them the news. I said, 'Boys, I've got something to tell you. I had a scan yesterday, I'm all clear.' I'd stood in exactly the same place six months earlier to tell them I had spots on my lungs, and there I was again, after a complete reversal. They all erupted. It's a moment I'll always treasure.

That moment also drove home how much things had changed. I'd played my last game at the end of 2015, and in the group that got around me to celebrate my good news there was no Jordy Lewis, no Sam Mitchell, no Brad Hill, no David Hale, no Brian Lake, no Matt Suckling. They'd all retired or gone to another club. Instead of those blokes, I was telling Tommy Mitchell, Jaeger O'Meara, Ricky Henderson – guys I didn't really know yet. It was just another example of how quickly things move in football.

———

I still hadn't kicked a footy in months. It was the longest I'd gone without putting boot to ball since I could walk. The first kick I had was in a session in December with the young kids – they start training before the older blokes, and when they hit the track I started back with them.

It was like that old saying about never forgetting how to ride a bike: I kicked the ball well and felt good. We weren't doing overly hard drills, it was about decision-making with our kicking. It wasn't super-hard stuff, but I did well enough for Brett Ratten to say about my efforts, 'They're the kind of kicks we need to do.'

I had this sense of freedom. I could just go out there with no great expectations and say, 'Right, let's see what I can do.'

I was training from day one of pre-season and started to think I was 100 per cent ready to go. In hindsight I should have known I wasn't – my knee was good without being great, and I certainly didn't have full strength back yet. My feet felt fine, but they weren't fully healed either.

I went to the camp before Christmas on the Sunshine Coast, trained well up there, and came back in good shape. I didn't know if I'd play round one, but I knew I was going to play again. That was enough.

While we were in Queensland there was a player vote on who would be captain. We all knew Hodgey was giving it up, and we each had to vote for our top six blokes in order of preference.

On 20 January, they announced that I was captain.

They'd had to go to the board first and they had discussions with me, too. 'Do you want to do it? You know it's going to be hard.' Behind the scenes they'd gone and seen Grant, asked if the extra pressure might even bring the cancer back. They went through a fair bit, and in the end they went with it. They just told me I'd have to be aware of my body language, stuff like that. I understood, but reminded them that I hadn't played for 18 months and they needed to be aware of that.

I wanted it. I knew it was going to be hard enough just playing again, that I'd have enough to concentrate on, but I wanted it.

I played all three practice games. The first was against Geelong in Tassie, and media crews were trying to follow me around. For a pre-season game. Please. Just let me go and play, I'll talk to you when I'm ready. Don't think you're going to get me pouring my heart out and telling my life story at an airport.

Two reporters fronted me when I walked into the ground in Launceston and I just ignored them. It feels like you're walking out of a courtroom, like you're on trial for something, and I didn't see why they couldn't understand that.

I never liked it and that's something I always struggled with when it came to the media – asking the same generic questions over and over isn't reporting, it isn't journalism. People say players are so robotic, well, don't be so robotic holding the microphone or the recorder in my face.

We played a ripper first half against Geelong – at that point I thought the year was going to be amazing. I think Kade Stewart kicked a goal on the siren to beat them. We lost to North a week later at Arden Street, then played Port at Noarlunga. I was alright against Geelong and North, didn't do much against Port. But I felt ready.

We had Essendon in round one in what was their first game after the suspensions. Dyson Heppell, who's another Leongatha kid, was captaining the Bombers. It was a pretty good story. I'm five years older than Dys, but I always spoke to him growing up. Sometimes when we were home we'd run or have a kick.

I had the chance for the fairytale return towards the end of the first quarter. I took a mark over Dys about 40 metres out – the script was perfect. I'd been hitting them pretty in the warm-up, so I went back thinking, 'Yeah, I'm gunna kick this.' City end, 45-degree angle, wrong side for a left footer but that's my better side. I could feel everyone lining up, ready to mob me. And I absolutely shanked it. Floated it through for a point.

I hadn't kicked a goal since the last quarter of the 2015 grand final win over West Coast. That's nearly 18 months – a long time without your bread and butter. I eventually got one a few minutes into the third quarter, which put us 13 points up.

After the game I got a video message from Jordy, who had gone to Melbourne that year, showing everyone jumping on me and him saying, 'It should be me.' It would have been nice, and it showed again just how much the team had changed since I'd last played. Mitch was in the stands – he'd gone to the Eagles, and they were playing North the next day – and as I came off after the warm-up he was there to wish me luck. That was nice. But it would never feel the same again; my closest mates were no longer there.

It took a while to stop being the footballer with cancer and go back to being just a footballer. The Sydney game in round 10 was the point where it really felt like I was back. We'd lost the first four games, including being pumped by Gold Coast and Geelong, and were 3–6 going to the SCG.

The game was tied up, 75 each, inside the last two minutes. Ty Vickery kicked it to me on the outer flank and I marked it right on the 50. Tommy Mitchell ran over and said, 'Just score.' He added, 'Can you get this?' And I was like, 'Yeah, I'm good.' A point would have put us in front, but I wasn't trying to kick a point.

As soon as I hit it I thought, 'That's not missing. No way.' That was the moment where I felt like I was back.

SARAH ROUGHEAD
Wife

For a long time Jarryd and I only knew *of* each other, rather than actually *knowing* each other. I was living in Loch but played basketball for Korumburra, and one of our big rivals was Leongatha, where Jarryd played basketball. I suppose I was about 15 or 16.

When I was 18 I went overseas and lived in London with a girlfriend. We had no money and were living in a hostel, paying our board by working in reception. While I was there, Jarryd added me on Facebook. He said he was coming to London at the end of the year, so that was the conversation starter. He was already playing AFL at that point, but I only really remembered him as a Leongatha basketballer, not really as a footballer.

We'd send Facebook private messages, talk about our days, what we were doing. It was almost like having a pen pal, but a Facebook pal. He came across as really genuine. Even though I had my reservations, it felt like I was just speaking to someone I'd known for a long time.

In 2008 he'd sometimes call me after a game, him ending his day's work at the MCG and me getting ready to start mine in London. They were winning and he was playing well; I think he was just feeling pretty happy with himself.

I got back to Melbourne in November that year, and we met properly at the Inverloch Pub on New Year's Eve 2008, but it wasn't until April that we began dating. It was a twelve-month courtship, if you could call it that! I had been wary, but when we met and talked and got to know each other properly, he was just a very nice guy.

We fell in love quickly in the end. It was so long before we even met that, when we did, it felt really easy. If you ask Jaz, he says he knew we were meant to be early on. I felt the same.

I am a Capricorn and Jarryd's an Aquarius, so as to whether we're similar people, yes and no. We're both stubborn in our ways – what we believe in, we believe in – but he compromises a lot. We value family and friends very highly – family is everything. That's even more evident now that we have our own family. He looks after his people; he's good to those he cares about.

Of course people have poked fun at his surname – they've said it suits. For mine, he's so handsome. I don't necessarily like a well-groomed man – I love his beard and freckles. I've got that surname now too. Both rough heads.

Jarryd isn't afraid to speak his mind. If an adult comes up to him and says, 'Mate, can I grab a photo?', the first thing he says is, 'Where are your manners?' That would mortify me, but he's just setting a standard that everyone should adhere to. That might come across as a bit grumpy. I feel like that's relaxed a lot over time – Pip's been a big part of that.

My memory of the spot appearing on his lip in mid-2015 is quite vivid. I remember looking at it and thinking I'd never seen anything like it, other than perhaps a cold sore, so that's what I initially thought it was. It was there for a few weeks – I look back at our engagement photos and it was there then, on the afternoon he proposed.

My Mum is a nurse, and one day I mentioned it to her during a phone call. What stood out was that it wasn't on the edge of the lip like a cold sore typically is, it was on the lip itself. And it wasn't healing, which is a sure sign of melanoma. Mum said straight away, 'He needs to get that checked.' I just thought, 'Hell, maybe it's just a sun spot, they'll chop it off and it'll be okay.'

When the diagnosis came back that it was melanoma, I was shocked. I guess we'd lived in this happy little bubble – life was great, planning a wedding in our home, which we were in the middle of renovating.

I hadn't prepared mentally for what he would look like after it was removed. I probably thought it would be a little stitch, but this was a huge incision. I was lucky I went with Cam to pick him up as I was really quite upset; it was frightening and made it very real indeed. Physically I felt he looked so different – a quarter of his bottom lip was gone and the scar went right down to his chin. I hadn't prepared for that visual at all, I was really shaken.

The recovery was quick – he only missed one game and then he was back playing. It looked worse than it was, in that sense. Fast-forward a week and he was in Sydney, playing really well, a patch covering the scar. Everything was back to normal.

At the time I was devastated, a lot of tears and fear, but once the stitches came out it didn't take long before I just didn't think about it at all. Not long after, they won the premiership for the third year in a row. We were preparing for our wedding. The sense was, 'Okay, we're done with that.'

The day he found out about the spots on his lungs, it was so strange. I was sitting on the couch in my PJs, wondering where he was – normally if he says he's home at 1.30 pm, he's home at 1.30 pm. We were going to order some takeaway for dinner, and I was texting him. I'd never known him to be at the football club so late. Eventually he texted back to say he was on his way home.

He walked in and just started crying. He said, 'It's back.' Initially I thought, 'What's back?' I'd lost all memory of it. And he said, 'The cancer's back.'

I could see he was devastated. He's not a crier – he didn't cry at our wedding. It was the first time I'd ever seen him cry.

He said, 'It's back, and it's in my lungs. They've found four spots.'

I was definitely in a state of shock. Cancer in the lungs. Lung cancer. You look at the statistics and they're pretty grim.

I asked him if he was going to die and he said, 'No.' I asked if he'd play football again and he said definitely. He said he'd be an All Australian again. That was just his response. We went from having a moment of shared emotion to, 'I am going to be fine.' So positive, and even having a laugh with family and friends when they arrived.

That night we went to bed and he was just exhausted, but I couldn't sleep. I probably only had a couple of hours sleep the whole night. He breathes so loudly when he gets into a deep sleep, and I'm a really light sleeper. It's always bothered me: pillow over the head or earplugs. That night I was wired, and I vividly remember thinking, 'I'll never get sick of hearing this.'

Jarryd is so extremely positive. I was quite the opposite – angry at the world. Life felt unfair. We were just married, I was 26, he was 29. I thought we didn't deserve this, that he of all people didn't deserve this. It's still quite emotional for me. I had a great network around me, but there's the quiet times on your own, when you research online or read books and get taken away on this awful tangent of what might be.

We had been thinking about starting a family. I remember thinking, 'Do we freeze his sperm?' I was really lost in it all and felt like I was barely keeping afloat. I wasn't sure if we'd ever get out of it, or how.

It definitely changed our relationship – not at all in a negative way, but it was just different. Here was this handsome, big, strong man, and then seeing him so vulnerable during his treatment – he'd lost a lot of weight. What I love about him is that he's well-kept, but he's a bit of a scraggy mess as well. He lost all of that, all of that spunk. I was scared. 'What if it never comes back?'

Jarryd never let any doubt or negativity enter his recovery, he was just so positive, like a determined steam train – no stopping, no distractions. If I was pushing some questions, some what-ifs – about his treatment, health, career or family – he would just shut off and not want to consider anything other than, 'I'm getting well, and life will be normal again.' What he did for himself was create this bubble, this place where there was no other reality than, 'I'm getting well – watch me get well.' Everything else was just white noise.

I don't think there was a time when I wasn't thinking, 'What if?' As much as you try to remain positive and keep a brave face, I thought, 'This really sucks.' You want to be able to talk it through with someone. To be able to say, 'It's not okay – it might be eventually, but right now it's crappy. How are we going to get through it?' That's where we're different in a sense. But that was just how we managed.

He didn't see his parents while he was sick. I know that seems strange, but again, that was just his mindset. 'I don't need a hundred people around to get me through. I'll be fine. Are you fine? I'm fine. Don't make a fuss. Let's get on with it.'

During his treatment, when he was really unwell, so thin and sweating so much that the bed needed changing daily, I'd go to work and my mind would be all over the place. I'd just started a new job, and they were so accommodating with time off when I needed it. I didn't progress very far in my career, those months that Jaz wasn't well. But work was good for me, a distraction.

There were days when I'd get a call and he would have driven himself to the hospital, to the Peter MacCallum Cancer Centre, because he was just so sick. Some of those times I didn't even know – he'd called Cam to take him, because he never wanted me to worry.

When they suggested the immunotherapy treatment, and how much it was going to cost, I just thought, 'How do people afford to do this?' But they do, they re-mortgage homes, they do whatever it takes. For us, it was incredible to find support in Geoff Harris and the Hawthorn Football Club. They financially supported us with a percentage of the cost. We were both blown away by the gesture and so grateful for the support.

I was still playing country netball every weekend; I made sure I stuck to that, and it was very good for me. It was tough early on, seeing everyone at the club. I never minded talking about it, but at the same time you don't want it taking over your lives, all of your conversations. I had my mum and sister to lean on, and some amazingly supportive friends. People are incredible in such times.

My first game back at netball, the girls all got in a huddle and they all started crying. It was just a moment of, 'We're here for you.' It was special and emotional, to see how it had impacted them. They were my teammates, not my best friends – I just played netball with them on a weekend and trained on a Thursday. But they made me realise there were so many people who cared. I was so grateful for that. We won the game somehow, too. I was an emotional wreck afterwards. I was so exhausted, I had to get Mum to drive me all the way home. But I needed to have that game, and see all those people who knew us and cared for us both.

We're quite private people; I'm shy in a sense. So those little things, like my first day back at work after it had been in the paper, were overwhelming. It was the same going back to the netball club – seeing all the girls for the first time after, it came with a lot of anxiety. It took a lot to build up the courage to do it. And again when I saw all of the girls from the football club. Every first, it made the whole situation feel very real.

The builder asked if we wanted to stop the renovation. I said, 'No way!' I thought it would keep us occupied. Even though it meant we were living out of two rooms, on a two-seater couch, cooking in an electric fry pan, washing dishes in the shower . . . And then I got a cat. Jaz hates cats! But I said, 'I need the cat.' It was funny; from the cat I got what I needed that I couldn't get from him.

The hardest part was the obvious part: no one could guarantee that he was going to live. I'm black or white: 'Is he going to, or not?' And there was no guarantee. We know now that if the immunotherapy hadn't been available, his chances of survival would have been dramatically worse.

Back then, I needed someone, anyone – a person on the street, even – to say to me, 'He's going to live, it's going to be fine.' I just wanted to believe something. So I went and saw a psychic.

It was a dark and dingy Wednesday night in August. My sister drove me to this house in the outer suburbs and waited in the car for an hour while I was inside. This woman read cards. I didn't tell her anything; I've still got the recording. She asked what was going on, and referred to someone being unwell. I started crying and she said, 'This is a tough year for you.' Then she said life would become better, it would be normal again.

I would have believed anything. My personality is a need-to-know personality. I'll start a series on Netflix or a book, and I'll get a few episodes or chapters in and I'll be googling the ending. I struggle not knowing.

The day Jarryd was told he was cancer-free was strange. We knew there had been signs of improvement, that the tumours were reducing in size. But even getting the all-clear, we weren't high-fiving. It was more or less like, 'This is great, but let's not get ahead of ourselves.' Jarryd still didn't know if he'd play football again. And there was so little known about immunotherapy, you start questioning whether it'll last. Maybe that's being negative, or maybe it's just being realistic.

Initially the tests every three months were worrisome. I could tell in the lead-up that he was edgy – sometimes I wouldn't even know, he wouldn't mention that he had the appointment, and then it would all make sense. He'd be quiet, not himself.

He manages it a lot better now. We both do. The tests have been bumped out to every six months and it's just routine. But I know he'll still be nervous, reliving that day when he found out. It takes a strong person to get on with life, and he's managed to do that.

I still have moments of reflection; you go back to that time. I've definitely dealt with it, but it was just a really dark, sad time. It wasn't just those six months, it's the 12 to 18 months afterwards, trying to get back to where we were before Jarryd got diagnosed. He's definitely a changed person – we're both different people because of it. We just focus on what's important, and the people who are important. And anything else out there that isn't, we try not to let it impact us.

Jarryd, maybe not so much now, but in the time afterwards, he lost his larrikin spunk, his charm. But it's come back, *he's* back.

I struggled with early parenthood, but Jaz was a total natural. A family is something he has always wanted and he's always been so wonderful with children. To see him and Pippa together, a dad and his little girl, it's so beautiful.

His mindset is very strong, which is amazing – and it does borrow a lot from being a professional athlete. What's the challenge, what do we need to do, how do we overcome it? It's helped him enormously, throughout his whole life. And now I know he's got this fierce way of approaching challenges, and together as a team, it's going to be fine.

Jarryd is definitely the leader of this family and, upon reflection, I guess that's why I struggled so much while he was unwell. As parents we're finally finding our groove and having such fun with Pip. We're all still here, making the most of this life, and that's the most important thing.

GEOFF HARRIS
Benefactor

I was born above the shop my father ran in Glenferrie Road after he came back from the war. Watching Hawthorn play at their little local ground was a huge part of my childhood – I was the kid with the autograph book, standing at the race after the game, looking up at the players thinking they were gods. Guys like Graham Arthur, John Peck, Ian 'Liberty' Law. I thought they were superheroes.

I had a fascination with John Kennedy Senior, the patriarchal elder who created an aura of leadership. It almost became a case study to me – that sense of discipline and team. He was there with his men, running and training in old tennis shoes, going home with his Gladstone bag every night to his wife, didn't drink, didn't smoke. He was almost the perfect role model.

That essence of leadership still resonates with me now, that uncompromising sense of team, where everyone's got a role to play – be it a volunteer, a president, a franchise player, a rookie – and it's all part of the club's success. Great leaders leave their values in organisations and Kennedy was a great leader who left his values at Hawthorn.

I've been very lucky in my business journey. I came back to Melbourne from London in the 1970s and three of us set up the first Flight Centre in Hardware Lane in 1982. I got involved with Boost Juice when it was a start-up and only had four stores then; I sold out when it got to 270 stores.

I've been lucky. In my fifties I stepped back and started looking at more philanthropic opportunities in the community. I joined the board of Reach, then STREAT, and also became involved in Whitelion. Helping at-risk youth, seeing them turn their lives around and find hope where they thought there was none, that's real reward.

When Jarryd became ill, the problem was the best treatment was a combination of drugs that were brand new to Australia and weren't on the PBS. It was going to cost about $400 000 for this life-saving drug. Sarah and Jarryd had just got married, they were planning a family, they'd bought a house that they were about to renovate – and then he gets this life-threatening illness.

I rang up Stuart Fox, who was CEO of Hawthorn, and told him I'd heard this treatment was a game-changer but would cost a fortune. I told him I was happy to go 50 per cent, and the club and Jarryd could kick in the rest.

Stuart went to the AFL and initially they said it would be counted as part of Hawthorn's total player payments for the 2016 and '17 seasons. We all thought that was ridiculous, Stuart kept negotiating, Gil McLachlan got involved, and eventually Ken Wood at the AFL signed off on a document laying out how the treatment would be paid and that it wouldn't fall within the club's salary cap.

The cost in the end didn't quite end up as high as we'd thought – because thankfully Jarryd got better so quickly. But the methodology was sound and we couldn't hang around and try to do a fundraiser, there was no time, he needed to start the treatment straight away.

I joined the Hawthorn board in 2005 and did three three-year terms. I started just after Roughy, Lance Franklin and Jordan Lewis were drafted and Alastair Clarkson started as coach. We went young on our playing list and reasoned that we needed a teacher as a coach. Bringing the 44 players together, walking the Kokoda Track with former SAS commandos critiquing them, that was a big part of that idea – they could advise us on who the natural leaders were.

The players adopted the values of the soldiers who were on Kokoda in 1942 – mateship, sacrifice, endurance, courage. It was one of the many things that helped galvanise the group. In four years we went from second-last and broke to making $1 million in profit and winning a flag. It's a classic example for any organisation on how to turn things around: creating a great culture by having great leaders in all the key slots.

I remember meeting Jarryd as a red-headed, skinny, shy country kid. I came to know him reasonably well – he was just a friendly lad. It took him a good couple of years to make it, but he always had that raw, country spirit.

He's a nice human being, and a Hawthorn person who was in desperate straits . . . I was fortunate enough that I could help, so I did. It wasn't an emotional thing, more that an elite athlete had got this disease, having just married, someone so young – that's tough. It was almost an unbelievable scenario. I knew he was a good person, and helping out was just the right thing to do.

Ron Walker had used a different immuno drug the previous year – what Jarryd was given was basically the next wave. We'd heard that treatment was compatible with melanoma, he needed it, so we fast-tracked it and made it happen.

I didn't actually speak to Jarryd at the time, just did it through Foxy. As soon as Jarryd found out he rang me, and it was a pretty emotional call. He knew his life was threatened, he was under stress, everything had come at once. To be given a leg-up was really important to him.

Whenever I see him now he gives me a big bear hug, just about breaks three ribs. I don't go out of my way to see him, but we text regularly to say g'day. There's obviously a real connection, you know you've helped somebody out, that's good. It was initially meant to be anonymous, but it got out. I don't mind doing it, there was never any feeling of debt. I could, so I did.

I didn't see Jarryd when he was really unwell during his treatment, I stayed clear. But I know he was very sick. I'd text to see how he was going, there was constant dialogue in that way. He had shocking nausea, like flu 100 times over, and of course there was the numbness in his feet. Everyone thought the treatment would take longer than it did, and we were pleasantly surprised how quickly the spots on his lungs went.

When he got the news that he was cancer-free he was on the phone quickly, and that was a pretty teary call too. It was a big day for everyone. Then to see him play again – it was just a great story of persistence. I'm proud of the footy club for standing by him and looking after one of their boys.

Jarryd stayed on just long enough and stepped back at the right time. We had spoken about that, leadership and timing. We talked about the old saying, 'You don't want to wait until they're saying you should go, you want to go and have them asking, "Why did you go?"' When you think of all our politicians, very few of them get that right. Shane Warne did it – he took seven wickets at the MCG in his second-last test, played at Sydney the next week, then finished up. Jarryd handed the baton of the captaincy on at just the right time.

I guess I've become a little bit of a life mentor for Jarryd, just someone for him to have a chat to. The leadership thing was an obvious one for me. One door shuts, another opens. Jarryd working at St Kilda now, that's great. He's still passion-ate about footy. I can see him as a player-welfare manager, list manager, that sort of thing. He's got good empathy for people – those country values shine through.

When I look at Jarryd now I see a really good person, someone who got the best out of himself. And simply as a footy fan, I'm grateful that he came to Hawthorn. He was a champion of the club. That draft he was in became the genesis of the greatest period in the club's history. You think about that journey together with Lewis and Franklin, they've become his great life mates. How fortunate is he?

And Jarryd's story shows how fortunate we are to live in Australia, where the government can make the sort of drugs that saved his life affordable to everyone. He was the pioneer, and he was bloody crook initially. But here he is now with a little child, and that little girl has got her Dad. It's a great story.

CHAPTER 12
'I Can See What's Coming'

In many ways 2018 was the best year of my life. I'd been cancer-free for almost two years. In February Sarah gave birth to Pippa, our beautiful little girl, the first of our new generation of Rougheads. Life was good.

My football life should have been good too. We'd only finished twelfth in 2017, with 10 wins and a draw, but I'd played every game on the way back from a year out, kicking 38 goals. I was captain of the club I loved. There had been big changes to the list and while we weren't blowing away sides, we were competitive. I could feel something building.

The last game of the 2017 season had been against the Bulldogs. It was both Bob Murphy and Hodgey's last game. We won and I kicked a few. In the exit meeting the next week the question was, 'What made you play well compared to the rest of the year?' I thought it was just time; after I did my Achilles in 2011 it had taken me 12 months to really find red-hot form again. Plus, in the game before, against Carlton, I'd put in a bad performance – I was determined not to go into the break on a downer. I wanted to finish the year enjoying footy. That happened against the Dogs, and I was feeling good about things picking up in 2018.

After all of the change we'd been through, there was excitement that this group was gelling together and going places. Jaeger O'Meara's knee was coming good, Tommy Mitchell had won a best and fairest and been All Australian in his first season as a Hawk, and we had some really good kids coming through. Looking to 2018, I was thinking, 'Let's see what can happen.'

Fast forward ten months. We'd just beaten Fremantle in Perth in round 19 and were sitting seventh with four games left to sew up a spot in the finals. It was a Tuesday afternoon, everyone was almost done for the day, and I was heading to see the physio and then out the door when Clarko asked if we could catch up. A few minutes later I was in a room upstairs, sitting across from Clarko and our list manager, Graham Wright.

Clarko said something I'd never thought I'd hear. 'What do you want to do with your footy life? Do you want to go to Gold Coast? Do you want to go to St Kilda? We can make it happen if you want to. We're happy for you to stay here, don't get me wrong, but do you want to go and help someone else?'

Clarko always said I either go silent or I go violent. The latter wasn't really an option, so I just sat there. The question was no longer 'What can happen?' but 'How did it come to this?'

———

Going into the 2018 season I hadn't given a thought to the finish line of my career. I had two more years on my contract and I was excited about the way we were tracking towards a tilt at more success.

We started the season well, beating Collingwood then Geelong by a point, lost to Richmond, beat Melbourne in round four – when Cyril did his knee in what ended up being his last game. We lost to North, won a couple, then lost three in a row to West Coast, Brisbane and Sydney. We were questioning why we weren't playing well, questioning the game plan. Luke Breust, Tommy Mitchell, Ben McEvoy and Blake Hardwick were playing well, but it felt like everyone else was trying to find their form again.

Six rounds in, after we beat St Kilda on a Saturday night in Tassie, I had heard some speculation in the media questioning whether I might be playing my last season. I just blew it off and thought, 'I'll prove you wrong.'

A lot had changed in the year I missed. In 2015 I had Hill, Hodge and Lewis kicking the ball to me, now it was Mitchell, O'Meara, Henderson, Morrison. I'd gone from knowing which foot the bloke with the ball would roll onto, knowing for certain that he'd see me and hit me, to leading for blokes I hadn't built an understanding with yet. It was hard, because in my mind I almost expected them to have a better understanding of how I played, rather than me having to work them out.

Clarkson is a systems-based coach: if you fit into the system then the 22 who play each week know exactly what's going to happen. That had fallen away, simply because there were so many fresh faces.

After that loss to North Melbourne, Clarko challenged me in front of the group. Tex Walker had played poorly for Adelaide the week before, then on the Friday night he'd kicked four and helped the Crows get over the line against Sydney. Clarko said something like, 'Look how Tex responded. How's our captain going to respond?'

I was fine with getting baked in front of my teammates; I'd been around long enough to see the old 'shoot one, scare a thousand' approach before.

Then in the review on the Monday, Jack Russell went at me in the leaders' meeting. Jack had been at the club for as long as me, so there was enough respect there that he could have his say where other fitness coaches might have bitten their tongue. But I was still taken aback by what he said.

In front of the leadership group, Jack asked me, 'Does it mean as much to you as it used to?'

Battling a life-and death-illness tends to give you some perspective. Faced with a question like that, I felt like saying, 'If you want me to answer honestly: of course it doesn't. I've got my health. I've got Pippa.'

But I knew there was no point to me talking – I wasn't going to get anywhere – so I just stayed quiet and agreed. They asked if I was going to say anything and I said, 'What's the point? What's in your mind, I can't change.'

I was angry for a week and didn't really talk to either Clarko or Jack. I knew I had the support of the rest of the leaders, the boys throughout the footy club, other coaches, but my relationship with those two – who I'd been with since I was 17 – was tested like it had never been before.

Looking back, was that the start of things going south? Maybe. If water keeps drip, drip, dripping on a rock, it wears it down eventually.

The season rolled on. By the time we beat the Bulldogs in round 16, the volume on the talk about my future had been turned up from the occasional murmur to full-blown chatter. Because Lewis, Mitchell and Hodge had all finished their careers in another jumper, the media was mad for speculating whether that was going to happen with me. After the Dogs game I did a TV interview in the rooms with Bruce McAvaney and Matty Richardson, and they asked about it. Then Jon Ralph from the *Herald Sun* grabbed me and told me he felt bad even asking because of what I'd been through. 'Why are we even questioning it?' he said. I was thinking, 'I couldn't agree more.'

Around that time Clarko was asked a question in a post-game presser along the lines of, 'Will Roughead see out his contract to the end of 2019?' His response was something like, 'Where we can, we like to see players finish their contracts.' I didn't think anything of it – I actually thought he'd done the right thing, pretty much said, 'He's got a contract, he's gunna play.'

But in the next day or so Lewy and Hodgey both called me to ask if everything was alright. I was like, 'Yeah, sure, why?' And Hodgey said, 'I've seen this, I can see what's coming.' That planted the seed and I started to get worried.

The next week I got on the front foot and told the club I wanted to do the weekly player presser. Even as captain I'd never had to do all that much media, simply because between our leaders and emerging leaders there were a dozen, maybe 15 blokes they could rotate in front of the cameras.

But whoever fronted the media kept getting asked the same question: how's Roughead's form? I just thought, 'Stuff this, I don't want people having to answer for me, I can do that myself. Stomp on it and put it to bed.'

I fronted the media at the start of the week with an attitude of, 'I'm here now, you can ask me, and after this it's done.' The first question was along the lines of, 'Are you thinking of finishing up this year?' I said, 'I've got a contract, why would I?'

I couldn't go violent in a media conference, and I couldn't go silent either, but I was pissed off and it showed. One, Clarko hadn't backed me up. Two, Hodgey and Jordy had been in my ear. And three, the media were coming in loaded and ready to fire. I know they all had to ask the question, but I never lied to the media, so I just told it as it was.

I didn't want to give them a headline, but I gave them enough for everyone to know that I was upset. People at the club thought I went too defensive and weren't too happy.

A couple of days later I said to Wrighty, 'I've known you for five or six years, we've been through everything and we always speak. Talk to me. Why hide stuff from me? If you guys are having the conversation, tell me now. I don't want to be blindsided like Lewy was.' He didn't really give much away.

That's where you start to understand the business more than ever. I'd seen enough following American sports, I knew how it worked, but until it happens to you there's no way you can prepare yourself for it. There's always emotion in it, you can't escape that. Imagine telling yourself at 17 that you'll have a good career – better than you could ever have imagined – but at 31, when you're captain, they'll come for you. You can't prepare for that. From the moment I arrived at Hawthorn everything had been good in my footy career, but they still came for me.

Sitting in that room with Clarko and Wrighty, being asked if I wanted to leave Hawthorn and finish my career somewhere else, I realised that footy life is like real life – when you start out you're like a baby, and by the end you're just about dead.

I wasn't ready for it, not at all. And my gut reaction stayed with me: did I want to play for someone else? No.

I was a bit dazed for the rest of the day, and by that evening and the next day I was no good. Sarah noticed, of course. My coping mechanism was to go quiet – silent rather than violent. I was as flat as shark shit.

It was no coincidence that the following Saturday against Essendon I did a hamstring in the first ten minutes. It was the first soft-tissue injury of my career.

Stress can do strange things to you – back in January Sarah had pranged her car, and luckily she was okay, but I was stressed about it, really worried about her. I went to the club the next day and ran a shit time trial. In terms of footy, I'd never had to deal with anything like that uncertainty over my future, and I'd never done a soft tissue either. Jack Russell, the doc and physio all agreed stress had played a part in me straining a hamstring for the first time.

It was a decent hammy too – there was a bit of tendon damage – so I had to be careful not to make it worse. When I missed round 21, against Geelong, it was the first time I'd missed a game since I came back. Including preseason stuff I'd played 46 games on the trot after a year off – I reckon I did alright in that sense.

I spent the time out talking to people and trying to figure out what I should do. I was walking along the street near home, up a hill, when Stuey Dew answered my call.

Dewy had almost pre-empted this exact situation when he got the Gold Coast job at the end of 2017. Back then he'd asked me if I thought there was a chance Clarko might do the same with me as had happened with Lewy, Mitch and Hodgey. I said it wouldn't happen, and Dewy had said, 'Well, give me a call if it does.'

When I rang him that day he knew straight away what was going on. We spoke several times over the next few weeks, and he was open to all sorts of ideas. Do you want a two-year playing, three-year coaching deal? Do you want one and four? I said, 'Look, mate, let's get through finals and see how I'm feeling at the end of the season.'

Obviously I spoke to Sars and she was open to having the discussion about leaving Melbourne. But it never got to the stage of, 'Let's go up north and have a look.'

In the end I just kept coming back to not wanting to start all over again. Yes, I could have gone to Gold Coast with the idea of helping to develop their kids, but I wanted to stay at Hawthorn and help *our* kids, rather than starting a relationship with a new group of players I didn't know. I also didn't know if I even wanted to help another team to do well, because I knew when I was done playing I'd still barrack for Hawthorn and cheer on the kids I'd played with. I thought about it for maybe a day, but I just couldn't do it.

There was speculation in the media that I was going here, there and everywhere – to Carlton, to Collingwood. Apparently I was seen with Luke Beveridge, so I was definitely going to the Bulldogs. I know how the game works, I'd seen it with other blokes. 'Should this team have a crack at him? Should he go to that team and help make them better?' But when it's you they're writing and talking about, it's bloody confronting.

It seemed like every time I was bathing Pippa, Mark Stevens or Tom Browne were on the TV screen in my living room saying, 'The jungle drums are beating, Roughy's leaving Hawthorn.' These blokes camp outside a footy club staring down a camera saying, 'Sources tell me this could happen.' They don't know.

I've always said that they should get a show going where players hide behind trees and nab some reporter while he's walking the Tan Track in tights on his day off – the player jumps out and asks the reporter a load of bullshit questions. That'd be better than some of the crap they do.

Everyone I was speaking to was saying, 'Why don't you just go around to Clarko's and talk it through?' Lewy initially said, 'Just go. If they don't want you, just go.' Lewy's the bluntest person I know. When I eventually said I was going to stay, he said he'd always wanted me to.

I'd already been having conversations about giving up the captaincy, purely because I wanted to enjoy my last year as much as I could. I'd been in a leadership role since 2008, when I was 21. That involves leadership group meetings and all the other little extras that come with that. By the time you're 32, that's a lot of extras. I looked at Shaun Burgoyne, who hadn't been in the leadership group for a couple of years, and at 36 he was preparing to go around again. He'd been able to focus on himself. For any footballer, as much as you say you don't want to be selfish, towards the end you've got to be.

So on a Wednesday night in August I grabbed a couple of Melbourne Bitters and put them in my little Esky with some ice. I knew Clarko wouldn't drink them, so I went via a bottle-o and grabbed a couple of Coronas for him. He knew I was coming, and I don't know if it was arranged, but Karen and the kids weren't home.

We sat down and it was comfortable from the start, I guess because I felt like I had nothing to lose. We talked about everything – family, life. Eventually I said, 'There's a reason why I'm here.' I told him my future had been constantly on my mind, that I thought I'd done my hammy because of the stress of the constant questions. I said, 'I want to stay. I know you've given me all these options, but I don't want to go anywhere. I want to help us get better here.'

He was straight up about how he saw my prospects for 2019. He told me I could end up out of the team, playing in the VFL for Box Hill. I said I didn't care, that I'd still rather be at Hawthorn. I looked at Lewis and Mitchell and Hodge, all Hawthorn greats who finished their careers in another jumper. I didn't want that, I wanted to stay and have it out.

We talked about how the next year might play out similar to when Buddy and I started in 2005, when Nick Holland only played three games for the season because they decided to get games into us young players instead. Would I be prepared go back into defence? Would I help Mitch Lewis take the next step to becoming a serious AFL forward?

Of course I was prepared to help him, and I understood he needed to be given a chance. But in 2005, when Buddy and I played 20 and 16 games respectively, the club hadn't been in a position where we could win a flag. In 2018, we were gearing up to play finals footy. I didn't think Mitch Lewis should be handed as many games as Buddy and I had been if I was still playing well, and Clarko and I had that conversation.

From that night on, he was like, 'Cool, we've made the decision, let's move forward.' His tone in media conferences was different too. It was a great example of how quickly Clarko gets over things.

The questioning still trickled along a bit. I went on *The Front Bar*, and of course they asked about it. I know they had to, I get it. Some people thought my response was a bit testy, but I had other people tell me it was the best *Front Bar* they'd seen. You can't please everyone.

At the start of the finals Clarko and I did a joint presser and no one asked. It felt like it was done then, that we could just move on. But then Mark Robinson did a pre-recorded interview with Clarko and asked the same question. Clarko said I had half a dozen options on the table: retire, keep playing, go to Gold Coast, coach, whatever else. That was the last question Robinson asked, apparently, and obviously they showed that one when it aired.

When we lost the semi-final to Melbourne and our season was done, Clarko said in the post-game presser that I would be playing at Hawthorn in 2019. For anyone who was still wondering, that should have finally been the end of it. He'd actually said the same thing on radio on the eve of the finals and a lot of people just hadn't picked it up.

He rang me after that interview and said he was sick of answering the same question too, so he'd been upfront. I felt like saying, 'You could have done that 10 weeks ago and saved us a lot of worry.'

Even in grand final week, when I did a couple of AFL and sponsor appearances, people were saying, 'You'd look good in such and such a jumper' or, 'Why don't you come to Carlton?' As if you would.

There was an upside to it. By the time I got to my end-of-season exit interview, when normally you might be wondering what's around the corner, we'd already been through the whole thing and there was no chance of being blindsided. If we'd waited until the end of the season to have that, maybe I would have thought about going, because I wouldn't have been around the boys anymore and suddenly they'd be asking me if I wanted to piss off.

Lewy had left at 30 and got a three-year deal with Melbourne. His football life was fine, and he had a fair impact with the Dees. Who knows – after one more year at Hawthorn he might have been done, whereas Melbourne gave him an extra couple of years on his career. He enjoyed the change.

I was looking at being 32 when the 2019 season started, and that's a tough time to leap into the unknown at a new club. The outcome I wanted all along was to stay, and I'll always be glad I did.

All up in 2018 I played every game, felt like I contributed, had my head chopped off and could have ended up somewhere else or been finished altogether. Funny game, footy.

On the Monday in grand final week I went to the Brownlow Medal as Tom Mitchell's date, and of course he won. I got in there about 3 pm, had beers until about 11, moved on to water, started fasting at midnight, got home about 1.30 am and was at the hospital at 6 am to have clean-up surgery on my ankle. Very rock'n'roll.

I went to four Brownlows where we were playing in the grand final on the weekend, so obviously I didn't drink at those. The other years we never really had someone who was a chance to win it, so being there with Tommy made it a great night. And I didn't go nude as far as votes went – I was worried I wouldn't poll a single vote, but I got one against Essendon. It meant I still hadn't been to a Brownlow where I went nude.

When I woke up to the pre-dawn alarm to get to the hospital for surgery I was still getting Facetime calls from the boys, who were still out celebrating Tommy's win. We had a room off to the side at Crown for the six blokes who'd been invited to the event, but someone had a room upstairs where another dozen or so of the boys watched the count on TV – they all came down as soon as Tommy won.

It's funny, the actual Brownlow Medal's not much bigger than your thumbnail, but we were all partying like we'd won a premiership. Credit to Tommy – in his first two years at the footy club he won two best and fairests, was All Australian both years, and won a Brownlow. If it all ended there, he'd still almost go down as a legend of the Hawthorn footy club already.

Even after all that to end the season, you get excited straight away about next year. After we lost to Brisbane in Tassie in round 17, Clarko's only mission had been to play finals and get some September experience into the kids. We'd done that in 2007 – beating Adelaide in our first final, then losing to North the next week. That gave us a taste of it and the next year we won the flag.

When we beat Sydney in our last home-and-away game of 2018 to sew up the double chance, seeing the smiles on the faces of Jaeger O'Meara, James Worpel, Harry Morrison, Teia Miles and Conor Nash, it made me wonder again, 'What could happen?' But we didn't play well against Richmond in the qualifying final and lost, then caught Melbourne at the wrong time when they were on a run.

But all in all, if you were a Hawks supporter you'd have been pretty pleased to get to the top four and see your team play two finals at the G. After that Sydney game, Conor Nash said that the 45 000 people at the SCG were the loudest crowd he'd ever heard. Then the next two weeks he played in front of 90 000 at the MCG! Things like that made you think we were taking significant strides.

We were getting Sam Mitchell back to the club as an assistant coach, Chad Wingard from Port, Tom Scully from GWS, Chris Newman was becoming a line coach, the VFL team won the granny, we'd played two finals and got that experience into our young blokes. There was more blue sky than grey, that's for sure. Those things make you want to hang around.

People were saying I wasn't the player I'd once been because of the cancer and the treatment. That's fair enough, but how many players are still at their best in their last couple of seasons? It frustrated me that in certain parts of the game I could do things that left me wondering, 'Why can't I do this all the time? Why do I have an impact in one quarter and then go missing?' In the past I could fix it – go onto the ball, go into the ruck. But things change. I was a big focus point for the team for eight years, but then I came back and it had changed, the team and how it played were different, and I had to find a new way to fit in.

Stuart Giles, a businessman who has done great things in cancer care and also donated a lot to Hawthorn's Indigenous program, had organised a golf trip to the States in 2017, and we went again in October 2018. During that trip the business of modern footy was really rammed home – you just had to look around the group that went. Matt Suckling had already gone to the Bulldogs, Hodgey to Brisbane and Lewy to Melbourne. Ryan Burton and Taylor Duryea were both on the trip, and by the time we came home they'd been traded and were no longer my team-mates. That was five blokes gone right there.

People we got chatting to in America would hear that we were footballers and ask, 'So you all play together?' And I'd be standing there with Lewy and Hodgey or who-ever and answer, 'Yep.' Five minutes later we'd be like, 'Well, actually, we used to . . .'

For the 2018 trip, 15 of us met in Los Angeles and flew on to Sage Valley, just near Augusta. The rumour was the owner of the course hadn't been able to get a membership at the famous Augusta National, so he bought 10 000 acres a little to the north and built a course that's even better. Whatever the real story is, it was a pretty flash place for someone who'd only taken up golf a year or so earlier to keep a connection with the young blokes.

We played a handicap tournament in teams. I got paired with Ricky Henderson, and no one gave us a chance – Hendo was playing off 20 and I was off 27. On the first day we knocked out Duryea and Lewis, who were just about favourites to win the whole thing. Then we beat Burton and

James Sicily, made the final against Liam Shiels and Ryan Schoenmakers, who's off seven. We lost on the last hole.

There was an individual competition too and I was equal leader after day one, in front by a shot after day two, then won by two after the third day. Hendo should have won the whole thing but he fell apart on the last two holes and even wiped one. If he'd scored at all he would have won.

They were all calling me a bushranger, but I finished with 108 stableford points, which was playing exactly to my handicap. Take it boys, take it.

Even before the trip I'd heard that Doc Duryea might be going to Sydney or the Dogs as a free agent – the club offered him a one-year deal for 2019, but Clarko had told him if he could prolong his career and get a longer deal somewhere else, why not think about it? He couldn't go to the Dogs under free agency because it would have affected the Luke Dahlhaus trade to Geelong, so he had to be traded. The pick we traded him for was used to get Tom Scully, so we basically got Scully for Duryea.

The big one was Burton, who was seen as a 'future of the club' player. Just before we left, Chad Wingard had nominated Hawthorn as his club of choice for a trade, and we had offered Burton to Port Adelaide in exchange. Burton wanted to stay, but that didn't happen. Again, business.

If I'd been traded to another club it would have been for pick 80. It wouldn't have been as hard as the Burton trade. But he's an Adelaide boy who barracked for Port. And in terms of his footy life, he went to Port on a five-year deal on better money than he would have got if he'd stayed at Hawthorn. He could set himself up for life. It made sense, as harsh as it seemed.

The trip to America was good for me, it helped me clear my head. Before we left, about 10 days after our last game, I was at the club and saw Jack Gunston doing a personal training session. I looked at Gunners, working hard to get ready for another season that was still six months away and thought, 'Stuff that.' In hindsight, it made me realise how much the 2018 season had taken out of me.

By the time I got back and started running on the AlterG treadmill, the footy club looked like it did at the start of every pre-season: players like Burton and Duryea were gone, Jack Russell had moved to Carlton as fitness coach. The business of AFL footy had rolled on. They preach loyalty to you for so long, but when you're done, when the use by date arrives, they'll lick the stamp and send you on your way.

That was the unhappiest year of my footy life, but there was upside. It made me more excited for what was next – life after footy. I got drafted on 26 November 2004; I graduated high school and the next day I was an AFL footballer. All I'd ever known was school and footy. Whatever was next, it felt more exciting than worrying about whether my skinfolds and time trial would stack up in November.

CHAPTER 13
'This is What Dad Used to Do'

Following my ankle surgery I had a good pre-season in 2019. I gave up the captaincy and all leadership responsibilities, just tried to focus on enjoying footy again. Clarko had been pretty honest in terms of what I had to do to keep my spot: key forward stuff, fly at the ball, take your chances, contribute on defence. I played well against Richmond in Tassie in a pre-season game, and the first couple of weeks felt good. We beat Adelaide in round one – I had three shots at goal without kicking any, but I was getting chances.

Against the Dogs a week later we should have got belted. We were five goals up at three-quarter time but they kicked seven in the last and got us by a couple of goals. Maybe it was just because I was last to walk into the changerooms but Clarko went at me straight away. I don't remember what it was for; I had enough of that over the journey, the specifics tend to get lost.

We played North Melbourne the next week and Chad Wingard cleaned me up the day before the game. I corked my thigh and couldn't get up to play. I got straight back the next week and was good in patches – really good in the first quarter against St Kilda, then had a decent game against Geelong, playing ruck and forward and kicking a couple. The review of my game against Carlton the week later was essentially that in crucial moments I should have done better. The next week against Melbourne, I only had eight touches, didn't take a mark, kicked a goal in the last quarter that put us in front but we couldn't hang on.

Clarko called me in on that Wednesday. We were up against GWS in round eight. He said, 'You're not going to play.' It was about 9.30 in the morning and I was just about to head off to Canberra for a sponsor's function. I'm sure dropping me was hard for him, but we'd had the conversation and I knew that if my form didn't stack up this was what would happen.

I had a lot of thoughts going through my head – is that it, am I done? – but it is what it is. I could have cried 'poor me', thrown the towel in, but I decided to make the best of it and enjoy playing VFL for Box Hill. I had to tell the boys myself that I was dropped – Clarko said it would probably be better coming from me. To be honest, there wasn't much dialogue between us over the next few weeks.

Logistically, playing VFL didn't change things too much. I'd train with the Hawthorn boys at Waverley on Tuesday and Thursday, then either Thursday or Friday night at Box Hill. I'd go in to the club Friday morning depending on when the game was, have a team meeting at Box Hill

Friday night, play Saturday or Sunday. The VFL build-up doesn't involve as many meetings, it's just knowing what you have to do and enjoying your footy. Sometimes I found myself wishing it was like that at senior level too.

I hadn't trained on a Thursday night for more than ten years and I was the oldest player by a fair bit. When we played Williamstown in one of my first games, the second oldest player in the forward line was 21. I was 32. Some of my teammates I'd meet for the first time on the day of the game, which was interesting – I'd usually remember their nicknames, but I wouldn't know everyone's actual name.

Maxy Bailey was coaching, and I'd played in the 2013 premiership with him. He was really good – I'm sure it was tough for him at times, coaching me, but I don't think I let the disappointment of going back poison the group; my attitude was good.

My first Box Hill game, against Footscray, got a bit of publicity because of the footage of me giving some advice to my opponent, Reuben William, who was born in South Sudan and had played with the Brisbane Lions before the Dogs. It was a Sunday curtain-raiser to the Hawthorn–GWS game – it might normally have been weird playing at the G with the stands virtually empty, but the crowd (just over 14 000) wasn't much different for the AFL game later on. Footy on Mother's Day is a tough sell.

I had to get there when the gates opened, at 10 am, for an 11.50 game. The last time I'd turned up that early was playing Box Hill twos in 2007. Back then, I'd been dropped from Hawthorn to Box Hill and there was no senior VFL that weekend, so I played twos and went back up to the AFL the week later.

I had no reason to go back to the VFL and try to rip blokes heads off. I wasn't going to make it a war against whoever we were playing – these were kids, 19-year-olds straight out of school who were just trying to play. I was one of them once. I knew that playing with me was an opportunity for them to learn a bit – whether it was my teammates or an opponent who had asked a question.

In the first quarter I kicked two on William, and after one of them I just told him, 'You missed the body there.' He was smaller than me, so it couldn't have been easy for him. I kicked a third up the other end in the next quarter and he asked, 'How'd you manage to read that and get out the back?' I told him I watched the pressure from the next bloke up the ground, saw that we were going to get the ball, so I went that way while he kept watching the ball.

I kicked 5.1 by three-quarter time, then we ran out of legs and it was a draw. Clarko had told me even if I kicked six I was unlikely to come straight back in. As I said, we weren't getting on like a house on fire right at that point in time. I felt like a wall went up and he stopped communicating. In hindsight, it was just a classic example that breaking up is hard to do, whether it's in sport or in life.

We played Richmond the next week at Punt Road, the first time I'd ever played there. There was a big wind going to the train line and even though we had it in our favour in the last quarter, we didn't learn and went down by seven points. But I enjoyed it – it reminded me of footy back home. You rock up, get taped, have a quick team meeting, a couple of lollies, out you go, warm up, into it. No bullshit. Good meetings, good messaging. I understood what I could do to help and vice-versa.

There were plenty of firsts in that last season, playing in the VFL – Punt Road, Windy Hill, Frankston. During grand final week a couple of months later, I drove past Frankston with Jordy Lewis on our way to a sportsman's thing we were doing in Mornington. 'I've got a 100 percent winning record there,' I said. And that's not going to change, either.

My third game was against Collingwood at Victoria Park, which I'd played on once for Vic Country in the under-18 championships. There was dog shit on the ground on a forward flank and I fell in it. That was another first. Thankfully it was dry and didn't stick.

Before the game, officials went around moving on homeless people. I was walking through the car park and this bloke came up and said g'day and wished me well. I asked him if he lived nearby and he said, 'Yeah, in the grandstand.' I was thinking, 'Jeez, right, enjoy your day.'

We were in front again, this time kicking with the wind in the last quarter, and still lost. We just had a lot of young blokes who were still learning how to win together, what to do in crucial situations, not trying too hard, not trying to do special things, just doing the easy things.

Then we were at home. It was my first game at Box Hill since 2007. We played Williamstown, coached by Andy Collins, who had coached me in my first year at Box Hill.

We beat them, and of course the boys were all trying to get me in the middle of the song, thinking it was my first win with my new team. I told them I'd won games for Box Hill in 2005, when some of them were in prep.

I'll always remember my last season fondly, and with no regrets that I played on in 2019. The scenario Clarko had flagged the year before came to pass, but I enjoyed my time in the VFL. I had a ball. Sure, some games for Box Hill were harder than others – for instance playing on a Sunday after Hawthorn had won the day before. Or they'd play Friday night and I'd be at home in front of the telly with a bowl of pasta getting ready to play the next afternoon at god knows where.

I remember driving down to Frankston. It was mid-July, rain pissing down, wind howling, sky overcast, worst day in the world. You get there and it's a seven-goal breeze to one end. And you're like, 'Why am I playing here?'

We started into the wind and by quarter-time they'd kicked seven goals and we'd kicked one behind. A day like that, you think, 'Okay, at least the senior coaches won't be here.' So we get into the quarter-time huddle, and there's Alastair Clarkson, Scott Burns, Sam Mitchell – they were all there! I looked at them and thought, 'Really?'

As it turned out we got up and won. I didn't do much, kicked 1.3 or something, but I played everywhere. When you're seven goals down at quarter-time, you end up play-ing loose in defence, ruck, forward, midfield, everywhere.

There's something about going back to that level that brings back the pure enjoyment of the game. The changerooms are small and basic – there's nowhere to hide like in the MCG rooms – and half the time you don't even have a locker, just a hook to hang your clothes on. I liked it. There aren't the time restrictions on when you have to get there like in the AFL, and you don't have to hand your phone in to the property steward.

When we played Werribee, we caught a bus there and back from Box Hill and had a couple of beers on the way home. Old-school stuff. I knew that as a 32-year-old I could either crack the shits or buy in to what they were about. For me it was just, 'Fit in, who knows what can happen?'

In the end I only played two more AFL games after I was dropped following the loss to Melbourne in round seven – against Sydney up there in round 14 and my last game, against Gold Coast in round 22. The rest of the time I was a VFL player.

There were days when I wished I was still playing for Hawthorn. Like the week Shaun Burgoyne broke the record for most games by an Indigenous footballer. That was a Friday night at Docklands, and we were playing the next day so I was stuck at home in front of the telly.

My last game with Grant Birchall was against Geelong – at Box Hill in the VFL. Birch was coming back from injury, playing his first game of the season, and went straight up the next week. When I played against Gold Coast in round 22 he'd done a hammy the week before, so for all we'd been through, my last game with Birch was a win over Geelong. Beauty. Except it's Geelong in the VFL.

I'd like to think I finished with better relationships with the young boys on the list than I would have if I'd played all of 2019 in the AFL. I'm really happy about that. I think they all became comfortable around me, and vice-versa. Kids like 'CJ' Jiath, Harry Morrison, Jackson Ross, Dylan Moore – it's nice to think you might have played a small part in their careers.

Easily the toughest thing about my last year was how strained things were with Clarko. For a long time after I was dropped there wasn't much dialogue between us – a token chat in the middle at training, ticking a box, but neither of us had much to say.

At one stage he got me in and asked what my plans were for the following year; he told me there was a 99 per cent chance I wouldn't be at Hawthorn. Craig Kelly, my manager, had already told me he wasn't going to let me play anywhere in 2020, and that I wasn't going back to Hawthorn either. When Clarko asked if I wanted a job at the club, I said it was probably best I go somewhere else.

Ahead of the Essendon game in round 13 he dropped Mitch Lewis. I was at the club on the Thursday, having a massage, and got called in to a meeting. Scott Burns and Maxy Bailey were there. Clarko told me he was dropping Lewis, but not picking me – even though when he'd first dropped me he said it was in order to play Lewis, and if Lewis wasn't playing I would be.

He said, 'Mitch isn't playing and neither are you.'

I shot back, 'I knew that yesterday when the text went out and I wasn't in the squad. You don't need to tell me that.'

He went back at me about a few things. We'd done mid-year report cards, grading ourselves on impact and effort. I gave myself a C-minus for AFL and an A for VFL. He thought that I meant C-minus for my effort around the footy club after I got dropped, which just wasn't true.

So Mitch Lewis and I ended up playing together in the VFL against Essendon at Windy Hill. The next week we played Sydney at the SCG and I went back up to the seniors. It was supposed to be wet up there and their thinking was to get a taller, experienced bloke who was okay in the wet. I kicked a goal just before half-time, then did the classic cricketer's side strain – I've got no idea how it happened, but in the rooms I was really sore, couldn't take off to run. They gave me a jab but it wasn't deep enough and I really struggled in the second half.

I missed the next week against West Coast, then didn't get in the following week against Collingwood. That's where things went a bit further south with Clarko – there was no communication from either of us, since both of us are stubborn buggers. He didn't talk to me and I didn't talk to him. It was almost like seeing who was going to flinch first. I thought that after 15 years together we might have been able to get beyond that, but we couldn't. I got the situation, understood it all, but you just want to know, 'Why isn't he talking to me?' It was hard. The whole place was fun, but there were issues with the boss.

It came to a head on a Thursday arvo about round 16, when we had a bit of a barney. I think the club pushed him a bit – 'What are you going to do with Roughead? How is it going to end?' So he sent me a text saying we should catch up.

He had Graham Wright in there and I brought Cam Matthews with me. When things are strained and you're having big conversations, it's best to have a couple of impartial heads in the room who'll remember what's said without being weighed down by the emotion of it all. I just told Clarko what I thought, said he'd hardly spoken to me, asked what the story was. He said, 'Well, you haven't come to see me either.'

It wasn't personal, I just needed him to know how I felt. And that was, essentially, that I didn't feel comfortable enough to come and talk to him. He was trying to say it was an open door policy, he was always approachable, but I didn't feel it was like that.

I needed to stand up for myself and from then on I saw a change in him – towards me, and towards the group. I think it opened his eyes up to changing. If after 15 years I was saying that I didn't feel I could come to him, what about the blokes who hadn't been there nearly as long? It's about good communication, no matter how hard the conversations might be.

A couple of months later Richmond won the flag for the second time in three years and they were all talking about the connection between players and coaches. In my last year at Hawthorn I don't think that was as good as it could have been, but after we thrashed it out I saw things improve. Our form improved too: we beat GWS, Geelong, West Coast. I don't reckon it was a coincidence.

At the Crimmins Medal night a couple of months later, Clarko gave an amazing speech. He talked about losing perspective. He said that after we'd won the three flags in a row, he made it too much about winning and forgot about fun, about seeing the things in the game that had made him fall in love with it in the first place. He referred to me a few times, but he could have been talking about Mitch or Lewy or Hodgey too.

'Lose perspective and the game becomes a prick,' Clarko said that night. That's how it felt at times during my last season, but thankfully we found a way through it. God knows we've been through too much together for things to go pear-shaped.

There was no guarantee I'd get a farewell game. They said it could happen, but also that it might not. Our last game would be over in Perth, so on the Monday before our last game in Melbourne – Gold Coast in round 22 – I had a meeting with Clarko, our CEO Justin Reeves, our head of communications Clare Pettyfor and Wrighty. That's when they said, 'You're gunna play.' Clarko told the boys in the team meeting, and that night it was announced in the media. It helped that Mitch Lewis had hurt his shoulder, opening up a spot and making it an easy decision.

The rest of the week was gold – I was able to enjoy being around the boys, hearing all the things that were said about me. Jordy Lewis and Sam Mitchell didn't get that at Hawthorn, because they'd moved to other clubs. Hodgey retired as a Hawk, and they did the whole farewell really well with him, but then he bobbed up and played another two years at Brisbane. I'll always be grateful I had the opportunity to say goodbye as a Hawthorn player.

I went into the Gold Coast game confident that I'd get a couple of goals. During the week all the midfielders were saying they'd be looking for me and I said, 'Well you didn't help me in the first seven weeks, there's no point now!' But I knew the ball would come my way often enough to have a fair impact.

The club had been planning for a crowd of 18 000 at Docklands – apparently they were going to shut level three and just have everyone down the bottom. When they announced I'd be playing they revised it up to 25 000, and there ended up being 31 331 there. All you could hear was Hawthorn.

All the boys were in the rooms – Bud, Hodgey, Lewy, Birch. There's a photo of us five in the rooms before the game, which is an awesome thing to have. It would have been great to have Mitch and Shaun in there too, but they had a game to focus on and it didn't happen. That's okay – I've got plenty of great photos from that week, they're just amazing, and I'll have them forever. I ran out with Pippa in my arms and made sure I had plenty of souvenirs to take home with me – I wore five jumpers that day, changing into a new one at every quarter break and wearing two in the last.

My riding instructions were simple: every forward stoppage, just go there and get the ball. And I did. My GPS tracking was as high as it had ever been in the first quarter, I was just running around trying to get the footy. When Chad Wingard got the ball out of the middle, swung on his right, then cut back onto his left so he could hit me for my first goal, I knew we were on.

When I got a second goal right on quarter time, roved it and kicked a right-foot snap from the square, it was like, 'We could have a bit of fun here today.' It was six goals to one by then.

I didn't touch it in the second quarter, but got a bit of momentum up in the third, kicked another and then got a free kick. A few minutes earlier, my opponent Charlie Ballard had held me when I went to lead; I reckon the umpire saw it and didn't pay it. I let him know, and he paid the next one.

After that I got run down by Lachie Weller running through the 50, just to remind everyone I was old, but then in the last quarter Poppy passed one to me for my fifth, and then I kicked the last of the game.

That sixth goal, people said it was like turning back the clock. To me it felt like all the structure of being a Hawthorn forward went out the window – normally I'd look for someone to run past for a handball, or I'd try and spot someone up. Instead it was like going back to having a kick in the park.

Gunners put it out in front, the defender went past the ball, I read it better and grabbed it, swung it onto my left foot like I would in the park, around the body, goal, go nuts. The photos of that goal and the celebration are just ridiculous – they're the shots I'll have in a frame for life.

After the siren Lewy interviewed me on the ground for Fox, which was nice. I was chaired off in front of all my mates, and Gold Coast did a terrific job with Stuey Dew and Dougy Evans there, two special people. All the staff, the crowd. Down in the rooms, Sewelly was there, Joe Ingles, a heap of mates who'd been in a box the AFL had given us. And that was it, my final moment as a player; it's like you die as a footy player and everyone celebrates the end.

So there it was – six goals in my farewell game. And of course, then the question they were asking Clarko was, 'Surely he plays again next week?' Everyone was saying how mad it would be to risk ruining the perfect ending, but I was up for playing. If we beat West Coast in Perth and the Bulldogs lost their game, we'd be playing finals. I wanted a crack at that. If I went over there and kicked one or none, it wasn't going to put a dampener on the week before. Why not have a crack?

On the Sunday night after the Gold Coast game we all headed to my local pub, had the whole place booked. We stayed there until they closed, then a few of us went to Richmond. I had to be back in at the club the next morning, because they hadn't put a nail in the idea of me playing the next week – I had to do recovery as if I was.

I was sore, but more in the head than the body. I was pretty lucky with that during my career; I never lay in bed feeling shithouse after games, and normally got going again by Tuesday.

On the Tuesday night Clarko rang me and said we should put a full stop to it right there, I wasn't going to play, and that was fair enough. I still trained on the Thursday, for the last time. Had a walk around at the end, a good look, just took it all in.

I had a mate staying over and had about eight beers watching the Friday night game with him. I think I had beers every day that week – leading up to round 23! It wasn't a normal last round of the season, that's for sure.

Sars was out on that Friday night and Pippa got crook, had really bad gastro and was spewing every 15 minutes. I sat in the shower with her for ages, and when Sars got home we took her to the hospital. I got home about 2 am, then flew to Hobart at 9 am to watch Lewy play his last game. This time I interviewed him for Fox, which was good, I had a bit of fun with him.

When the boys ran out against the Eagles on the Saturday night I was on a plane flying home from Tassie. I listened on the car radio on the way home from the airport, and by the time they won I was in bed. The boys caught the red-eye home and on the Sunday we all went to The Rose in Fitzroy to watch the Dogs–Adelaide game. We knew that if it was over quick we could start enjoying the week and sure enough the Dogs were five goals up at quarter-time – we weren't going to be playing finals.

Mad Monday was at the Union Club in Fitzroy, which meant we dodged the TV crews who camp out at the same old haunts in Richmond to get vision of footballers in silly costumes. We never did dress-ups, so there was nothing to see anyway.

I had a medical on the Tuesday, which was actually bigger than any I'd ever had. In your exit medical they have to document every little thing that's possibly wrong with you that might be from playing footy, in case you come back at them in the future.

They ordered MRIs on both ankles and knees. I never had any issue from the hips up, nothing at all, but over the journey I had one knee operation, a PCL, three knee scopes, two scopes on the right ankle, and two Achilles repairs on the left. You know as a bigger fella that's what's going to cop it, in terms of the impact on your life after footy, and that you're probably only going to get heavier.

The exit interview was fine, because we'd already had the conversation. It was only Clarko and me, whereas before there would be assistant coaches in the room, and it was just a chat – what are you thinking of doing next year? Do you need a hand with anything? Almost like back to a few years ago, caring Alastair. I hadn't made a decision on where I was going to work, but I was open with him. By then we were fine; I sat next to him at the Brownlow, all good.

Clearing out my locker wasn't a big deal – I had grabbed things over the last few weeks but it was always pretty clean, nothing in there that needed to be thrown out.

I think I chucked out my toothbrush and my mouthguard, took a couple of pairs of boots and swimming goggles home, took a couple of footys, and that was it. Left two coat hangers in there and the code for the safe. Done, gone. Fifteen years, time to move on.

The absolute end – when you walk out the door for the last time – hits people in different ways. But for one reason or another I kept finding myself back at the club. My thumb print on the buzzer still worked, which made me smile.

The Tuesday of grand final week, all us blokes who'd played in the three flags from 2013–15 were out there having photos taken with our kids and the cups, recreating shots of us celebrating at the time. There were seven of us with kids – Hodge, Burgoyne, Mitchell, Roughead, Hale, Lake, Puopolo. It was the first time I'd had a photo taken with all four cups, which is a nice thing to have.

Pippa hadn't been born for any of my premierships, and there she was, hamming it up, sticking her head into one of the cups while they were taking photos of her and me. They'll be nice to look back on and say to her, 'This is what Dad used to do.'

CAM ROUGHEAD
Brother

I was born with a hole in my diaphragm. I contracted a bug inside the womb, Strep B, and that ate away at my diaphragm, which is one of the muscles that helps you to breathe. I was airlifted to Monash hospital two hours after I was born, and I was in there for a month and a half. They told Mum and Dad to expect the worst. From what I've been told, I was pronounced dead three times. Born a fighter, hey?

When I got out, I had 60 staples running from my chest down to my navel. These days if I take a big hit in my stomach, I'll feel it, but other than that the only real side effect is I've got asthma. And I've got a bed scar from where my head was resting – I didn't move for so long that no hair grew in that spot.

The only thing I remember from that time are the constant trips to the paediatrician, every three months, when I was maybe three or four. Mum kept a diary when I was in hospital and gave it to me for my twenty-first birthday. I still haven't read it – I don't know that I want to.

My strongest early memories are Friday nights, in the back of the car, travelling to Dandenong for Jarryd to play basketball. They could be 9 pm games, even 10 pm; some weeks we wouldn't get home until after midnight. On the way home we'd always stop at Encore Pizza in Cranbourne – $5.90 for a large pizza – and the rule of thumb was that by the time we got to Tooradin, only about 15 minutes down the road, there would be three empty pizza boxes in the back of the car.

I'm four years younger than Jarryd – five school years – and Em's in the middle. Jarryd and I shared a bedroom from when I was born until he was drafted, when I was 13.

We were just like any young kids in what we got up to – we loved our wrestling, imitating our favourite superstars. It was the 'Attitude Era' of what was then still the WWF, and we were always pretending to be The Undertaker or Stone Cold Steve Austin. We'd put a spare mattress on the floor and use that and our beds to land on, but once Jarryd did a Russian leg sweep and I cracked my head on an old VCR. Another time, playing footy in the backyard, he knocked out a couple of my teeth – pretty standard brother stuff, nothing too bad.

We were lucky that Mum and Dad never held us back in sport. They let us try anything we wanted and were prepared to put in the miles to get us there. It wasn't probably until Jarryd was really 16 or 17 that I started to think he was alright at sport. Before that we'd play in the backyard and he'd beat me, but only because he was older. I'd go to school and compete against kids my own age and I was fine – then I'd go home and get a touch-up.

Dad was a really good cricketer – and he'll tell you, too. He was a left-arm bowler. We'd be out for a family drive and go past some ground, Outtrim or somewhere like that, and Dad would say, 'I took 8-for there . . .'

Jarryd and I were both handy cricketers; he was good at whatever he wanted to play, really. That story about the 227 he made using my new Michael Clarke V900 Slazenger, when he hit 19 sixes – I bet he didn't include that it was on a ground the size of a postage stamp. Like, a junior oval. It was embarrassing. Really, it was barely worth a hundred. I'd made a first-ball duck: big 'Gooch' from Wonthaggi got me with a big inswinger. A few hours later Jarryd walked off and said, 'At least your bat's knocked in now.'

I think you always idolise your big brother, especially when you're so close. I never won anything against him, but I absolutely looked up to him – I wanted to spend as much time with him as I could, and do whatever he and his mates were doing. He allowed me to do that, which left me with a pretty strong relationship with everyone that he grew up with. There's guys his age that I'm still close friends with now.

They got up to some mischief that I was never a part of, like that thing with jumping fences. I remember being told years later by school teachers that there was a handful of boys who were the worst group of Year 12s they'd ever had, and Jarryd's name was in that lot.

He'd probably like to think he was right in the middle of it, but I think he got dragged into a lot of it and just went along for the ride. They did some pretty dumb stuff, but they got away with it and nobody got hurt, that's the main thing. On the back of it they've got a very, very close group of five to ten mates, all from that time.

It didn't seem to me that he was popular – he was still a skinny, pale, freckled, redhead kid from Leongatha. I don't know how popular you can be when you look like that. But I guess when you're in the local paper every second or third week, through basketball, footy, whatever it might be, people get to know you. We knew no different. Nan always collects the clippings out of the papers: Jarryd's got three big books of clippings, Emily and I have about half a book each.

I think Jarryd and I are similar, we've got the same mannerisms. A lot of people say I don't really have a filter compared to him – I'll say what I think, do what I want. But because he's always been my idol, and has helped me through so much, I'd pick up on his good traits and always want to replicate them. I'd see how good a person he is and want to be the same.

We've both got the same passion for sport, especially American sport, but we can talk for an hour about anything. During his career I never rang him and asked, 'How's the footy going?' It's the last thing he wanted to talk about.

Em's different to us, she has different interests. She's a good netballer and swimmer, but I just don't think it interested her as much. She was a hairdresser for quite a while, and lived in London and Edinburgh for a couple of years.

Initially, I thought Jarryd wasn't going to make it as a basketballer, but that he was playing too much basketball to become a footballer either. Then, when he was playing senior football at Leongatha and Dad was coaching the fourths, I realised he was going to be pretty good at footy. I'd go to those Gippsland Power games and he'd kick five or six and I'd think, 'Oh, okay . . .'

Then he played for Vic Country at the MCG. We used to go there maybe once or twice a year for a game, but it was a long way from Leongatha back then. To see your brother out on the G, in the national championships, that was like, 'Wow.'

I was probably too young to realise what it meant. And the internet wasn't in your face like it is now; everyone knows who the number-one pick is going to be these days. They've got people at the AFL who are employed just to talk about the young kids coming through. That wasn't there back then, which was a good thing – you could still be a normal kid before you were recruited.

Everything changed when Jarryd got drafted. The next night Alastair Clarkson and Damien Hardwick knocked at the door and took him to Melbourne. I had a room to myself for the first time in my life, and it was shithouse. These blokes who you don't even know rock up and take your best mate away – it sucked. I bawled my eyes out a couple of times to Mum. 'Who am I going to hang out with? Em's not a great kick of the footy, and she doesn't like wrestling!'

That first season he played I was a bit of a nuffy. Mum made up a big sign for his debut against Essendon, I can't even remember what it said, 'Go Rough' or something silly. You'd think that being in Year 8 and having a brother playing AFL would have some kudos about it, but early on there were times I hated it. I'd get compared to him in everything I did. 'Your brother's playing AFL, why aren't you any good at footy?' At that stage I was a little fat kid who got hidden in the forward pocket and played fourths.

I took a year off footy because I couldn't deal with it – he was playing at the elite level and I couldn't match that. But at the end of the day you are who you are, you just live with it. He's got skillsets that I don't, and I've got skillsets that he hasn't. Once I matured and understood that, I was fine. I had a growth spurt in Year 11, going from the little fat kid to a ruckman; now I've got Jarryd covered by a couple of centimetres.

I remember one win I got out of Jarryd being gone: we had to get pay TV to watch him play. That meant we also got the wrestling and American sport. I loved it. Another win was that once I hit 16, Dad would let me drive to Jarryd's games on my Ls, which meant I got my 120 hours up pretty fast.

In those first couple of years, when the fixture suited, Jarryd would say, 'I'm coming home,' and I'd think, 'Great, we get to hang out again!' But he'd be home all of five minutes and then go off to see his mates; I'd hardly see him at all.

But school holidays were good, I'd come down to Melbourne for a full week and stay with him. For a while he was living in Burwood with a mate who he'd played basketball with. Naturally it was all jokes on me: they'd offer me $50 to eat a tablespoon of Vegemite, or a sandwich with whatever they wanted to put in it. I'd always do it, and they'd always pay up. It was for their enjoyment, but hey, I was a 15-year-old kid – 50 bucks? Bring it on.

At the start it was pretty cool meeting Jarryd's teammates, hanging out with them. I'm lucky, working in talent management, dealing day-to-day with some of the biggest athletes and personalities in Melbourne. It reminds you that we're all people, no one's really any different to anyone else.

I'd done my Year 10 work experience at Elite Sports Properties, which became TLA Talent Management. They've managed Jarryd from day one; Brad Lloyd was his first manager. Then I did a degree in sports management at Vic Uni and did some placement work TLA. When they offered me a job, I jumped at it.

To start with I was in the memorabilia program; one of the first things I did was the 2013 Hawthorn premiership program. After that it was memberships: scarves, stickers, whatever you get in a footy club membership pack. I absolutely hated it. I stuffed something up for Melbourne footy club, got the wrong red apparently. How many different shades of red are there? It just looked like red to me.

I've always been a hard worker, always had a good work

ethic, but when I was in that role, I was like, far out, I can't do this. Somehow I weaselled my way into the talent area from there. The relationships I'd forged over Jarryd's career – just understanding how to deal with the talent – it's put me in a pretty good spot in my career, and I'm grateful for that.

When Jarryd first told me he had something on his lip, I just said, 'Mate, get some cold sore cream and fix it!' That's what it looked like. Not long after that, he rang me and said, 'I'm not playing this week – I'm getting a melanoma cut out of my lip.' He was pretty relaxed about it, they were just going to get rid of it and that would be it.

I'd been living with Jarryd and Sarah for four years at that stage, and had just moved out into a place with Emily and my partner Vonnie. Sarah was a bit shaken up, understandably. He had the day procedure at the Epworth and I drove Sarah to pick him up. Just seeing his lip, it was like, 'Shit!' He looked like the Joker out of Batman, his face all cut up. Think about taking off half of your bottom lip; he looked like a cat's arsehole.

He played a week and a half later, and from there we pretty much forgot about it. We'd see him back on the footy field and think everything was rosy.

The day he found out about the spots on his lungs, I knew he was going for a check-up. I got a missed call from him in the afternoon, and already suspected something was going on. Then he rang back and said, 'I need you and Emily and Vonnie to come over.' Then I knew for sure something was up. He never just said, 'Come over.' If you wanted to visit, you'd have to book it in three days earlier.

Sarah was in tears when we walked in. Jarryd just said, 'The cancer's back. It's in my lungs.' I always think you've got to stay positive, because if the person in the middle of it all sees weakness, they can go that way too, so instantly that's what we had to be. Any sign of defeat from others, he might have taken that on board.

I lived five minutes around the corner, so if they needed anything, I was there. And I was lucky with work – if I had to drop everything to help Jarryd, they were okay with that. It's nice to be able to be called upon, because it means you're trusted.

We didn't talk about him dying, and I didn't think about it either. Not once. The docs said they were going to try this new treatment, immunotherapy, and that the results had been really positive. Ten years earlier, he'd have been in a lot of strife, but now the outlook was okay. So I thought, 'Alright, strap in, let's go.'

He was pretty crook at times. There was one day where he called me at work and said, 'I need you to take me to Peter Mac.' I asked if he was okay, and he said, 'I just need you to come home, get me, and take me to Peter Mac.' He can be blunt, but it was obvious he was really struggling. Effectively all he was ingesting then was juices and smoothies – he was just too sick to keep things down, and even those drinks were coming back up.

When I walked in he was on the couch, white as a ghost. The heater was blazing, because just keeping his body temperature at a comfortable level was a challenge. When I saw him, I just thought, 'Shit he's crook.'

That was the worst it got. I drove him in there, and we didn't say a word. He could hardly even speak, he was so weak. All he could focus on was keeping warm. He'd lost more than 10 kilos and just looked so frail. By then he'd lost all feeling in his feet, so he was barefoot. It was just so confronting.

While he was undergoing treatment, it was his decision not to see anyone – not even Mum and Dad. Of course they were there for him, but he felt that them driving down from Leongatha wasn't going to achieve anything and would probably be more of a hindrance than a help; we all know what parents can be like. And Jarryd's a private person, he wants his own space, deals with things his own way.

It's hard to look back and think about how other people were coping. Em and I were living together, which was a good thing for me because it gave me a family member to talk to. She was always positive too – it must be a genetic thing! The support Jarryd got was amazing, but that's just what we were brought up with. Coming from the country, if something like that happens you just band around each other and get through.

The footy club was unbelievable too. They didn't know if he'd ever play footy again – it was a serious possibility – but the support that Clarko, his teammates and the docs gave him, it was so humbling. It showed that whole 'family club' thing isn't just a gimmick, it's real.

———

To be given the captaincy when he came back was a pretty special thing for him. He overcame something that was horrific, but just to see him back doing what he loved, that was the best thing for me. We had 50 or 60 people there when he made his comeback. It was a special day.

Jarryd's last season was tough for him. When he got dropped, there were blokes playing worse footy than him, but he was the oldest one. They weren't doing that well, and someone needed to make room. He knew that was a possibility, going into his last year, but he backed himself to finish at Hawthorn.

His last game was just so perfect. I played a final for Inverloch that day – we lost – and afterwards I jumped straight in the car and came up. The AFL kindly gave Jarryd a box for the game for close friends and family. When I got there most of the guys had been there for a while, and the consensus was Jarryd would go out with a bang. No disrespect to Gold Coast, but you just knew he would.

The boys were looking for him every time they had the ball, and I don't think he ever kicked straighter. A few things fell his way, a dubious push in the back in the third, but you make your own luck. I started thinking, 'Imagine if Clarko had played him out of the square all year . . .'

Going down and having a beer with him after the game, you couldn't have seen a happier bloke. The smile was ear to ear. It was just the perfect way to finish.

It's not until his playing career was over, seeing everyone heap so much praise on him, seeing all the highlights packages, all the nice things everyone said about him, that you actually look back and go, 'Far out.' It's pretty amazing.

Chris Judd didn't play 283 games, and how good a player was he? Nick Riewoldt never won a flag – and how good was he? Jonathan Brown only played 250-odd, how good was he? Jarryd won four flags and played in one of the great teams of all time – he's in pretty elite company.

Cancer has changed Jarryd, for sure. It's opened him up to understanding there's more to life than footy. So much of his life had been determined by footy, by the routine of playing at the highest level. Before, he was very narrow-minded. I'd always butt heads with him on that – when we lived together, I wasn't allowed to do certain things because he had to prepare for footy. He'd say, 'Just remember: you're living with me, I'm not living with you. We don't share – this is my house, and you're living with me.' He's a lot more relaxed now, he sees life through a different lens.

It's changed our relationship, too. I was a turd when I was younger – between 18 and 22, I was just a shit of a kid, but I guess everyone is at that age. The more you mature, the more respect you have for things in life. To watch him go through what he did, it's definitely changed all of us.

Everyone's had Jarryd wrong, though, which is pretty funny. The public have this idea that he's this laid-back, easy-going character who's always fun – for such a long time he was actually a prick. His way or the highway. Not so much anymore, but the littlest things used to set him off. If something didn't go his way, he'd crack the absolute shits.

Having a daughter has also changed him as a person – Pippa has forced him to be even more relaxed. Because the other thing about Jarryd is he's a shocking clean freak. I never really noticed when we were kids, but I guess when you get your own place and your own stuff, things can change. He's really bad; he'll brush the suede on the couch so it's all going the same way.

And I've never seen a bloke go through as much Spray n' Wipe as Jarryd. As soon as Pippa's finished playing with something he'll put it away and the Spray n' Wipe will come out. But when you've got a little one you soon realise you can't have the house spotless, you've just got to deal with it.

He still tries to have a routine, even with Pippa, but it just doesn't work. Once she came along we started seeing a lot more of him – he'll need to get her out of the house, so he'll walk around to ours and sit on the couch so we can deal with her. She'll tear up my place instead of his place. We don't mind. It's great having them around.

JORDAN LEWIS
Best mate

Every time I get asked about finding out that Rough had cancer – that there were spots on his lungs and he was in real trouble – I get choked up. He can talk about it, but for some reason I find it really difficult. It's weird. My wife Lucy and Roughy would both say I'm not an emotional person, but this gets me. I guess it's because, of all the people I've met through football, he's the number one.

Our paths first crossed at an under-16 basketball camp in Ballarat. His version of events is that he saw this kid who was wearing NSW basketball shorts (I'd come home from a tournament against NSW with a pair, just because I liked their blue more than the blue of the Victorian shorts), and thought to himself, 'That guy looks older than the rest of us, I'm gunna team up with him.'

I don't know what it was, but we got on instantly. He was the only kid there from Leongatha and he was looking for a mate. He says he spotted me and thought, 'I need to hang around with him.' I thought it was just my basketball ability that drew him to me.

As a basketballer he was a forward – too short to be a centre but too big to be a guard. I was a left-handed point guard. He was probably more likely to kick on as a basketballer than me – he made more representative sides – but you never know. When you've gone through a professional career, and learned all the lessons that come with that, you do sometimes think, 'Imagine if I'd known what I know now and applied it to basketball. Would I have made anything of it?'

We didn't keep in contact – 16-year-old kids didn't have mobile phones back then, and I can't remember ringing him at home. For the next couple of years we didn't see each other, then our paths crossed again through footy. I was top-age TAC Cup, he was bottom-age; I was Geelong Falcons, he was Gippsland Power. When we played against each other he'd be in the ruck or in the forward line, and I'd be on the opposition saying, 'Just tap it down here mate and I'll take it from there.' There was a bond already there.

When we spent a week in Melbourne, playing for Vic Country in the 2004 national championships, there was a day where there was no game and they said everyone could go home to their family for a night. Roughy and I were like, why would we want to do that? We lived in the country, why would we knock back a chance to hang out in the city? We were the only kids who stayed in Melbourne. We didn't get up to any mischief – there was certainly no alcohol consumed. I think we caught a tram for the first time and got lost – that was as exciting as it got.

We just enjoyed each other's company. I met Buddy Franklin at draft camp later that year, through Roughy, and the three of us all hit it off from the start. Even though we'd all grown up in different places, it just felt like we were mates who'd known each other forever.

Roughy was supposed to be going to Richmond, and I was going to Port Adelaide. He was more certain he was going to Richmond than I was about Port, but the night before the draft Port sat down with me for an hour and a half, so I knew they were keen.

I decided to stay at home on the day and follow the draft on the internet – it wasn't on TV back then, and I didn't fancy driving more than three hours back to Warrnambool after it finished. When Rough's name was called out as going to Hawthorn, I heard it clearly. But then there was a glitch in the system and I missed my own name getting called out. I was trying to get back online when messages landed from Roughy and Bud – we must have had mobiles by then – saying, 'I can't believe we're all going to Hawthorn together!'

For the first week, the three of us were billeted with the family of Gary Buckenara, who was the club's recruiter at the time. I was the only one with a licence, so I drove us around in an old Ford station wagon that Bucky leant us. We'd go to training, come home, sleep for an hour and a half until dinner, get up and eat a meal Annette Buckenara had made for us, then we'd go straight back to sleep. We were totally cooked from training.

Roughy was a bit shy – we didn't pick on him, but Bud and I would do stuff that we knew would wind him up. If we had the weekend off we might say, 'Let's go to Lorne.' And he'd be like, 'Nah, I don't wanna.' He liked everything to be planned, and that hasn't changed – if he hasn't processed something, worked it through in his head and got himself ready for it, he's no good. So we'd just rock up at his house and pick him up anyway. He'd get down there and have the time of his life, but the next time it would be the same all over again.

But he matured quicker than Buddy and me – the three of us all liked to go out and have a few beers, but he switched on a bit sooner. That said, he had this thing as though he had to prove himself, maybe because he was from the country and thought he had a reputation to live up to. If you were having a couple on a road trip, for instance, he'd finish a beer and make sure you heard the empty bottle rattling on the floor of the car. Or he'd crush the can, just so you knew he was ready for another one.

Early on he had a bit of a tight-arse streak, but that got knocked out of him. Midway through our first season the WWE came to town – Roughy and his brother Cam are huge wrestling fans, and Bud and I went along with them. We got tickets for Hawthorn's box at Rod Laver Arena; for 18-year-olds we were on a good wage, so the cost wasn't a big deal.

Halfway through the show, we heard Roughy say to Cam, 'Have you got that $60 for the ticket?' Bud and I looked at each other, thinking, 'Did he just ask his younger brother – who's still at school, who doesn't have a job and is still living at home – to pay him $60 for a wrestling ticket?!'

Now he's a sharer. We shamed it out of him, right then and there.

Roughy's always had his quirks. We roomed together on every interstate trip as teammates, and he was like a robot. It was the same thing every time: he'd get into the room, unpack his bag, line everything up, fold his clothes, grab the bag that'd been used to line the bin and take it with him to training so he could put his dirty clothes in there afterwards. I never got tired of it – we were given the option of rooming by ourselves, but it would have been so boring if I didn't have Rough there to keep me amused.

He's got an amazing memory, which is part of why I like hanging around with him – he remembers everything we've ever done, which jogs my own memory and brings all that good stuff back again. Early on I was the person who didn't care about much, whereas Rough was a deeper thinker who let things affect him more than Bud and me.

As a footballer, his competitiveness was a big part of what made him so good. He had a group around him who were all competitive people too, and that suited him perfectly. He's got this really strong trait of not wanting to let anyone down, and that drives his performance. In essence he just loves the game, and he wants to prove himself, but the main reason he was so good is that he just didn't want to let anyone down.

After those early years as a forward, he created a position that hadn't really been utilised: playing as a key forward, then having a run in the middle of the ground and being a ruckman at 193 centimetres. After that, other people started doing it. He always had versatility, which no doubt came from the basketball side, but he revolutionised that role of the power forward going on the ball and then back to forward.

To be alongside him in the middle and at stoppages when he was rucking, it was like you had an extra midfielder. His vertical leap prior to rupturing his Achilles in 2011 was massive, and he had football smarts that ruckmen tend not to have (a big shout out to all my ruckman mates).

Rough and Buddy both had that ability to really have an impact as soon as the ball hit the ground. On the surface you might think Bud overshadowed Rough, but if you watch the games, look at the stats and see how they played out their careers, I don't think so. Buddy's one of the 10 best players to ever play the game, and through those premiership years Rough was right beside him and pretty bloody close to his level, if not matching it. Together, they were an unbelievable combination.

When Bud left, and Roughy had those four or five years where he was the main forward, maybe it made people realise how damaging he was as a player. But because Roughy has that selfless part to his make-up, they worked perfectly together. He was happy for Bud to be that number-one forward, the key, and he'd just join in to complete the picture.

I remember we were driving past a pitch-and-putt golf course when he took the phone call to say the spot on his lip was melanoma. My reaction – 'at least I know someone with cancer now' – who even says that! But what do you say when someone has just been told they've got cancer? He laughed, so at least it broke the ice.

Even when it was much worse, and there were spots on his lungs, he never allowed the thought that he might die to enter his head, and neither did I. I think that's what footy does for you, it teaches you to really break things down and work systematically towards getting a result.

To see him at his worst was just terrible. He willed himself to get to the ground for Sam Mitchell's 300th, because he just so wanted to be there, but when he came into the rooms before the game he looked exactly like you'd imagine. Just a shell of a man.

During the treatment he came up to Sydney for a game, just to feel part of it, and we roomed together as usual. That's when I woke up in the middle of the night to find him in the bathroom with his feet in the bathtub try-ing to cool them down. Those moments made me realise how sick he was, but he always just got on with it, never complained.

It's amazing how he dealt with it; I don't know how I would have coped. Perhaps similar, because football teaches you to be like that. It was like the game prepared him for it – you just shut all of the negative thoughts out. It was harder for Sarah, because she had time to think about it, to look things up on the internet, how long he might have to live. None of it would have been good reading.

When he was going through treatment he just wanted to get on with it, then as soon as he stepped outside the hospital he didn't want to think about it or talk about it. He knew that if he went back home and saw his parents then it would be the topic of conversation, so he just avoided it. He was a bit of 'out of sight, out of mind' about it.

I got comfort from knowing that he was getting the best treatment in the world. The times I saw him were still good times. Once he dealt with the initial treatments and started getting a bit better, it gradually became easier. And he always knew exactly how many days he had to be dry; he loves a beer, Rough.

Even today he never talks about how he's going. I'll always speak to him after he's had a scan, which feels like a coincidence. He'll call me and I'll ask, 'What are you doing?' 'Oh, I've just been for a scan.' Then there's the waiting for the results, which must be hell.

Nobody really saw what he went through to get himself up to play again once he had the all-clear. If someone has something like a broken arm, you know about that, you can see it; this was different. For him to go through what he did in 2016 then come out and play every game the next season, it was extraordinary. I'd left the club by then but even watching from afar, for me, that was massive.

I did tell him not to take on the captaincy. My advice, from the bottom of my heart, was not to do it. I just thought that coming back after a year off, after the illness he'd had, and be captain of the football club, it was just too much to take on. Playing that year was enough of an achievement. They were renovating their house, trying to have a child, it just felt like too much. He didn't need the extra workload. I thought it was a mistake.

It's great to be captain of a football club, of course, but if he had his time again I don't think he'd have done it. But he didn't listen to me, and he's a Hawthorn captain – he'll have that forever. He didn't do it for himself, he did it because he thought it would make the team better.

I don't think cancer has changed him, because I don't think he's let it. He's always been sun smart, although he's taken that to another level. He used to enjoy the occasional smoke with a beer – that can't happen anymore! I think he just tries to forget about what he's been through and move on.

There are people who know Roughy and people who *know* Roughy. He's absolutely a grumpy old prick, always has been. He always had a short fuse at footy clinics, if the kids were mucking around or weren't respectful. Or with supporters who'd come up and ask for an autograph by just barking, 'Sign this.' He's a big manners person – he'll wipe you if you don't use your manners.

He always found it hard to adapt if things weren't as he had pictured them, but Pippa has certainly helped with that. Having a child made him chill out a bit. It's not as though he's walking around behind her with a bottle of Spray n' Wipe, but I'd still say that if you walked into their house you wouldn't know there was a small child living there. I'm sure there's a room somewhere with toys and shit piled halfway up to the ceiling, but I haven't found it yet.

One thing that he's developed over the years is expensive taste in clothing and shoes. It wouldn't be out of the ordinary to see him in a pair of shoes that cost four figures – not even necessarily dress shoes, they could be casual shoes worth over a grand. That's certainly different to when he arrived in Melbourne with horrible dress sense.

Lucy has been massive in moulding and shaping me, and Sarah's been the same for Roughy. I guess we've been that for each other, and it's great that our wives have become such good friends too. It feels only like yesterday that we walked into the footy club; we still think we're the same people who left Leongatha and Warrnambool, and deep down we are. We still love getting back to the country and the simple things we've always enjoyed.

What would those 18-year-old kids have thought of who we've become? I'd never heard of red wine, so the idea that I'd have my own label one day would have been a stretch. I don't know what 18-year-old Roughy would have made of him wearing $1000 shoes! But we're pretty modest people, pretty humble. Hopefully good fun to be around, and we don't take ourselves too seriously. I think we'd be happy with the people we've become.

Parenthood has been great for us. It's beautiful to see him as a father. To have children of similar ages, knowing we've got years and years ahead of us of going away together with our families, that's a nice thing to look forward to.

We were so close before he got sick, I don't think our friendship has changed at all. But I do sometimes catch myself and think how lucky we are to still have him.

CHAPTER 14

'What Foot Do You Kick With, Amos?'

Fifteen years as an AFL footballer exposes you to a lot of things. It was probably only when I was done that I realised how much it broadened my horizons in ways most jobs wouldn't have. One experience I'm forever grateful for, that would never have happened without footy, is that being a Hawthorn footballer taught me a lot about Indigenous Australia. Through footy, I met Aboriginal people who made me a better person. Some are up there with the best footballers I played with and some are mates I'll cherish forever.

Growing up in Leongatha, I didn't know how sheltered I was in some ways. The first Indigenous blokes I met were two kids from Moe who I played against in the under 16s, Malcolm Dow and Geoff Yates. 'Mouse' Dow was later a teammate in the year I spent at Gippy Power. I played underage football against Chris Egan, who went on to play footy at Collingwood, and in Canberra against Patty Mills, but 'Mouse' was the first Indigenous person I met properly.

Between arriving at Hawthorn in 2004 and retiring, I'd had a couple of dozen Indigenous teammates. Three of them – Buddy Franklin, Cyril Rioli and Shaun Burgoyne – would arguably be in the best 10 Indigenous players of all time, actually just outright three modern-day greats of the game.

I knew Bud from the AIS stuff we'd done in 2004, and we were close from the start. But looking back, it's embarrassing how naive I was in those early days. To call it racism would be a stretch, but I'd make jokes and say things that I shouldn't have said. I'd muck around with Bud and say stupid things – not trying to put him down or be hurtful, just silly stuff that I didn't realise could leave a mark.

It was stupid, immature ignorance. But it didn't happen for long – 'Changa' Bateman made sure of that.

Percy Cummings was Hawthorn's first Indigenous footballer, playing five games in the mid-1960s. Willie Rioli, uncle of Cyril, was drafted in 1990 but didn't play a senior game. Then, in 1999, Chance 'Changa' Bateman came to the club. For a whole heap of reasons, Changa became a huge figure in Hawthorn's history.

I can't remember what I'd said – another dumb joke, probably – but one day very early in my career Changa pulled me aside and said, 'No, you don't say that sort of thing.' He nipped it in the bud then and there, which I'm really grateful for. I soon realised how uninformed I'd been growing up, and over the course of my career I saw examples of how hurtful even little things could be.

Changa changed the way his teammates thought about Aboriginal Australia. He brought the education to us, told us stories, gave us an understanding. He spoke about his grandparents being part of the stolen generation. When Shaun came over from Port Adelaide, we had three years with him and Changa at the club – two of not just the most highly respected Indigenous boys in the game and the broader AFL community. It wasn't their job to educate us, but they were extremely generous and open, and we just learnt so much.

When he was in his second year at the club, Changa lost his sister, Candice, in an awful train accident back home in York, just north of Perth. She was 15. He asked for a trade back to West Coast or Fremantle to be near his family, but the club talked him into staying. He set himself the goal of becoming the first Indigenous footballer to play 50 games in brown and gold; he finished in 2012 with 177 games and a premiership.

I reckon that's just amazing. Bud played 182 games for Hawthorn, Cyril finished too soon with 189, then Shaun broke through as the first Indigenous bloke to reach 200 games for the club, finishing with close to 400 all up, more than half of them as a Hawk. Before Changa started, Percy Cummings had been Hawthorn's Indigenous games record holder – with five games!

Changa could play, too. He was one of the best runners I've seen in the game, a huge part of the way we played in 2008. He set really good standards for professionalism, and he was one of the main conduits between the leadership group and the young boys. He'll have a special place forever in Hawthorn history.

Alastair Clarkson was a big part of the change at Hawthorn, opening the door and welcoming Indigenous players in. Clarko was like me to an extent – he's from Kaniva, near the Victoria–South Australia border, and I don't think he came across too many Indigenous boys growing up. He talked about being embarrassed by how uneducated he and his teammates at North Melbourne were. He played with the Krakouer brothers and said he learnt so much. He saw the way they reacted to being racially abused – they'd just smack on – and he could see how much it hurt them.

When I got to the club there were three Indigenous boys on the list – Changa, Mark Williams and Harry Miller. Harry was from Port Lincoln in South Australia, the same club as the Burgoyne boys; he and Shauny are close even though their Hawthorn careers didn't overlap. Harry is a good fella who had strong ties to home and plenty of flair. It would have been interesting to see how he'd fared if he came to the club even five years later.

Willo played on raw talent, and he was bloody good. He kicked 60 goals in a shit team two years in a row, in 2005 and '06. He was barely six feet tall, weighed maybe 85 kilos, but he knew exactly what to do as a leading forward and didn't miss goals. It blows me away that in 2008, when we won the flag, Bud kicked 100, I kicked 70, and Willo kicked 46 as a third-string forward. Amazing, really.

By the time I arrived at the club, Clarko had put an end to Willo's shotgun celebration, but he was still a very confident bloke to be around. I learnt things from him; he was great to play with. He was also the first bloke to have his kids around the club after I got there – he's got four now, and loves bringing them out to the footy club. These days he's got a garden business that he calls Garden Hawk Maintenance. It's a shame he only played 111 games, which doesn't get you life membership. It's a shame, too, that he ended up going to Essendon on a three-year deal and getting cut after two, his body letting him down. He was better than that and deserved a better end to his career.

Amos Frank came to us at the end of 2011 as one of the most speculative rookie draft picks ever. We were told we might be getting this bloke who'd been playing seconds footy with Woodville-West Torrens in the SANFL, but was still living in the Anangu Pitjantjatjara Yankunytjatjara lands (APY) in far north-west South Australia. Apparently he'd catch a bus from the middle of nowhere, change buses a couple of times, eventually land in Adelaide, play footy, then go home. It would take a day to get there and a day to get back.

If you put a circle around where WA, SA and the Northern Territory meet, that's basically where Amos is from. His local team was Fregon; they played footy on dirt grounds and even at the grand final there'd be a goat or some other animal wandering around on the ground.

English was his third language, and he was very quiet. We knew he had a family – a wife and three kids. Everyone made an effort to help him fit in, but you soon realised how far he'd come. Most of the boys ended up learning a few words of language just to have a conversation with him – asking if he was okay, was he sore, parts of the body, boy, girl, simple things. We never made it to long sentences ourselves, but Amos's English improved pretty quickly with the help of a tutor hired by the club.

After we drafted him he lived in Caulfield with Leon Egan, who was the club's Indigenous liaison officer. Amos would be on the phone to back home, and I'd just sit there thinking, wow! This wasn't like Spanish or French, where I'd heard the words before and could get a bit of an idea – this was like nothing I'd ever heard.

Amos is an elder back home. He'd been initiated, and we'd try to ask about that but never got told. Maybe we shouldn't have even asked, it's that personal.

He was a lot of fun, great energy for the boys to be around. But the amount of training that comes with elite sport was just so foreign to Amos, and you could see by how tired he was that it was taking a toll on him. After a while he realised he could get out of training by saying he was sore in certain spots. 'How much is that pain?' 'Oh yeah, very sore.' You'd call him if he was late, 'Where are you?' 'I'll be there in a minute.' An hour later he'd rock up. 'Where you been?' 'Went the wrong way, bloody traffic.'

There were times when we'd all be sitting around and Amos would ring home and play the guitar to his family over the phone. He could seriously play. He'd be going for a while, then he'd stop and talk, play some more, talk some more. Before you knew it he'd been on the phone for two hours. Phone plans were different then, and calling the outback wasn't cheap – his bill was in the thousands. The club would say, 'Amos, what's going on?' He'd be like, 'I've just been ringing home.'

He played a couple of VFL senior games with Box Hill. He was tiny – only 169 centimetres tall – and he got knocked around a bit, but he showed flashes of real brilliance. He didn't even know which was his preferred kicking leg. You'd ask, 'What foot do you kick with, Amos?' He'd say, 'Both.' Brilliant. You just let him go.

If you asked blokes to name their favourite teammates over the years, I reckon a lot would say Amos. He was just great for the group, so much fun. In a sense we were the outsiders in his world. That's what you forget.

When he left us he moved to Adelaide into an Indigenous development job with the SANFL. We'd see him sometimes when we'd go across for games, and he'd come to say g'day to the boys. We'd ask, 'How many tickets did you get for the game, Amos?' And he'd say, 'Sixteen.' He was a beauty.

The AFL Indigenous Round hadn't been going for long back then, and that acknowledgement wasn't as great as it is now. When Amos was at Hawthorn, someone had the idea to start an Indigenous night. Cyril's uncle came in and cooked in the kitchen of the café downstairs at Waverley, other members of the boys' families helping him, then we'd all sit down to eat and Amos would play music. Because of that I've tried wombat and kangaroo sausages, turtle, you name it.

———

You can't buy experiences like that, and I've been lucky to have a lot of them thanks to my teammates. When Cyril got married in Darwin, I went up a few days early with Shaun Burgoyne, Brad Hill and Jed Anderson. Sars came up for the wedding, but in the days leading up to it, it was just me and the boys, and we went shooting for magpie geese. Best fun I've ever had.

Cyril's more into fishing and spears, Jed is shotguns. He can shoot from both sides. His shoulder was crook once, so he started off shooting from his right shoulder then said, 'Nah, I'm no good here,' and swapped to his left shoulder. Didn't miss a thing. He learnt off his dad, who's passed away.

Jed would call the magpie geese by making this sucking sound through his lips, and then they'd be flying overhead everywhere. Jed married into a Greek family, and they're very particular about how you cook them: they crumb them to make a schnitzel, using only the breast. The Indigenous people build a fire of coals and use everything, every bit of the bird.

I've been to the Territory a couple of other times with Shaun – fishing for barramundi, catching mud crabs, shooting. Jed's family cooked up an amazing feed of fish one time we were there, called numus. It's queenfish pickled in vinegar, chilli, garlic, ginger, soy sauce and olive oil, and you eat it like sashimi. It's unreal.

When Shaun came to Hawthorn from Port at the end of 2009, he lived with me for a while in Burwood. I remember him walking in on one crutch – people reckoned his knee was shot – hobbling upstairs, leaving me standing there, thinking, 'What have we got here?' The club signed him to a three-year deal, thinking it would be a miracle if he saw it out. He's played for another 11 years, and more AFL games than any other Indigenous player.

When he moved in with me his wife, Amy, had just had their second child, Percy. I'd speak to Amy on the phone and she'd say, 'You know all he can cook is apricot chicken?' And I was like, cool – I can do the spaghetti, he can do the apricot chicken and rice.

Shaun was 27 and I was 22, but we got on straight away. We just talked about anything. He's like a big brother to me now.

I saw how family-oriented he is, the number of times he'd quietly drive back to Adelaide with the kids in the school holidays to see family. He and Amy have got four kids now: Ky, Percy, Leni and Nixie. The boys are just like their Dad – love their footy, love all sport, really.

Shaun's the same as you see from the outside – just an incredibly impressive person. Blokes were always taking the mickey out of him because he'll tell a story and it'll go on forever. I mean, *forever*! When he played his 350th game, Mitch popped up on the video and said, 'Two things, Shaun: I'm sorry that I retired and can't still be playing with you. Second, I'm sorry that when I left you were halfway through a story and I never got to hear the end of it.' It's really not an exaggeration. He'll tell you a story and you're like, 'Okay, come on . . . get to it . . . get to it!'

Shaun loves routine and hates change, which in my view is a big part of why he's been so good for so long. When something changes, he gets his back up. They'd announce that we were doing a training session somewhere different, off-site, and Shaun would say, 'I'll just stay at the club and do my stuff there if that's okay.' I've got no issue with that, I'm the same. I understand the power of routine – most footballers do.

Brad Hill is another bloke I just feel lucky to have played with. He was similar to Amos – the smile and energy he brought, the laughter. You can't help but love him. He was a kid when we played together, although he'd grown up a lot by the time he went home to WA. He lived down the road from me so I'd pick him up for training or games, and he was so confident in himself.

Hilly could play, but he could also run. When you chuck him in the conversation with Izzy Smith, Changa Bateman and Tom Scully, I had some of the best runners in the game as my teammates. After we won the 2015 grand final, when Hilly was flaked out on my couch on the Sunday morning, I took a photo and captioned it, 'Finally stopped running.'

Hilly's got a lot of tattoos, and among them are the initials of people who've played a big part in his life. Cyril's are somewhere on his body, and Shaun's, and mine. That's an amazing thing. It was hard to see him go back to WA, especially as I lost him, Mitch and Lewy in the one off-season. But the last time I played with all three of them was a winning grand final, so I don't mind having that as my last memory of us as teammates.

Many other Aboriginal blokes came and went during my time at the club, and they all brought something different. Cameron Stokes had a rugby league background; he was a good player and only missed out on the 2008 premiership because he hurt a hammy. He ended up getting shoulder and knee injuries and not really having the chance to be as good as he might have been, but he was great support for Cyril in his early days at the club. One hilarious thing was that, right from the start, Bud had Stokesy and Cyril mixed up. He'd call one the other and we'd say, 'Bud, that's not Stokesy, it's Cyril.'

Derick Wanganeen was another bloke who told great stories, came to us from Darwin via Adelaide, and was good enough to play a lot more than the one game he managed, down in Tassie. He was just there at the wrong time and couldn't break into the side.

Carl Peterson's background was different again – he's from Kununurra and grew up playing footy in the Kimberleys. He told us sometimes the opposition wouldn't turn up on a Saturday, then they might get there two days later. We called him 'Grooky', after Marngrook. He was only 183 centimetres tall, but could jump so high he sometimes played in the ruck.

He'd spent a year with Richmond without cracking it, played up in Darwin, and was 22 when he made his debut with us in 2010. In his first half of AFL footy he had 15 touches and kicked a goal. In his first season he played 17 games; he didn't manage another one after that. It was another example of how hard it is to make it in the game, especially when you come from the most remote parts of the country.

Of course I also had front row seats for a decade to watch Buddy and Cyril.

Bud did things no player had ever really done before and Cyril was the same, plus he had a really strong defensive side to his game. Bud wasn't so much a chase-down-and-tackle player, but Shauny and Cyril, the way they tackled and hit – they're two of the best I've seen.

You heard commentators say all the time that Cyril could be best on ground with 12 touches. A lot of what's said about footy from the other side of the fence is bullshit, but that was spot on. I can't really remember blokes like Scott Pendlebury and Gary Ablett getting caught from behind, but Cyril got them both. Out on the ground, you'd hear opponents saying, 'How did he do that?' No one was safe when Cyril was around, that was the thing. He could make people look silly and feel small, just by being Cyril.

He'd do it to blokes at training too. Or the coaches would be talking about how some set drill played into our structure and systems, and they'd ask him, 'Cyril, what do you want to do here?' And he'd say, in that quiet voice of his, 'Just leave it to me, I'll do it.' Everyone would be pissing themselves laughing, but then you'd realise he was being serious. He had it covered. He hardly ever spoke, but when he did it meant something.

Modern footy is all about getting goals through structure, but sometimes you just need goals that come from pure talent. Chad Wingard does it now. Sometimes the coaches who've been drilling structure don't get a say – the game demands something special, and blokes like that can make it happen.

Cyril retiring at 28 was a massive shame – not just for Hawthorn, but for footy overall. He decided to move back home to Darwin after his dad had a heart attack.

In 2016 he'd kicked 47 goals and was All Australian for the third time. Then eight rounds into 2017 he hurt his knee, a PCL. His dad had that heart attack on grand final eve that year and Cyril rushed back home – we didn't see him again until the next year.

He came around to my place in January 2018, a few of us caught up, and Cyril said, 'I want to come back.' No worries, we'll have you. Then he played the first three games of the season, did his knee against Melbourne in round four, and never played again.

If not for footy, I'm sure I wouldn't have had as much exposure to Aboriginal Australia, or been able to count so many Indigenous people as friends. It's opened my eyes big time – to those friends' culture, understanding what the world was like for their forebears, what it's like for them now. It made me feel embarrassed at times.

To meet some of the older people through my teammates – Changa's old man, Cyril senior, the families – it's been an honour. Some of the stories they carry can be confronting and hard to hear, but I know I'm a better person for being exposed to them and knowing the people who've lived them. Stories like that should be told at school, they're so important. They should be something all Australians know growing up.

CHAPTER 15
Mates You'll Have Forever

Around the time I was hanging up the boots after 15 seasons, and Luke Hodge was finally retiring after 18, our little brothers Cam and Dylan became neighbours at work. They went to the same university, became accredited sports agents, and then ended up with desks next to each other at the TLA Talent Management offices in Hawthorn.

Every now and then I get a call or a message from someone saying, 'Hodge and Roughead have been getting up to mischief,' and I'm like, 'Hang on, I wasn't even there!' It's a reminder of how times have changed, but also how we're one big family now – my old teammates, our siblings, our wives, our kids. Life has moved on, but in a good way.

They say you get five or six good mates out of footy. I've been lucky, I've got more. For 15 years, the safest place in my world was the Hawthorn footy club. It was my second home. You spend more time with the boys than you do with your family, so of course they're the thing you miss most once it's over.

When I look at our wedding photos, there are 20 players there, the CEO, coaches, other staff. That doesn't happen in too many jobs. There are so many blokes I played with who I know so well. I know exactly how to make them smile. When we see each other now, especially those of us who played in premierships together, it's always the same: big smiles and even bigger hugs. I know it will be like that forever.

Footy brought us all together, but in a way it's the thing that means the least to us. I played with some football-ers who will go down as AFL legends – Franklin, Hodge, Lewis, Mitchell – but to my daughter, Pippa, even when she's older, they'll just be Bud, Hodgey, Jord and Mitch.

If I was lucky to come out of the game with great mates, I'll always be grateful that I had some terrific mentors going into it. When Bud, Jord and I arrived at the club in 2004, Shane Crawford had just given up the cap-taincy to Richie Vandenberg. Between those two, Hodgey and Mitch, and blokes like Trent Croad and Ben Dixon, there was an understanding of where the club was at – that is, down the bottom of the ladder – and what was needed to change things. They knew they had drafted a couple of forwards and a midfielder who could help them improve, and they understood that the quicker they got us used to Melbourne and feeling part of the team, the better for everyone.

That first pre-season, when I was living with the Buckenaras, Jord was with a host family and Bud was with his parents in Box Hill. We'd turn up at a Saturday training session with our bag packed for the weekend because as soon as we were finished we'd all go and stay at Croady's.

Those older boys were like big brothers to us. We'd go through our allowance for the week and ask Croady for a loan. They'd take us under their wing when we went out, and in return we'd eat their food, drink their drinks, wake up Sunday and go home.

But they knew how to be the bad cop when they needed to be; they could come down hard on us if they thought we needed a kick up the arse. There was a midnight curfew in those early years, with the footy club working on that old theory that nothing good happens after pumpkin hour.

We'd push it when the mood took us, working with that kid's mentality, 'We can get away with this, no one will know.' But we were going out to spots where there were footy fans, so of course it got back to the people in charge. It probably didn't help that Bud was a six-foot-six Indigenous kid, and that there was a six-foot-four freckly redhead next to him. In a sense we were destined to stuff up, but at times we were happy to do so.

Arriving at the club at the same time as Bud and Jord was gold. We'd first met when we were 16, and we were already comfortable in each other's company. We got to know each other's families; Lance Senior and Ursula lived in Melbourne for a couple of years to help Bud settle in, we saw a lot of Shane and Judy Lewis, and even went to Shane's fiftieth birthday in Warrnambool, on the day of the

2009 Black Saturday bushfires. We were all just great mates right from the start.

Now Sars and I have Pippa, Jord and Lucy have three boys, and Bud and Jesinta had Tullulah in February 2020. The three of us have grown up together and we're blessed that our wives all get along as well as we do. It's more than footy – the game has given me my two best mates.

With Hodgey and Mitch it's the same thing – they were the older brothers who were hard on us, but you love them for it. We used to get together all the time because that was just how it was. Now Sars and I will bump into the Mitchells walking down Glenferrie Road on a Sunday morning and stop to chat for 10 minutes, wishing it could be longer. Every time it's a reminder of how our lives have changed, how different they were before.

Jord is the person I ring first for everything – sometimes before I ring Sars, which probably isn't great. But we've been like that for so long, it happens without even thinking. When I'm invited to something and it's got a plus one, I've been known to ask him before I ask my wife or brother.

Jord talks about how, as a kid, the highlight of his week was going to bed on Friday night knowing that the next day he'd get to play footy, do the scoreboard, run the boundary. He was doing that with Dennington (where his old man coached), and then Warrnambool, at the same time I was doing exactly the same thing in Leongatha. We're just similar people I guess, knockabout country boys.

With Bud having his parents in Melbourne in those early days, Jords and I were basically each other's support.

When Bud moved down St Kilda way, Jord and I lived not far from each other, so we'd be in the car on the way to the airport for interstate games, we'd room together. It felt like we were always together; we knew each other inside out.

We were all together in Byron Bay in 2007 when Jord first met Lucy, who was up there for a twenty-first with about 10 of her girlfriends. We met them out one night and Jord and Lucy clicked straight away. When he was getting married and asked me to be his best man, it wasn't something I even had to think about. A year later he was standing next to me at my wedding.

Jord's best quality is also his worst quality: he feels no guilt. He can say something and move on faster than anyone I've known. I don't think he has regrets, he's just so strong-minded. You can see it when he talks about getting traded, how he met with Clarko and was given the option of, 'What do you want to do: park or explore?' He walked out of that meeting thinking, 'Well, I'm a Melbourne player now.'

He moves on that fast, just thinking, 'Well, I can't change anything, better get on with it.' No baggage, just move on. That's how he lives. It can piss you off as a mate – you're like, 'Come on, show some emotion!'

I never really saw him get emotional, not until he had to talk about me getting crook. Every time, he just breaks down and can't do it. In the weeks after we'd both retired we did a few sportsman's nights for Hawthorn supporters' groups, and every time he couldn't get through the question. Which is nice, I suppose – it shows how scared he was, how much we mean to each other.

Opponents used to think we didn't get on, the way we spoke to each other on the field. From about 2008 onwards, when were established in a team that was on the rise, if one of us didn't do the team thing that was expected of us, the other would give it to him mercilessly.

There was a game against GWS where we were screaming at each other. Eventually it just ended as, 'Shut up, I'll deal with you later.' We could see the Giants players thinking, 'Do these blokes actually hate each other?' But it was about our expectations of each other, our standards, which was a big part of how good we became as a team. Intimidation doesn't have to be physical – we had a lot of blokes who were intimidating with their voice, and Jord was one of the best.

If you were picking a team, he'd be one of the first names you'd write down, for sure. He was so durable – he never had lower leg surgery, just a couple of fingers, wrists, a shoulder. Never the knees or ankles, the stuff that can end your career. To see his body change – he started around 94 kilos and finished at 85 kilos – was amazing. He was able to adapt with the changing game, all the while playing half-back, half-forward, midfield, wing. He was selfless. Until they outlawed someone going third-up in a ruck contest, he was arguably the best at it going around.

And in terms of aggressive, unsociable play – setting the tone for the group – you only had to ask opponents to know they hated playing against Jord. Absolutely hated him. When I spoke to the Geelong players, the conversation would always land on how much they hated Lewy. He was tough, and he could back it up.

As for Bud, he cares more than observers will ever realise – about people and about footy. His passion for the game is ridiculous, his knowledge and love for it. He has Fox Footy on in the background all day, watching and learning.

He's had to deal with more than anyone I've seen as far as pressure from football goes. He got such a high profile so quickly, he was forced to grow up fast. When we met at the AIS in late 2003 he was a big smart-arse and I was the same; we were always going to be mates. We're close, and I treasure that.

When Bud left Hawthorn he was texting me, 'I want to tell you something.' I was like, 'Mate, I don't care – you know I care, if you want to talk I'm here, but I'm not going to judge you.' He came around to my place the Tuesday after we won the 2013 flag, got Lewy to come over too, and said, 'I'm going to Sydney.' We'd heard the rumours he was going to the Swans and not the Giants, like everyone had thought was a sure thing, but we played dumb and said, 'Oh yeah, GWS, we knew that,' so he had to be all like 'No, no, the Swans.'

I didn't begrudge him moving, at all. For starters you couldn't knock back the deal he was offered, it was just too good. And of course there was Jesinta, who just makes him so happy. I'd love to have played my whole career with him – and Jord, and Hodgey and Mitch for that matter. But we don't always get the perfect ending.

As a footy fan, I can say I played with and against the best player who's ever played the game. I rate him that highly.

You can't do what he's been able to do for that amount of time – in today's game – and not be considered one of the very best ever. The night he ran away from Cale Hooker at the MCG, the goal of the year in 2010, that was just normal shit for him. We'd see stuff like that at training all the time.

And this was from a bloke who could walk in 10 minutes before we were due to run out, get changed, touch his toes, and say, 'Right, I'm ready.' Then he'd go out and kick seven.

In the early days he'd run the Tan Track with Crawf and keep up with him – over two laps – having been out the night before. You'd just shake your head saying, 'Look at this bloke!' He's just special, really special.

Our first day of training, in the gym at Glenferrie, Buddy couldn't do a proper push-up. Not one. They used to talk about Jason Dunstall and the big blokes from his era bench pressing 170 kilos, and Bud couldn't do one push-up! I've never seen him bench press 100 kilos, and yet he's the strongest player I've ever seen, hands down. That lower-body strength, the strength through the core. He'd just nudge blokes and they'd fall over.

Playing against him was weird. The first time, at the Olympic Stadium in Sydney, he kicked two goals seven, but we couldn't even really give it to him because we still lost. The next time was my 200th game, and the time after that was the 2014 grand final. We went as hard as we could for two hours, like our friendship didn't exist, then as soon as the siren went it was back to normal. At one stage in that granny he went to take a drink, and I was close enough so

I just cracked the bottle out of his hand. A week later we were in Jord's wedding party together.

The mental health difficulties he had in the 2015 finals, where he basically stopped playing footy to get himself better, that was hard to watch from afar. We were all worried for him, asking ourselves if we could have done something sooner to help him.

He put himself on the line by stepping back from the game, which took courage. To see where he's got to a few years later, how happy he is, that's all you want for the bloke. It wouldn't have mattered if he didn't play footy again, because you want to be mates and see him for the next 50 years, and that's got nothing to do with footy.

Sam Mitchell was there the day we got drafted, waiting at Glenferrie Oval to welcome us. I've never forgotten that, or the text he sent me saying, 'Hope I'm kicking it down your throat for the next ten years.' In the end it was twelve years, and goodness knows how many lace-out passes.

Mitch was misunderstood. He's incredibly professional, for sure. He used to do things like not drink from 1 January until the end of the season. That was just him. Some people pass judgment on a bloke because he doesn't drink, but I couldn't care less. At the start I struggled a bit with how hard he could be on anyone who wasn't as driven as him. But his dedication was something to see, and it worked: he's a Brownlow medallist and a premiership captain. He proved everyone who thought he wouldn't make it wrong.

There was the perception from the outside that being driven meant being selfish, but Mitch helped the young blokes massively – helped us understand footy, but also life. He's all over politics, so if you needed a crash course on an issue that was in the news, you'd ask Mitch. Problem solved. Some people can find that they either like Mitch or they don't, black and white. I'm glad I stuck with him, he's a great fella and someone I'm proud to call a mate.

Hodgey and I laugh at how, now that our footy lives are over, our Dad lives are well and truly here. We play phone tennis regularly: '40–30, your turn to call back'. Our conversations are no longer about how we can win on the weekend, they're, 'How are the kids?' And the answer is: 'I work, I pick up the kids, I go to school sports, I take them to a party.' Massage and ice baths don't get in the way anymore, there's no more, 'I can't do that, I've got training.' Now our normal is Dad stuff, and that's great.

Hodgey's so caring, that's his strength. If you're in trouble, you ring Hodgey. He'll reassure you, make you feel better, and then he'll have an answer. Similar to Clarko, he does things you don't hear about, stuff for people's families, no fuss, just to help. He's always put everyone before himself, that's why he's so loved. When I was sick, he had a lot going on – three young boys, people trying to write him off as a footballer – and still there'd always be a lasagne that turned up on the front step from Loz and Hodgey.

Playing with him was as good as it looked. He was great for me, letting me set things up in the front half while he controlled the back half. That was his expertise; when he'd come down my end he'd ask, 'Where do you want me to go?' When I played midfield the first voice I'd hear was Hodgey's. 'Go left, go right, push up, roll back.'

Late in his career they miked him up for a game and people were amazed at how much he spoke, but that's what he was like the whole time. I was lucky to play with him.

His oldest son, Cooper, was slow to warm to me, so I asked Hodgey how I should tackle that. He told me to just come in and play with his little trucks and cars. I was driving a silver ute at the time, and Coop used to say, 'Roughy's got the shil-va ute!' It's no surprise that an adult and a child can bond over cars and trucks, but Hodgey just knows how to connect people. He knows how to bring people together, no matter who you are or how different you are.

He's always been the older, wiser, big brother or Dad type. He and Loz have been together since they were 15 – they're a great story. Although sometimes Hodgey does make you shake your head. One time we were around at their place when Sarah was pregnant with Pippa and Hodgey was cooking. He prides himself on his barbecue skills, and then he goes and serves pregnant Sarah raw chicken! She cut it open and it was half-cooked! 'Maybe a little bit longer mate, don't you reckon?' Fair dinkum.

Hodge, Franklin, Lewis and Mitchell all had multiple coaches over their careers, but I only had one – Alastair Clarkson. The way my last season panned out, getting dropped seven rounds in and only playing eight games, there were times when I wished someone else was calling the shots. But even over the weeks and months where we weren't speaking much, digging our heels in like two old blokes, I knew things would be okay between me and Clarko. We'd been through too much not to be.

Clarko is the most caring bloke you'll meet. He does so much for people that you don't see. When I was crook in 2016, and Sars played a season of netball back at home to help keep her mind off things, he turned up at her grand final in Moe without telling anyone. I actually saw his car on the freeway driving down there and thought, 'Where's he going?' Then I looked across the court and he was sat on the hill watching. After they won he went over and congratulated Sars without making a big deal of it, then he drove back to Melbourne.

We just had a communication breakdown in 2019, pure and simple. Perhaps because I'd had him as a coach for so long I became like him, or at least became as stubborn as him. When you've got two egos being that pig-headed, you're going to clash. At the time I didn't consider that it was probably just as hard on him as it was on me – I was like one of his kids, and that's real. Buddy, Hodgey, Jord and Mitch had all left. I was the only one he had to drop. That must have been hard.

I was shocked when Mitchell and Lewis left in 2017. They'd come first and second in our best and fairest the previous season. Losing Brad Hill to Fremantle at the same time, I think it backfired on the club to a degree. But it just shows that Clarko can be as ruthless as he is caring, and that's what you have to do to succeed as an AFL coach.

I reckon he changed in the back half of my last year, because he needed to. I hope the experience helped him become better at handling those difficult situations, including when the next bloke who regards the place as home comes towards the end. But I wouldn't change anything – it worked out alright, and we'll always be fine.

That same ruthlessness kept us on edge from 2012 to 2016. He got us up for games against ordinary sides, made you feel like your spot was up for grabs if you didn't play well. He drove an incredible hunger, which was a hallmark of that group. They were teams with hall of famers on every line, but we'd come out against Gold Coast playing like everyone's spot was up for grabs.

Clarko's storytelling was famous. About Kaniva, where he's from, and about his old man's attention to detail as a carpenter. His guitar playing became a thing as my career went on. He wrote songs about players, played tunes in the rooms after games, pretty much always coming back to Bruce Springsteen. If he had a theme going he'd dress up. One night, before a game against Sydney, with the first team he'd coached that didn't have Hodge, Mitchell or Sewell, he turned up to the meeting at our hotel dressed as a Buckingham Palace Beefeater with the tall hat, to illustrate the changing of the guard. We lost, but it was pretty funny.

He goes to all the boys' weddings, and if I was getting married next week he'd be invited, for sure. We had a rough patch – at the time you're pissed off and angry, questioning why he's acting that way – but what's the point of holding a grudge against a bloke who's given you the opportunity to do so much? He was right in the end, I was done. There's more to life than footy. He's like a second Dad to me, always will be.

Clarko was big on travelling to America and Europe to see how professional teams in other sports went about it, always with an eye to making Hawthorn better. I was fortunate in that I had a couple of mates who gave me a window into life at the top in my first sporting love, basketball. That gave me a reason to regularly get away to America to catch up with them and see the best go at it in the NBA.

I met Joe Ingles and Patty Mills at a junior basketball tournament in Albury in 2001; Patty was ACT, Joe was from Happy Valley in South Australia. We crossed paths a bit over the next couple of years; Joe was the South Dragons' first signing when they started in the NBL in 2006 and we'd catch up either at the footy (he's a Hawks man) or the hoops when I went along to watch.

Joe's got a British passport through his father's mother, which meant he could play in Europe and not be considered an import. He went to Granada in Spain in 2009, Barcelona in 2010, Maccabi in Tel Aviv in 2013 and has been in Utah playing NBA with the Jazz since 2014. Salt Lake City's like a big Adelaide, so he's alright there.

Joe's married to Renae now, their twins are Jacob and Milla, and they've bought a place in Beaumaris for when they're home. But before all that, he used to come and stay with us. He'd come back with all of his bags from Barcelona or Tel Aviv, or from playing with the Boomers at a world championship or Olympics, and he'd land in our front room. The address on his licence was our address, which he didn't change for ages. He'd be back for six weeks and after he'd gone parking fines would keep arriving in our mailbox.

When Patty broke his foot in 2009 he came to a few Hawthorn games and we got to know each other better. Then one off-season I told him Sars and I were looking to go to America, and he said, 'Come to San Antonio.' I asked where there was a good hotel to stay in and he said, 'Nah, just come stay with us.' We weren't close at that stage and didn't know his partner Alyssa, but we went and stayed for five nights and it was unreal. Patty was in-season when we got married and couldn't make it, but Alyssa, who's a California girl, flew out and had a great night without really knowing anyone.

I've been to Texas a few times since, just playing the fan. Patty takes me to training and I'll sit in the corner watching how arguably the best NBA team of the past 20 years go about their business. One year, on an end-of-season getaway with a few of the boys, I took Hodgey and Lewy to Utah to catch up with Joe. He got us in to the shootaround, which is like our captain's run – except it's the morning of the game and it goes for three hours!

They let the media in for 10 minutes, then there's stretching, vision, and they work through offence and defence relative to their opponent that night. They do walkthroughs on the court to show how it will look, then rehearse things at a higher tempo against the coaches. There's individual shooting, recovery for 45 minutes, then they go home, have a nap, and then it's game time.

It's fascinating to see how elite athletes from another sport prepare, and Joe was very generous in having us there – especially given how little luck I brought him. At one stage, between my brother Cam and me, we'd seen Utah play eight games for eight losses. When they lost the night Jord and Hodgey were there, Joe walked out of the locker room and said, 'Never again. No more Rougheads.'

His mood wasn't exactly lifted when we were out to dinner a while later and Cam sent him a message: '0-8 – the streak lives on!'

What's good about both Joe and Patty is that they haven't changed. Joe doesn't get recognised much in Australia even though he's in the top handful of Australian athletes in the world by any measure – the profile of the sport he plays, the money he earns, whatever. In 2018, Joe and Patty both signed four-year, $50 million deals. That means each of them is earning an AFL club's full salary cap every season. But when Joe comes home and goes out to dinner with me and Ben Stratton, nobody recognises him – all they want to do is get a photo with Stratts and his mullet.

Patty's a big Crows man; Shaun Burgoyne has a connection to Patty's mum. He's introduced a 'Mad Monday' at the San Antonio Spurs where he gets all the players and staff on a bus, they all get kitted out at a costume shop and then they pub-hop around town. It's a bit of Australian culture that he's responsible for, which is cool.

I'm probably a bigger basketball fan than those two are footy fans, but I think they've enjoyed being able to chat with someone who's playing another sport at the highest level, who happens to be a mate and who you can reach any time on Skype or Facetime. I'd pick their brains on certain things, and I think it's been good for them to have an Aussie connection. Anytime I say, 'I'm thinking of coming across,' they're quick to say, 'Hurry up then!'

I've already mentioned that in my last couple of years I started playing golf. If anyone ever asked, I'd tell them it was my way of trying to stay relevant to the young blokes. I used to be of the 'perfect way to ruin a good walk' school of thinking; I could hit a ball, but not well enough to lose four or five hours of my day chasing it around.

But we're all suckers for peer pressure. By the time all my old mates had left the club, I was surrounded by golfers. Gunston, Breust, Schoenmakers and Suckling are all low-handicappers, Tim Mohr and Mitch Lewis play off scratch. I saw how playing golf helped James Sicily become a real part of the group and around the time I became captain, I became a golfer too. Funny – the best way to lead was to follow.

What it did for me was highlight how much I loved being around the boys. Their annual tournament had been going for six or seven years when I parachuted in at the end of 2018 and won in South Carolina, playing off 27. They'd been to Barnbougle in Tassie and raved about it, so when they went back during the mid-season break in 2019 I was all over it.

I was playing VFL for Box Hill and also had the following weekend off, so when the boys headed to Brisbane to play the Lions they left their golf bags in their cars at Tullamarine, I met them there on their way back, and we flew straight down to Launceston.

We were there by mid-afternoon, drank until midnight, then got up at 6 am and were through 18 holes by lunchtime, played the other course in the afternoon, then settled in for the night.

We could have been Hawthorn or Leongatha, what mattered was that we were together. We were in our golf spikes until 1.30 am; it was like being back home at the local on a Saturday night, still in our cricket whites when they called 'time'. There was banter, drinking games, and the odd casualty. Punky Breust, who was eight shots clear going into the last day, didn't prepare as well as he might have – he fell into an awfully big hole.

Luckily Roughead – handicap by now wound in to 18 – stepped up to save the day, winning by a shot from Sicily. I'd won a vase for taking out the American tournament, and at Barnbougle it was a red jacket that you get your name embroidered on the back of.

I reckon if you're talking about a day with the boys, it would be hard to go past golf in the morning, meet at the pub for lunch, put a quaddie on, make your way home when it gets dark to have a pizza for dinner. It's worked for Australians for a long time, why change it now? But things do change, and I'm good with that too.

By the end of my career I had young blokes at Box Hill telling me I was like a big brother, and James Worpel called me 'Dad'. That's pretty touching. If I was able to teach them something about perspective – 'you played a shit game on the weekend, move on, it doesn't matter' – then I'm happy with that.

Even if a footy career lasts 15 years like mine did, it doesn't define you. But the people you meet along the way, the mates you'll have forever, they're part of who you are.

Conclusion

On a Friday evening in February 2020, about five months after I'd emptied my locker and left my football home of 15 years behind, I drove back out to Waverley to present the number 2 guernsey to Mitch Lewis. It was pouring rain and the end-of-the-week traffic on the Monash Freeway was so heavy the drive took me an hour. Some things don't change.

The place that started out as VFL Park will always hold special memories for me, yet as soon as I walked in and saw so many new faces, I realised I was okay with not being a Hawthorn player anymore. I'd taken an off-field role with St Kilda a few months earlier, and that night I realised I really had moved on. Looking around as we had dinner – at staff, players and parents who I didn't recognise – made me understand that footy clubs are an evolving beast, and that the evolution happens fast. I kept nodding towards people wearing club polo tops and whispering to ex-teammates, 'Who's that?'

The following Thursday night, at Moorabbin, St Kilda played their first pre-season game – against Hawthorn. My new football world was meeting the old.

The game didn't start until 7.10 pm, but with the Saints' new AFLW team also playing a game there the following night, there was plenty of work to be done around the ground in preparation. So from just after lunchtime, with my new workmates, I spent the afternoon setting up the temporary bars and trestle tables and tents that were dotted around the outer. The weather was pretty warm, but we resisted the temptation to tap a barrel.

The game itself highlighted how much my working world has changed. I was down on the bench, regularly speaking on the phone to coach Brett Ratten and the assistants, talking to the players as they rotated through for a rest, walking along the boundary line with them, offering reassurance and advice. As much as anything, my aim was to keep the players relaxed and make the environment cruisy and a good place to be.

That night, I knew I'd made a good decision and that I'd enjoy my new life. I could see how much I was helping the boys, from a young forward like Max King who I worked closely with from the start, to defenders who'd picked my brains about their Hawthorn opponents. When blokes came up to me after the game to say thanks, it gave me a sense that however my role panned out, it was going to be worthwhile.

Gold Coast had been keen on me, and Melbourne came hard late, but from the time we first met up, St Kilda's willingness to offer a flexible role and find the best way to use me was appealing. My role is officially Football Operations Assistant. It's a bit of everything: help the leaders, help the talls, help list management, help out on the bench on match day. It's a three-year contract, and their pitch was that we'd pretty much have a year to work out where my passion was. I liked that – it showed they were determined to get the best out of me.

In saying yes to St Kilda I had to say no to Gold Coast and Melbourne. It was the first time I'd had to make that type of phone call. I sat down on a Saturday morning and rang Stewy Dew, then his boss at the Suns, Mark Evans, and then Simon Goodwin and Gary Pert at Melbourne. Dewy was the hardest, because we're such good mates, but they got easier after that and within 20 minutes I was telling St Kilda's General Manager of Football, Simon Lethlean, that I was taking up the offer to become a Saint.

In no time I had a security pass that got me into Moorabbin, a computer and a work email address, and was getting fitted for a St Kilda suit. I checked my email a few days after I got the computer and there were 70 messages. Welcome to your new world! My desk is upstairs in the admin area, next to the Melbourne Storm legend Billy Slater, who helps out part-time with tackling and leadership. He too was recruited by Simon Lethlean, in line with his approach of getting people in who've known sporting success.

From the outset I liked the variety of the job. If the boys were on the track, I was on the track. Afterwards I'd go upstairs, have a shower, get changed into chinos and a polo top (it's amazing how much easier red, white and black are to work with than brown and gold), and sit at my desk in an open-plan office. I might be working one-on-one with Max King, Tim Membrey or Rowan Marshall one minute, then sitting in a list management meeting the next. I felt comfortable having input in different areas. They got me in because I was recently retired and came from a successful environment. It made me feel relevant, which was nice.

Initially I missed the banter of the locker room – to an extent I have to separate myself from the playing group. I'm not a player anymore. The staff don't use the same facilities as the players, and I don't have a locker; my boots and runners sit under my desk, and because there's a full-sized basketball court at Moorabbin, I keep a basketball there too. That's a bonus.

St Kilda is different to Hawthorn in lots of ways, but that's what I expected. Certain resources aren't what I was used to at Hawthorn – the numbers of trainers or ball collectors on the ground during training, how many footballs you have to work with and how long you use them before they bring out new ones. But the simple fact that things *are* different makes it interesting. The facilities are still great, and from day one the excitement about the season ahead, including the first year of the AFLW team, made it a buzzing place to be.

I've got three years to work out what I'm best at, but from the day I signed on I've seen my role as a simple one: help make St Kilda better. Before COVID-19 rocked the world and shut down footy, I was due to write a 100-day report and present it to the board, detailing my impressions. I was going to say that when you walk into Hawthorn, straight away you see the premiership cups that the club has won, and an empty glass cabinet where the next one will go. That's not getting ahead of yourself – it's creating a vision, an understanding of what you're playing for.

St Kilda has one premiership cup, and it's in the museum. I consider it my job to play a part in getting number two.

After I stopped playing, it didn't take long at all to feel calmer, as if I wasn't under as much pressure. I'd heard people say you sleep better after retiring from playing, and it's true. I wasn't stressed, I wasn't worried about form, or wins and losses. It was just better – I was more present, I could go out for dinner with friends on a Friday night and not worry that I had training or a game the next day.

The week I took the job at St Kilda, Sarah and I flew to Perth, then up to Exmouth for eight nights. We went there with my old teammate Ben Stratton and his partner Laura, who had been one of Sarah's bridesmaids. It was the first week of the finals, and we were 360 kilometres from the nearest town.

Laura's parents live up there; her dad's a former fisheries and wildlife inspector who's got a boat and all the toys. We saw sharks and turtles, humpbacks breaching 30 metres from our boat. We went snorkelling, and on the last day caught our dinner: tuna for sashimi, two decent-sized squid and four goldband snappers. I properly relaxed.

If that was a window on life after footy, I'm going to be happy. Would I have thought of going somewhere like that at 19? No chance. But it was incredible, we had a ball. I was retired, happily. I was ready.

Back in Melbourne, grand final week drummed that home. On the Friday I did a speaking gig with Jordy Lewis and Brett Deledio, the three of us from the same 2004 draft, but three different stories. I felt for Lids, who'd done his calf in an elimination final and missed his chance to win a premiership. He's a life member at Richmond, played 243 games, and left because Dimma Hardwick told him, 'Go. You can win a flag at GWS.' A year later the Giants lost the prelim final to Richmond, and the Tigers went on to finally win it. Then in 2019 it was the Giants v Richmond in the granny, and he's not there.

On grand final day I was in the Ryder Room at the MCG, having a beer with Lids and Bob Murphy, when an old great of the game came up to us and said to me, 'G'day, Jordan. How are ya?' I looked at the others and they were all downing their beers in one go to stop from pissing themselves laughing. You get forgotten pretty fast.

You get AFL life membership at 300 total games, which I got to with 283 games plus pre-season and International Rules. That gets you into a room at the MCG on grand final day for the rest of your life. I'm sure I'll make better use of the hospitality in future than I did at my first appearance; Richmond were dominant, and I just couldn't get into it.

I ended up leaving at quarter-time, catching a cab, and was home halfway through the second quarter.

I asked Sars, 'Is this what it was like when we won? Do you lose interest that quick when one team's so far in front?' Pippa was in bed at 5.30 pm, Sars at 6.30, me at 7.30. Grand final day over, everyone asleep by 8 pm. Very different to some previous grand finals, that's for sure.

On the Monday night after the granny I played a game of basketball with Bob Murphy in his D-grade team. I was tonguing it after a few minutes, and at one stage I even thought I'd done a hammy. I ended up standing on the court doing the test where you drag your foot along the floor to see if the hammy's gone, which was a laugh for the blokes I was playing with.

I was okay, but I'll admit my first summer with no pre-season training looming over my head wasn't exactly an ordeal. I walked the dog, I played golf, but I didn't go for a run – I just didn't have the motivation to, and that was fine. I'd hardly missed a training session in 15 years, other than when I was crook. It was okay to have a break. Before coronavirus hit, the plan was to play a couple of games alongside Cam at Inverloch, maybe one back home for Leongatha. But I wasn't yearning for it.

I'm happy with my lot. If my football story only read 'four premierships', that would be enough. I also ended up ninth on Hawthorn's all-time games list, with everyone above me playing 300 games or more. I'm sixth in goals behind some pretty decent names. Bud got me by two in the end: 580 goals for Hawthorn to 578. Two more goals would have been perfect, but I'm not complaining.

I don't get too wound up in records, but as a 17-year-old getting drafted, if someone said you'd finish your career in the top 40 on the game's all-time goalkicking list, and be part of one of the greatest teams of all time, would you take that? Would you ever. I'm content, very much so.

I've got a lot of people to thank for that, but no one more than Sars. No partner should have to go through what she has. She's lived the most incredible peaks and troughs. Snapped my Achilles, she was there. Came home with a scar where quarter of my bottom lip used to be, she was there. Gave her the news that I had cancer spots on my lungs, she was there, every breath and step of the way.

As the partner of a professional footballer, she's been respectful of the job and understanding about how selfish being an athlete can make you. There were times when I know I pissed her off, just not being able to do normal things because I was more worried about what it would mean for my footy than my family. Being a sporty girl helped with that, I'm sure, but it can't have been easy. I can't thank her enough.

I admire how strong-minded she is, how family-oriented. She's always been determined to be her own person, not just an athlete's wife. She studied, she worked full-time, and she sacrificed a lot too. She put her career to one side to let me flourish and let us grow as a family.

There's absolutely no doubt having Sars and Pippa helped me. That's what you're looking at the clock for, what you race home for after training – dinner time, bath time. Time with my girls.

Seeing Pippa grow into a little girl has been amazing. Having to work out ponytails has been fun – it's not like I can practise! The smile on her face when she wakes up, seeing how much she's changed in no time – you can't put a price on that.

I don't tell Sars often enough how much she means to me, how much I'm looking forward to everything that's ahead in our lives. We're in our early thirties, not even halfway there, and our little family is growing. We found out during the summer after I finished playing that Sars was pregnant with a little brother or sister for Pippa. That's the best retirement present anyone could wish for.

What we've been through has made us stronger, for sure. I might not have been here, and now we talk about the future. Where will we live? Where do we want to go on holidays? We're not handcuffed to a footy club anymore. I still work for one, but I don't have to be constantly worried about skinfolds, fitness, what I eat and drink.

It's that old line about athletes dying twice. I've died as an athlete, and now we've got our whole lives as 'normal people' ahead of us. You hear ex-players say their career was just a part of their lives, ten or fifteen years. I've only just started the next part, but I get that already. You grow up as a kid, then you're a footballer, and at 33 you start all over.

People ask how I reflect on what I've been through, and the truth is I don't. I hardly ever think about it. I've been told by the best people in the business to go on with life as normal. They haven't said, 'don't drink', 'don't exercise', 'don't do whatever'. I don't hide from the sun. I have a check-up every six months, but it's just one day. I'm first cab off the rank on a Monday morning and I get the results that afternoon. I have to fast beforehand, but that's about it. A four, five-hour window of thinking, but I keep busy and it's over in no time.

If people still think of me as 'that footballer who had cancer', that's okay. It's only when I go into detail, show them photos, that they get an idea of how bad it was. I was the lead story on the six o'clock news, but that was only for one day too. Things move on pretty quickly.

Did it change me? Definitely. I've done a couple of things I probably wouldn't have done if I hadn't been crook. Bungee-jumping in New Zealand while still a contracted Hawthorn player, which I did on a bucks trip, probably wasn't a great idea. But I think I always managed to let my hair down when the chance was there. Sometimes I got the balance wrong, but you've gotta live. I wanted to do Oktoberfest before I turned 30, and I got there at 30. Now I play basketball, cricket, tennis, golf, whatever, without a thought for what it could mean to footy.

I don't look back, only forward. I'm not missing anything, I'm not thinking, 'What if . . . ?' If I'd never won a grand final, if I'd lost five instead of one, of course I'd be thinking that way. But I don't have any what-ifs with footy. I don't know what more I could have done.

When I look forward I see opportunity, excitement, the unknown. I see life, and all of its possibilities. And that's enough.

A Note on the Co-Author

I want to thank Peter Hanlon for his help in writing this book. The respect you showed for me and my family made working together a pleasure, and the book wouldn't be what it is without your expertise and way with words. Couldn't have done it without you, mate.

Index

2005 season 54, 55, 56–8, 59, 203
2006 season 59, 60
2007 season 61–3, 206
2008 season 67–76, 227
  grand final 72–6, 258
2009 season 77–8
2010 season 78–80
2011 season 81–2, 83–4
2012 season 86–7, 88, 93
  post-grand final breakfast 85–6, 88
2013 season 89, 90, 93–4, 227
  grand final 93, 235
2014 season 94–7, 227
  grand final 96
  post-grand final breakfast 96–7
2015 season 97–100, 104, 105,
  108–10, 227
  grand final 2, 99, 111, 264
2016 season 2, 167
  watching team play 168
2017 season 147, 157–8, 170–3,
  193
  captaincy 170, 193, 238
  return to AFL 170, 191
2018 season 194–7, 204, 206–7
  contract, speculation about 197–9

2019 season 211, 217, 221, 294
  being dropped from AFL 212,
    217
  last game 222–4
  VLF games for Box Hill 212–17

Ablett, Gary 92, 266
Adelaide Crows Football Club 51,
  62
AFL Life Membership 294
AFL Victoria 35
All-Australian team 35, 44, 179
Anderson, Jed 262
Archer, Glenn 45
Arthur, Graham 187
Atcheson, Matt 31, 33
Australian Institute of Sport 35,
  44–5, 46

Bailey, Max 81, 213, 218
Ball, Luke 84
Ballard, Charlie 223
Banky, Jeremy 104–5
Baquie, Peter 103
Barker, Johnny 56, 60
Bartel, Jimmy 91, 92

basketball 31, 33, 35, 36, 243, 244, 282
  NBA shootaround 283–4
Bateman, Candice 257
Bateman, Chance 'Changa' 63, 256–7, 264
Beckham, David 83
Bell, Kevin 7, 8
Betts, Eddie 111
Beveridge, Luke 201
Birchall, Grant 74, 100, 112, 217, 222
Bogut, Andrew 126–9
Bolton, Brendon 95
Box Hill Hawks Football Club 95, 203, 261
  2005 season 56, 61, 216
  2019 season 212–17
Boyd, Col 21
Boyle, Tim 54, 60–1
Brereton, Dermott 92
Breust, Luke 80, 94, 95, 101, 112, 167, 195, 285
  All Australian 2014 95, 100
Brisbane Lions Football Club 61, 77
Brown, Campbell 64, 66, 74
Brown, Jonathan 240
Browne, Tom 201
Brownlow Medal 73, 205–6, 226
Buckenara, Annette 53, 55, 246
Buckenara, Gary 50, 53, 55, 245, 270
Burgoyne, Amy 263
Burgoyne, Shaun 62, 80, 89, 90, 100, 101, 122–3, 202, 222, 256, 257, 262, 263, 284
  350th game 263
  Indigenous player, most games 217, 257, 263
  Jarryd, relationship with 262–4
Burns, Scott 216, 218
Burt, Jason 4

Burton, Ryan 208, 209–10
business, sport as 208, 209–10

Campbell, Adrian 38
Campbell, Robbie 123
cancer
  immunotherapy treatment 116, 155–6
  Jarryd, reaction to 142, 149–50, 161, 165, 180
  lung biopsy 120
  melanoma see melanoma
  Sarah, reaction to 161, 178–9
  side effects see side effects of cancer treatment
  skin cancer 1, 104
  spots on lungs 115, 119, 155, 178
  steroids 137
  talks given at Peter MacCallum Centre 158–9
  treatments 116, 121, 123–4, 133, 134–7
Carlton Football Club 39, 41, 44, 77, 153
Casey, Clinton 48
Ceglar, Jonathon 95
Chapman, Paul 91
Cheney, Kyle 95
Clarke, Tim 63
Clarkson, Alastair 4, 52, 53, 54, 60, 67–8, 69, 74, 70–1, 78–9, 97, 112, 194, 195–6, 216, 233, 279–82
  conversation about Jarryd's future 202–3
  Crimmins Medal 2019 speech 221
  father figure, as 282
  Guillain-Barré syndrome 94–5, 110
  Indigenous players, encouragement of 258

kindness of 280
straining of relationship 196–7,
    198, 218, 219–20, 280
Clarkson, Caryn 53, 202
clinical trials 145, 159
Cloke, Travis 46
Collingwood Football Club 19, 43,
    62, 71, 72, 80
Collins, Andy 215
contract, 2018, speculation about
    197–9, 201
Cousins, Ben 78
Cox, Adrian 55
Crawford, Shane 54, 55, 56, 63, 77,
    86, 103, 270
Crimmins Medal 80, 221
Croad, Trent 56, 61, 65, 66, 71, 77,
    103, 271
Cummings, Percy 256, 257
Curry, Steve 127
Curtis, Catherine 14–15
Curtis, Michael 14
Curtis, Sarah 14

Dahlhaus, Luke 209
Daniher, Neale 50
Deledio, Brett 43, 44, 51, 294
Dellavadova, Matthew 126
Dempsey, Gary 22
Dew, Stuey 68, 73, 75, 100, 101,
    200, 224, 291
Dixon, Ben 54, 56, 60, 103
Docherty, Sam 110
Dow, Malcolm 'Mouse' 255
draft, 2004 48, 49–52
Drum, Marcus 43
Dunkley, Andrew 38, 39, 40, 41
Dunstall, Jason 50, 87, 147
Duryea, Taylor 80, 208, 209, 210

Egan, Chris 255
Egan, Leon 260

Ellis, Xavier 72, 77
Enright, Corey 74, 92
Essendon Bombers Football Club 21,
    44, 61, 172
Evans, Mark 'Dougy' 61, 224, 291
Everitt, Peter Spida 53, 54, 56
Exmouth holiday 293–4

Fagan, Chris 4, 83, 93, 165
Fairlie, Gwen (Nannie) 8
Fletcher, Dustin 57
Footy Flashbacks 92
Fox, Stuart 125, 128–9, 188
Frank, Amos 259–61, 264
Franklin, Jesinta 272, 275
Franklin, Lance (Buddy) 44, 45, 48,
    49, 51, 52, 64, 65, 189, 222,
    245, 246, 256
    2005 season 55, 56, 57
    2006 season 60, 61
    2007 season 62, 63
    2008 season 68, 72, 75, 78, 258
    2009 season 78
    2010 season 79–80
    2011 season 84
    2012 season 86
    2014 season 96
    friendship with Jarryd 246, 247–8,
        270, 271–2, 275–6
    games for Hawthorn 257
    Kokoda Track 53, 54–5
    mental health difficulties 277
    parents in Melbourne 55, 270,
        271
    playing against 276–7
    statistics 44, 248, 295
    Sydney Swans, move to 94, 275
Frawley, James (Chip) 98, 100
Fremantle Dockers Football Club 43,
    93, 99
The Front Bar 203–4
Fyfe, Nat 108

game reviews 1, 4, 67, 89, 196
games played 59, 61, 68, 101, 200, 204, 240
Gartside, Phil 69–70
Geelong Football Club 52, 61, 63, 67, 73–4, 90, 93, 98
  Hawthorn and 90–3
Gibson, Josh 80, 90, 94, 100, 110, 111
Gilbee, Lindsay 70
Giles, Stuart 208
Gilham, Stephen 77, 81, 83
Gippsland Power Football Club 233
  TAC Cup 2004 40, 46–8
Glenferrie Oval 52, 85
Gold Coast Suns Football Club 97, 290, 291
Goodwin, Simon 291
Graham, Mark 55
grand final games
  2003 Leongatha 41–2, 72
  2008 72–6, 258
  2012 85–6, 88
  2013 93
  2014 96
  2015 99, 111
Griffen, Ryan 48, 51
Grimley, Sam 5
Grundy, Heath 47
Guerra, Brent 66, 74, 77
Gunston, Jack 88, 94, 95, 100, 210, 224, 285
GWS Football Club 43, 97

Hale, David 80, 81, 169
Hardwick, Blake 195
Hardwick, Damien 52, 63, 68, 233, 294
Harley, Tom 75
Harris, Geoff 181, 187–92
  financial assistance for immunotherapy 181, 188, 190

Hart, Royce 22
Hawkins, Tom 91
Hawthorn Football Club 2, 21, 44, 50
  coaching team 63, 207, 216
  contract with, speculation about 197–9
  Crimmins Medal 80, 221
  curfew 64, 271
  draft 2004 51–2
  exit interview 204
  exit medicals 226
  family club, as 158, 238
  financial support for immunotherapy 181
  Geelong and 90–3
  golf trips 2017 and 2018 208–9, 286
  grand final 2008 72–5
  grand final 2012 85, 87
  grand final 2013 93–4
  grand final 2014 96
  grand final 2015 99
  Indigenous liaison officer 260
  Indigenous Program 208
  milestone videos 135
  premiership games 2, 72–5, 85, 88
Hay, Johnny 56, 57
Henderson, Ricky 169, 208
Heppell, Dyson 172
Herald Sun 197
Hill, Bradley 94, 169, 262, 264, 280
Hill, Grant 127
Hodge, Cooper 279
Hodge, Dylan 112, 269
Hodge, Lauren 67, 112, 278
Hodge, Luke 56, 62, 63, 65–6, 67, 68, 90, 100, 112, 125, 193, 222
  2015 season 98–9, 111
  Brisbane, move to 208, 222
  friendship with Jarryd 202, 270, 272, 278–9
Norm Smith Medals 96

Holland, Nick 54, 56, 203
Hooker, Cale 276
Hudghton, Max 62
Hudson, Paul 39, 41
Hurn, Shannon 44

immunotherapy treatment 116, 118,
    121, 123–4, 155–6, 190, 237
    cost 117, 181, 188
    financial support for 181, 188, 190
Indigenous Australians 255, 267–8
Indigenous players 255–66
Indigenous Round 261
Ingles, Joe 83, 125–6, 133, 168, 224
    career 282–3, 284
    friendship with Jarryd 282–3
injuries 122–3, 226
    2009, Hawthorn players 77
    Achilles, rupture 81, 82–3, 122, 168
    ankle surgery 205, 211
    broken collarbone 40
    hamstring injury 199–200, 202
    posterior cruciate ligament 2, 110,
        113, 226
International Rules tests 46, 111–12

Jacobs, Danny 56
James, LeBron 127
Jiath, CJ 218
Johnson, Mick 41
Johnson, Steve 92
Johnstone, Travis 58
Jones, Luke 31
Judd, Chris 240

Kelly, Craig 218
Kelly, James 82
Kennedy, Josh 44
Kennett, Jeff 79, 91
Kennett Curse 90, 91, 92
King, Max 290, 292
Kokoda Track 53, 54, 189

Ladson, Rick 60, 62, 75
Lake, Brian 95, 100, 169
Langford, Will 96, 98
Langstaff, Daniel 37
Latrobe Valley Football League 22,
    38–9
Law, Ian 'Liberty' 187
leadership 187–8, 189
Leongatha 9, 12–13, 19, 21
    cricket clubs 33–5
    football ground 22–3, 37–8
    football team 21
    golf courses 30
    Leongatha Tennis Club 31
    Parrots Football Club 22–3,
        39–41, 43
    premiership tradition 41–2
    Roughead Street 12–13
Leongatha Parrots Football Club
    22–3, 39
    2003 season 39–41, 43
Leppitsch, Justin 50, 57
Lethlean, Simon 291
Lewis, Jordan 4, 47, 52, 53, 64, 65,
    66, 90, 100, 104, 169, 189, 222,
    224, 243–53
    250th game 118
    2005 season 55, 57–8
    2007 season 62, 63
    2008 season 68
    2014 season 95, 96
    cancer, feelings about 4, 243, 249,
        273
    coaching skills 281
    draft 245
    friendship with Jarryd 243, 246,
        270, 271–4
    last game 225
    Melbourne, move to 172, 199,
        205, 208, 280
    player as, Jarryd's opinion 274
Lewis, Lucy 243, 252

Lewis, Mitch 203, 218, 219, 221, 289
Lewis, Shane 271
Liberatore, Tony 165
Ling, Cameron 92
Lloyd, Brad 235
Lloyd, Matty 78
Lowden, Luke 89

McArthur, Dr Grant 3, 108, 115,
   116–17, 147, 153–9, 169
McAvaney, Bruce 197
McEvoy, Ben 95, 195
Mackie, Andrew 90
McLachlan, Gil 189
McLean, Ray 89
McMahon, Sharelle 83
McQualter, Andrew 46
Maffra Football Club 22, 40, 41
Makdissi, Dr Michael 2, 3, 105, 106,
   108, 115, 158
Mansfield, Matty 38
Marshall, Rowan 292
Matthews, Cam 220
Maxwell, Nick 62
Meagher, Jill 87
media attention 118–19, 120, 166,
   168, 171
Meesen, Johnny 51
melanoma 104, 109–10, 154, 155,
   236
   diagnosis 1, 104, 105, 106
   removal surgery 1–2, 106–7,
      177–8, 236
Melbourne Cricket Ground (MCG)
   4, 46, 207, 290, 291, 294
Membrey, Tim 292
Merriman, Phil 167
Meyer, Danny 51
Michael, Mal 57
Miles, Teia 206
Miller, Greg 48
Miller, Harry 56, 57, 258

Mills, Patty 168, 255, 282, 283, 284
Milne, Donna 115, 121–2, 123, 133,
   136, 141–51
   Sarah, relationship with 143, 150
Milne, Lewis 147, 148
Mitchell, Sam 52, 56, 63, 66, 68, 75,
   90, 94, 100, 108, 111, 112, 169,
   216, 222, 277
   300th game 135, 249
   Brownlow Medal 277
   friendship with Jarryd 270, 272,
      277
   West Coast, move to 172, 222, 280
Mitchell, Tommy 169, 173, 194,
   195, 205–6
Moe Football Club 22, 39, 255
Monfries, Angus 44
Monkhorst, Damian 29
The Monthly 25–6
Mooney, Cam 74, 75
Moore, Dylan 218
Morrison, Harry 206, 218
Morton, Mitch 44, 46, 49
Morwell Football Club 22
Mundy, Dave 111
Murphy, Bob 112, 133, 193, 294
Murphy, Gerard 31
Murphy, Justine 133
Murphy, Marc 46

Nash, Conor 206, 207
National Health and Medical
   Research Council 159
NBA finals trip 2015 125–9
Newman, Chris 207
North Melbourne Football Club 45,
   61

O'Meara, Jaeger 169, 194, 206
O'Reilly, Josephine 14
O'Reilly, Tom 14–15
Osborne, Michael 66, 75

Peck, John 187
Pendlebury, Scott 266
Pert, Gary 291
PET scans 2, 108, 113, 137, 149,
    183
  cancer-free scan 169, 183
Peter MacCallum Cancer Centre 1,
    2, 115, 123, 148–9
Peterson, Carl 265–6
Pettyfor, Clare 221
Pike, Martin 57
pneumothorax 130
Port Adelaide Football Club 44,
    61–2, 68
posterior cruciate ligament injury 2,
    110, 113, 226
Puopolo, Paul 80, 227

Quinlan, Bernie 22

racism 256, 258
Ralph, Jon 197
Ramakrishnan, Dr Anand 106, 107
Ramanauskas, Adam 124
Rath, David 70, 80, 135
Ratten, Brett 110, 170, 290
Ratten, Cooper 110
Reeves, Justin 221
Renouf, Brent 81
Rice, Dean 39
Richardson, Matty 197
Richmond Tigers Football Club 43,
    44, 48, 51, 220
Riewoldt, Cath 112, 133
Riewoldt, Nick 112, 133, 240
Rioli, Cyril 68, 74–5, 94, 95, 99,
    100, 195, 256, 265, 266–7
  All Australian 267
  games for Hawthorn 257
  retirement 267
  wedding 262
Rioli, Willie 256

Robertson, Russell 83
Robinson, Mark 204
Rooke, Max 74
Ross, Jackson 218
Roughead, Ann (Nan) (née Griffiths)
    9–10, 13, 26, 28, 232
  children 15, 18
  farm days 15–17
  Griffiths family history 9–12
Roughead, Brendan 15, 16, 19
Roughead, Cameron 5, 7, 13, 27, 36,
    94, 107, 136, 229–41, 269
  career 129, 235, 269
  childhood 230–1
  health 28, 229
  Jarryd's cancer and 163, 181, 236,
    237–8
  NBA finals trip 126–9
  relationship with Jarryd 231,
    232–6, 240
  support given by 163, 181, 238
Roughead, Christine 14, 15, 19
Roughead, Emily 5, 7, 27, 28, 36,
    232–3, 236, 238
Roughead, Greg 15, 16, 19
Roughead, Jack 19–20
Roughead, James (Jim) 15, 16, 17,
    18, 20
Roughead, Jarryd 25, 26, 102
  Achilles, rupture 81, 82–3, 122,
    168
  All Australian 100
  ankle surgery 205, 211
  basketball 31, 33, 35, 36–7, 82,
    230, 244
  broken collarbone 40
  cancer see cancer
  captaincy 170, 193, 238, 251
  captaincy, stepping down 191,
    202, 211
  career statistics 44, 295–6
  childhood 27–32

Roughead, Jarryd *continued*
clothing taste 252
competitiveness 247–8
cricket 31, 33–5, 231
Cyril's wedding 262
draft 48, 50–2, 210, 233, 245
effect of cancer on 240, 298
family, relationship with 163, 176
family heritage 7, 12–15, 19
football injuries 226
Fox, interviewing for 225
friends from AFL 270–82
friends from basketball 282–4
golf 208–9, 285–6
hamstring injury 199–200, 202
Hawthorn Club, feelings about
    269–70
high school graduation 48, 50, 210
house renovations 131–2, 177,
    180, 182
Indigenous Australia 255
last game 222–4, 239
memory 144, 247
organisation 247
parenting 184, 241, 252–3
post-player life 294–7
psychologist appointments 164
retirement 151, 222–4, 239
Rising Star nomination 2005 59
St Kilda, Football Operations
    Assistant 191, 290–93
travel post-2008 season 76
USA trip 2016 168
wedding 2, 113, 270
Roughead, Jordan 19
Roughead, Professor Libby 12, 14,
    15, 164
Roughead, Michael 7, 15–19, 20–2,
    26–7, 33, 35, 37, 39
Roughead, Paul 15, 19, 20–1
Roughead, Pippa 14, 115, 143, 151,
    184, 193, 222, 227, 241, 297

Roughead, Sarah 104, 107, 115,
    132, 175–85, 252, 296, 297
cancer recurrence, reaction 4–5,
    161, 178–9
family support 181–2
meeting and early relationship 175
melanoma 177
netball 162, 181–2
pregnancy and parenthood 143,
    184
psychic, visit to 183
support for 142, 162–3
wedding 2, 113
work and career 162, 168, 180–1
Roughead, Sheryl 8, 9, 22, 30–1, 37
Roughead, Vincent 9, 15, 19
Roughhead family history 12–15, 19
ruckman role 81, 247
Russell, Andrew 'Jack' 4, 68, 76, 79,
    165, 196, 200, 210

Sale Football Club 22, 41
Salmon, Ian 21
SANFL 259, 261
Schoenmakers, Ryan 95, 98, 100,
    209, 285
Scott, Doug 57
Scully, Tom 207, 209, 264
Selwood, Joel 92
Sewell, Brad 72, 78, 90, 96, 224
Shiels, Liam 80, 89, 100, 209
Sicily, James 209, 285
side effects of cancer treatment
    131–2, 138–40, 146, 156–7
eye inflammation 157
feet nerve damage 138–40, 146,
    156, 167
hepatitis 157
lung inflammation 157
pneumothorax 130
Sim, Lachy 47
Simpkin, Joffa 95, 96

Slater, Billy 291
Smith, Isaac 80, 94, 167, 264
Smith, Joel 56, 62
Smith, Ross 63
Solomon, Dean 57
Spangher, Matt 98, 100
St Kilda Football Club 39, 61, 72,
    77, 78, 80
  AFLW team 292
  Football Operations Assistant role
    191, 290–93
Standfield, Barry 38
Stevens, Anthony 45
Stevens, Mark 201
Stewart, Kade 171
Stibbard, Neville 45
Stokes, Cameron 265
Stratton, Ben 80, 86, 94, 284, 293
stress 199–200
Stribling, Toby 45
Stynes, Jimmy 154
Suckling, Matt 80, 169, 208, 285
The Sunday Footy Show 86
Sydney Cricket Ground (SCG) 207
Sydney Swans Football Club 44, 62,
    86, 87, 96
  Buddy, move to 94, 275

TAC Cup 2004 40, 46–8, 244
Tambling, Richard 51
Taylor, Harry 75, 92
Taylor, Simon 56
Templeton, Kelvin 22
Thomas, Dale 43
Thomas, Isiah 127
Thompson, Nathan 55
Thurgood, Josh 53, 56
TLA Talent Management 235, 269
training 39, 295
  All-Australian under-16s 44–5
  Hawthorn, with 53, 56, 59, 71,
    73, 112, 170, 245

post-diagnosis 118
St Kilda, at 292
Tszyu, Kostya 45–6
Tuck, Shane 78

Vanderberg, Richie 54, 56, 63, 66,
    270
Vic Country AFL team 35, 43–4, 46,
    49, 233, 244
Vickery, Ty 173
Victorian Football League (VFL)
  2005 season 56
  2019 season 212–17
Viney, Todd 63

Walker, Ron 124, 148, 154, 190
Walker, Tex 196
Wallis, Steve 21, 56
Walsh, Phil 108, 110
Wanganeen, Derick 265
Warne, Shane 191
Weller, Lachie 223
West Coast Eagles Football Club 44,
    61, 98, 99, 111
Western Bulldogs 19, 21, 38, 51, 72,
    167
Wheeler, Terry 44, 46
Wigley, Ted (Poppy) 8, 9
William, Reuben 213, 214
Williams, Mark 57, 74, 75, 77,
    258–9
Williams, Mark (Choco) 49–50
Williams, Tom 52
Wingard, Chad 98, 207, 209, 211,
    223, 267
Wonthaggi Football Club 39
Wood, Ken 189
Worpel, James 206, 286
Wright, Graham 194, 198, 220, 221

Yates, Geoff 255
Young, Clinton 77

Discover a
new favourite